PRAISES FOR B

"I bought the book and read it straight through. So glad to see this piece of history so lovingly preserved."
Ceil Damschroder, Larimer County Genealogical Society

"Without this book I might not have found my grandfather!"
Nathelle Stollens, Longmont, Colorado

"It is so great after all these years to find out some history about our great grandfather and his children."
Doris Compton, Florence, Oregon, great-granddaughter of John B. Provost

"My work on behalf of young people in Larimer County emphasizes the importance of making every effort to preserve Colorado's proud Spanish heritage, wherever it can be found. A great deal of it can be found between the covers of this book. Nearly half of those buried in the little cemetery on the hill are of Hispanic descent. This is a wonderful tribute to a part of history all too often ignored and overlooked. It will be an excellent resource for future generations looking into their genealogy. It is a must for anyone really interested in local history."
Richard Payne, M.A. E.C., community activist, educator and writer

"Colorado Preservation, Inc., has awarded Rose and her work on the Bingham Hill Cemetery a well-deserved State Honor Award."
Mary Humstone, neighbor of the cemetery and assistant director of the Mountains/Plains Regional Office of the National Trust for Historic Preservation

"Rose Brinks' *History of the Bingham Hill Cemetery* is a valuable historic resource; it ties many of the cemetery's people to stories of the Laporte area's colorful past. Much of Laporte's history lies beneath the sod of this picturesque country burial grounds—and Rose has uncovered their stories!"
Wayne Sundberg, Fort Collins historian

"This book represents a real service to the community."
Ida Pennock, author of Happy Hardships

"May the Lord bless Rose Brinks in her effort to write the history of the children of Bellvue Cemetery."
Maria Esquibel, sister of baby buried in 1938

"I found the book absolutely fascinating, and read it cover to cover without interruption. It was very poignant that somehow these everyday working people buried in that cemetery had part of their lives brought back for the rest of us to remember.
James S. Warson, MD.

"Bingham Hill Cemetery has been used extensively by the local history archive patrons at the Fort Collins Public Library. An excellent source on Laporte and Fort Collins personalities based on meticulous research."
Rheba Massey, Fort Collins local history librarian

"For years Rose Brinks has been researching cemetery records, interviewing and compiling information. She is intensely committed to doing a great job. Everyone should look forward to this new edition."
Arlene (Briggs) Ahlbrandt, former president of the Fort Collins Historical Society

"I appreciate the many hours spent in researching the history of the Laporte families, with particular gratitude with respect to the Rowland Herring family...."
Doris Sarchet Atkinson Bice. granddaughter of Rowland and Nettie Herring

"The book looks like a big winner."
Allene Niehaus

"We enjoyed our tour of Bingham Hill Cemetery. It was difficult to drag the girls away when it was time to go."
Kathleen Edmiston, Brownie leader

"It was wonderful to finally see the grave of my great-grandmother—Jenny McGaa Brown. The book is so interesting. I've shared it with so many. God Bless Mrs. Brinks for what she has done."
Delores McGaa O'Daniel and Bob O'Daniel. Rapid City, South Dakota

"This book sets a lofty standard for those who want to do cemetery research."
Richard H. Sweetman, Professor, University of Colorado

"Rose is terrific (and so is the book!)"
Bob de Baca, Huxley, Iowa

"*Bingham Hill Cemetery* is a success. Several local families have used the book as a supplement to their Sunday drives or picnics in the hills. A useful and informative guide!"
Eliza Schmidt, former librarian at Wellington, Colorado

"The book is super."
Clara Rodgers. sister of three siblings buried in 1911

"Mrs. Brinks has spent many hours researching and interviewing to complete this important historical work dear to the hearts of many natives of this area. Mrs. Brinks and her family have also done much work to physically improve the condition of the historic old cemetery and have encouraged many others to help. Those interested in local history will find the book of utmost interest."
Dick Baker, Fort Collins historian

"I count myself fortunate to have obtained a copy of this book. What a marvelous volume. It is giving me an expanded knowledge of early-day Laporte and some of the contemporaries of my ancestors."
Raymond L. Owen, Santa Rosa, California, descendant of James Barr of early Laporte

HISTORY OF THE
BINGHAM HILL CEMETERY
Laporte & Bellvue, Colorado

ROSE L. BRINKS

A humble-looking, woebegone pioneer cemetery lies nestled between two farms south of Laporte, Colorado. No burial records were ever kept and no one had ever seriously sought to determine who lies under all the unmarked stones.

Not only has the author achieved the near impossible by finding the identities of over 150 persons, but her diligent and persistent research has almost brought them to life. The reader may be surprised, as were living relatives of the dead, to discover exactly who is buried there.

Visitors to the cemetery will be greatly aided by taking this book along.

BINGHAM HILL CEMETERY
1st Edition May 1988, 88 pages
2nd Printing, Revised April 1990, 114 pages

Library of Congress Catalog
Card Number 88-71244, First Edition
Card Number 90-081184, Second Edition

Renamed:
HISTORY OF THE BINGHAM HILL CEMETERY
3rd Printing June 1998, 210 pages
4th Printing November 2005, 212 pages
5th Printing, July 2015, 230 pages

ISBN 978-0-692-47236-1

Published by:
Rose L Brinks
P.O. Box 710
Laporte, Colorado 80535
(970) 221-4261
rosebrinks@gmail.com

CONTENTS

This book is dedicated to my husband,
James S. Brinks,
the greatest guy in the world.

January 2, 1934 – June 11, 2015

And also, to the late **Father Thomas Merton**, whose inspirational words kept me going on this long and difficult project:

*Do not depend on the hope of results, when
you are doing the sort of work
you have taken on. You may have to face
the fact that your work will be
apparently worthless and even achieve no
worth at all, if not perhaps,
results opposite to what you expect.
As you get used to this idea, you will start
more and more to concentrate
not on the results, but on the value, the
rightness, the truth of the work itself.*

AUTHOR'S FOREWORD

My personal association with cemeteries began when I was twelve years old and my dad was buried in one. For the next several years my mother and I tended his grave, planted trees and flowers, carried buckets of water and, like all good Catholics, knelt and prayed for his soul. Then my mother died, my first husband was killed, and both were buried in the same country cemetery near Stratton in southwestern Nebraska. Therefore, I have had enough cemetery experience to know the comfort that can come from visiting the graves of loved ones.

Years passed and I found myself living on a farm near Laporte, Colorado, with a second husband and our collecton of nine children. For the next ten years, the weedy old cemetery along Bingham Hill Road was of no personal interest to me except that it was visible from my kitchen window. The few names on headstones meant nothing and my husband even thought the red unmarked stones must be for soldiers from the early Laporte fort. In 1987, as a gift to my husband, who was always curious about the names on our land's abstract of title, I researched the history of our farm and wrote a 145-page book about it (1). Our farm was an important part of early Laporte, and since the cemetery was part of the original farm, my appreciation of it grew. Through time, one family after another tumbled through this land, and finally the stories of those who lived and were buried here motivated me to write *Bingham Hill Cemetery, Laporte & Bellvue, Colorado.*

That book, small but packed with information, was published in 1988. New information immediately came in from readers. All copies of the first printing were quickly sold, so I compiled the new material and photographs and simply added 29 pages at the end, an insert in the middle, and a new cover for a 1990 updated version. Ten years after the first publication, due to a plethora of yet more information, happenings and photographs, I felt that another, longer version was required. This time the book was rewritten from front to back, which should make for easier reading.

In this new book, some of the material on previously mentioned buried persons is more detailed, and especially if not printed elsewhere, family stories are expanded. There are newly discovered inhabitants such as Mr. OUDERKIRK, Mr. CLARK and Mr. SHAFFER, buried long ago, and I found names of others buried in Laporte and later moved, like the LESHERS. There is also a chapter on recent burials up to 1998.

New mysteries surfaced and were solved, such as where Mrs. FOIDL lies after her body was brought here from the countryside near Steamboat Springs. An old mystery was solved—the identity of the red-headed J. THOMAS, buried by the ditch bank. An access problem is discussed and errors in the first two editions corrected.

Though the inhabitants rest in peace, there is plenty of activity at the old pioneer cemetery. Several Eagle Scout projects were completed. More than 10,000 visitors from every state in the union and over 20 foreign countries have signed the guest book. Money was raised to buy a memorial stone large enough for the names of all known to be buried; the deteriorating LAROCQUE gravestone was replaced. A dowser found indications that more graves than previously thought might be inside and outside the cemetery fences. A surveyor made a plat with each significant stone and structure marked. Sometimes "wiccans" hold candlelight vigils to pay their respects.

All told, there is real reason to re-write the book. Because of what happens to me when I write about this cemetery, however, I was reluctant to get involved in the project again. It isn't just the horrendous amount of time it takes or that unanswerable questions agitate me. It's that no matter how I try to avoid being obsessed, I am pulled deeper and deeper into the cemetery cauldron until my thoughts are all back amongst the Provosts and Binghams, the McBrides and the McGaas, the Apodacas and Pachecos. I "see" the Indian women walking around Sarah Jane Hardin's cabin when she died. I cringe to remember three little Robertsons dying so quickly; I shiver from cold in the shacks at Ingleside; I puzzle over "Evil Eye," and ache for the mother who walked from west of Laporte to the hospital carrying her sick child; I agonize about the drowned child who was pulled from the irrigation ditch. I know how the woman with 14 kids struggled!

As I research and write, then, I live amongst these characters and think of them constantly. Perhaps all writers become obsessed. I wouldn't know; I never claimed to be a writer (except letters of admonition to my kids), and certainly wasn't trained as a historian; I just did what needed to be done, and this book—a product of my labor and so many deaths—is worth it, I think.

I try to write dispassionately—nothing but the facts—but occasionally I need to insert an opinion or a guess. At times I went into detail about how I found information and did so for the benefit of a reader who might be doing similar research. It was probably good that information was brief and sketchy, for I'd never be able to finish if I knew anyone's whole story. Just a glimpse into each life was enough and sometimes too much.

My rewards have been many. The book brought over a thousand fourth-grade pupils on local history tours with their teachers; years later they tell me how much they learned. I was honored to be given a recognition award in 1995 by the Fort Collins Historical Society. In 1998, preservationist and Laporte resident, Mary Humstone, nominated the cemetery restoration project for the Colorado Preservation, Inc., State Honor Award, and it won! Ten other state awardees and I were honored at a dinner in Denver on June 10, 1998. I have a stack of letters of gratitude from relatives of the deceased and new friendships with wonderful people and I feel pride in the memorial which grew from an idea in my head, to a sketch on paper, to enough donated money to order the granite. I watched the sandblasting and final placement in the cemetery. All those who donated money for the memorial (names listed in the chapter on volunteers) should know that people come from all over the country to touch it and run their fingers along the names of their loved ones.

None of the excellent projects which have stabilized or enhanced the cemetery or proclaimed its historical importance would have been carried out without first spreading the word that there was a cemetery here and that it was crying out to be recognized.

So to my readers, thank you for your interest in this small part of Laporte history. It is not a morbid necrology, but a celebration of ordinary lives. None of the dead are just names any longer. They are the relatives of many fine people; they are the unsung and unwitting characters who played roles in Laporte and Bellvue history; they fill my imagination. My gift to them is that they now have a place, however sketchy, in printed history, and will not be forgotten.

Rose L. Brinks
Laporte, Colorado
June, 1998

ACKNOWLEDGEMENTS

The following people deserve sincere thanks for their help in one way or another with one or more versions of this book. Many have died since I first contacted them and it is obvious that had I not started researching when I did, a great deal of information would have been lost. Many have become dear friends.

Richard Baker (died at age 79, 8/20/1989) was so generous in sharing his scrapbooks, a sketch of Mountain Home Cemetery plots, and memories of watching the bodies of his grandmother and young aunt being moved from the Laporte cemetery to Grandview Cemetery in Fort Collins. He was a fine historian. His daughter, Marcia Dowdy, relinquished his scrapbooks and other historical material to Bill Schneider.

Bill Schneider found a letter in the Baker scrapbooks which reveals who is under the J. THOMAS headstone. Schneider also found a newspaper photo of Bill Howell, the last adult buried (1940) before a new owner of adjacent land closed the gate to the cemetery.

Dr. Michael Charney (d. at 87, 5/2/1998), Colorado State University's famous professor (emeritus) of forensic anthropology, examined and wrote a description of the bones of J. THOMAS.

Local newspapers helped a lot! Every single article about the Bingham Hill Cemetery brought forth new information from readers which aided in the writing and updating of this book. Periodicals, writers and dates include:

Fort Collins Coloradoan: **Faith Kuhns**, 9/1/1987; **Cara Neth**, 6/15/1988; **Jill Shadick**, 3/19/90; **Teresa R. Funke**, 2/28/1993; **J. Lewandowski**, 8/6/1994; **Dan Haley**, 11/7/1994; **Susan Harness**, 9/3/1995; a letter to the editor from me 2/24/1998; and **Robert Baun**, 3/6/1998;

The Triangle Review: **Dan MacArthur**, 5/10/90;

Inside Fort Collins: **Dan MacArthur**, 11/3/94;

The North 40 News: **Jim Brookman**, 5/1995; 4/1996; and

Colorado Country Life Magazine: **Wil Huett**, 9/1991.

Joe (Angel) and **Anna Garnica** from Holy Family Church reassured me that this was a worthwhile project and directed me to the right people.

Television Channel 4 from Denver, in May, 1995, aired an excellent piece by **Julia Sandige** and **Stephanie Riggs** about "Witching for Unmarked Graves in an Old Cemetery" and our attempts to prevent development.

In 1998, **Mike Elliott** surveyed the cemetery and plotted each structure and significant headstone. **Tom Yip** helped with computer enhancement of one photograph. **Platte River Power Authority** donated the aerial photo.

Wayne Sundberg rescued years of bound copies of the *Fort Collins Courier* from the State Historical Society, which planned to take them to the Denver dump. He loaned them to me and is always liberal with his time in promoting the endeavors of local historians.

Neurosurgeon **Dr. James Warson** performed a cervical laminectomy on me in October 1987 and, by removing a bone spur, freed me from years of pain which allowed me the energy to begin this book in the first place.

Louise (Mondragon) Aragon's own first child was buried in Laporte and she remembered so many parents and godparents of little ones.

Clara E. Rodgers (d. at 93, 10/29/1996) and her half-sister, **Rose Hoffman**, who was 100 years old on March 8, 1998, solved the mystery of the three Robertson children and described their deaths which took place 87 years ago. Clara also furnished the photo of E.A.E. Robertson.

Cecilia Beecher, now of Hanna, Wyoming, related to both the Vigil and Torres families, helped time and again with family information.

Henry Kingman and **Ann Ryan** shared the poignant diaries and letters of Nettie Garbutt Herring written from 1874 to 1894 and diaries and letters of Ed Garbutt written from 1867 to 1895.

Henry Moore, a great-grandson of John Provost, found documents at the Pine Ridge Reservation and shared them.

Margaret Isaac of Denver has worked on Hardin and Hand genealogy since 1937 and, at age 88, has decades of information on the tip of her tongue.

Dr. Ken Goldsberry, president (1987 to 1998) of the Pioneer Association of Fort Collins (which purchased a 1990 edition of my book for every public school in Fort Collins), always expresses his helpfulness in cemetery matters.

Several City of Fort Collins employees gave of their time to ensure the accuracy of historical data: **Phil Carpenter, Alyce Mierman, Steve Comfort** and **Patricia Windmuller** at Grandview Cemetery; **John Q. Carr** from the museum; and **Rheba Massey** in the local history area of the public library.

Maria F. De Chaparro (Holy Family) and **Belle Benzel** (St. Joseph's) allowed me to go through old baptism records; **Greg Hays** from the Loveland cemetery looked up records, as did **Debbie Reisdorf** at the county coroner's office.

The Allnut (previously Goodrich), Reager, and Warren-Bohlender Funeral Homes let me research old records in 1988. Without their kindness, a great deal of information would have been missed. **Lynn Phillips** and **Paul Telleen** at Allnut, **Darren Gunn** and **Michelle Bernhardt** at Reager, and **Gwen Bohlender** helped track down more information in 1998.

Harold Warren told many anecdotes to a 4-H Club when he visited the cemetery on December 10, 1987, and remembered burials he conducted there.

These people furnished photographs:

Nora Castellanos loaned the photo of her sister, Lucia Trujillo, buried in 1927, and also supplied family information.

Mary Dinkle (d. at 85, 7/27/1990) told me about the death of her newborn baby in 1942 and furnished a photograph of him in his little homemade coffin.

Dora and **Lorraine Vigil** furnished the portraits of Jacobo and Acacio Trujillo and of Donaciano Vigil and Crisanta Herrara and stories of the Vigil families.

Nathelle Stollens of Longmont provided the photo and story of William Ouderkirk.

Frances Bujack (d. at 62, 4/21/1996) loaned the photograph of Ida Louise McNally and furnished information about her great-grandmother's brother and sister.

Eva Martinez (d. at 94, 10/7/1997) attended her little sister's burial in 1913 and donated a photo of it. She and her son, Daniel Martinez, also pointed out relationships between various families and corrected spelling of Hispanic names.

Ruth Brubaker of Riverton, Wyoming, found a picture of Abner and Florence Spragg, her husband's grandparents.

Frances E. VerStratten (d. at 75, 1/5/1996) loaned the photo of Barbara Bingham; she and her friend, **Mickey Ethridge**, also shared stacks of Bingham material.

Frances VerStratten's pictures and story were furnished by her two daughters, **Leslie Moore** and **Janet Iverson**.

Louise Allen of Loveland sent information and a photo of her son, Danny Allen.

Judy Gonzales and **Helen Alcorn** supplied photographs and information about Bill Alcorn.

Raymond Owen of Santa Rosa, California, sent a photograph and some history of Crawford Shaffer.

Maria Tamayo Esquibel of Cheyenne loaned the picture of the funeral of her sister, Maria Tamayo, and wrote a tribute to her family.

Marian Vigil furnished the photo and information about Leroy Vigil.

Also a special thanks to the following for information they shared:

Laporte residents: Merilyn and **Dean Roberts** (d. at 58, 6/21/1997), **Mary McNally, Florence Krickbaum Vigil, John Garcia, Jim Hyde** (d. at 74, 9/27/1996), **Billy Porter, Harry Dunlap** (d. at 78, 12/19/96), **Peggy Dunlap Simpson, Duayne Canfield** (d. at 94, 5/31/1995), **Fred Heustis** (d. at 78, 11/5/91), **Bill Thompson, Georgia Maxfield** (d. at 83, 5/20/1991), **Theresa Brookman, Jim Brookman**, and **Lala Nauta** (d. at 87, 6/4/1994).

From Bellvue: Dennis Brubaker, Lily Hout, Glenn Pennock, Helen Bland and **Vic Tamlin** (d. at 79, 1/26/1994).

From Fort Collins: **Pat Corrigan, Ellen Allen, Sadie Gallegos, Clara Pacheco, Preston Farrell** (d. at 86, 7/8/1988), **J. Raymond Kissock**, (d. at 101, 3/6/1994), **Florence LaBadi, Darlene McQuire** (moved to Texas) and her mother, **Florence Williams** (died, date unknown), **May Apodaca, Cleo Furones Holsinger, Tina Gallegos, Charlene Hicks, Delphine Garcia, Iola Pennock, Lois Johnson, Ivan Pennock** (d. at 84, 7/31/1997), **Walt Little** (d. at 88, 3/11/1995), **Berniece Collamer Kelly, Hazel Wexler,**

Dr. Bob Pike, Alan and Kathleen Dean, Jose D. Gonzales, Jim Yockey, Steve Mosqueda, Esther Dixon Moore, Hazel Kern, Art Collamer (d. at 93, 12/19/1986), Mary Wessels, Mabel Burns, Frank McConnell (d. at 89 on 11/13/1994), Rosalie Rohrbacker, Jacqueline Michie, Carol Throckmorton, Irene Gibbens, Stella Gallegos, Mary Romero Gallegos, Larry Newman, Don Woeber and Bob Rupp.

Other Coloradoans: Edwin Brown of Longmont, Bessie Asbury of Delta, Don and Gerry Hinkle of Yampa, Elizabeth Allen and Celia Trujillo Silva de Compos of Colorado Springs, Esther Roberts Armstrong of Englewood (died, date unknown), Anna Bryant of Briggsdale, Zethyl Gates of Loveland, June Krakel of Red Feather Lakes, and Carol M. Yockey of Wellington.

Out-of-State People: Judy Hall of Independence, Kansas; Doris Compton of Florence, Oregon; Bill Howell, Jr., of Gainsville, Florida; Wilma Cathy Stowe of Abilene, Texas; Margaret Potts of Lebanon, Illinois; George and Angel Armijo and Carlene Heath of Cheyenne, Kate Moon of Encampment, and Carmen Torres Grass of Hanna, Wyoming; Hal Collier of New York, New York; Cathy Funkhouser of Bonner's Ferry, Idaho; Betty Jean Spencer of Ogden, Utah; Betty Amatur of Springerville, Arizona; Annie Mondragon (d. 4/20/1998) of Hemet, California; Hazel L. McGaa-Cuny of Rapid City and Sister Genevieve Cuny of Pine Ridge, South Dakota; and Adele Brown Tries of Kent, Washington.

And last, thanks to my daughter, Laura Pritchett of St. Paul, Minnesota, and daughter-in-law, Kathleen Dean of Fort Collins, both fine editors; Al Alkire from Citizen Press who guided me through the printing of this book three times; and above all, bless my best bartering friend, Steve Silva, who printed all these pages on his laser printer. Many times.

A lot of people have had input into this book! Without them, there wouldn't have been one.

I

INTRODUCTION

FIRST WE WERE **COLONA**, then **La Porte**. The post office opened here in 1862, discontinued in 1864, and was re-established in 1866; 17 postmasters and 32 years later, in 1894, we were designated **Laporte**, one word. Only 13 postmasters but 104 years after that, in 1998, we are still **Laporte**, and **Laporte** we shall remain. No matter how engulfing the rapidly-growing Fort Collins becomes, we will still be Laporte, and though we may not be much, it will always be true that we were here first. First army camp, first settlers, first courthouse, first saloons, first school, first mill, first county seat. First cemetery, too.

In 1862, just four months after the July 15 opening of the post office, and the July 22 establishment of Camp Collins along the Cache la Poudre River in Laporte, the first burial took place on the John Provost farm in a spot which later became known as the Bingham Hill Cemetery. Since then, two cemeteries were started and then abandoned in Fort Collins, but ours in Laporte stayed put. The Laporte Cemetery has been vandalized, reduced in size, ostracized (at least 15 bodies were moved out of it), and presently it is impossible to drive to, but it will stay a symbol of our proud heritage. Tough people were buried there; we will not abandon them.

The cemetery lies about one-half mile south of Laporte, somewhat inconspicuously squeezed between an irrigation ditch and a field. There is a large sign on poles proclaiming BINGHAM HILL CEMETERY, black on white, but the cemetery can be easily missed if, while driving west on Bingham Hill Road, one fails to glance up at the right time. Many local people did not even know it existed and for 45 years between 1942 and 1987, there were no burials and few visitors except for deer, rabbits, badgers and skunks.

No one ever paid for burial space, no one kept burial records, no one is responsible for its care. A little information about the cemetery was easy to come by, as there are names and dates on a few stones. But who are the people under all the unmarked stones and the sunken places with no stones at all?

1

My husband, James S. Brinks, a retired Colorado State University professor and small-time cattleman, purchased 100 acres of river bottom land north of and adjacent to the cemetery in 1977 and for the next ten years we were occasional cemetery visitors. You couldn't get to it without climbing through weeds and barbed wire fences unless you drove past the house of our neighbor, Roy Juhl.

As I talked to local people, I realized others would like to visit the unkempt, peaceful old place, so in September of 1987, after talking with Jack Loucks of Larimer County (regarding parking), Shawn Hoff (the ditchrider), and Roy Juhl, my husband and sons removed barbed wire and built two gates which opened walking access from Bingham Hill Road. Local publicity brought help and the chapter on volunteers recounts those who were involved in the early months of hand-blistering labor. Within two months, over 130 visitors had signed a guest book.

Now that the cemetery was free of weeds and brush and people were able to visit, my mission seemed accomplished. Yet, the big question remained about who was buried there. There were 25 professionally-made headstones and many small, irregularly-cut and spaced red sandstone markers, some with initials or names. Due to chaotic burial patterns, it was difficult to determine which were headstones and which might be footstones, but a conservative count in 1987 indicated about 130 graves. However, since it was known that some bodies lay outside the present fence boundaries and that vandals and livestock destroyed some stones (old-timers told me the hill was once white with stones between the cemetery and Bingham Hill Road), a reasonable estimate would be higher.

Having a curious nature, I embarked on some serious research. In Laporte, I went to bars, the Plantorium, the hardware store and to homes. I was afraid that too much time had passed as few of the old-timers knew anything about specific burials. Finally someone mentioned a baby "Jesse," then a "Freddie" and someone's "baby aunt." One by one, I picked up names of possible burials. Then I received a solid clue about "a guy named Robertson who'd stand on the street corner in Laporte swinging a gold watch." Maybe he was the father of those three 'Robertson' children whose headstones indicate they all died in 1911?

My next visits were to local funeral homes. From their records, I learned that Bingham Hill Cemetery was actually called "Laporte Cemetery" or "Bellvue Cemetery." In fact, it was never called "Bingham Hill Cemetery" until after burials were no longer conducted there. In this book, the three names are used interchangeably. There were no morticians here before 1900, but mortuary records revealed the names of over 40 persons buried at Laporte after 1900. It was a sad discovery as most of them were children. The names of Jacobo Trujillo and Maria Rosa Sanchez turned up; they were two who had homemade stones. I found records for " Baby Jesse" and "Freddie." I learned that 2-2-4 after a name meant the person lived two years, two months and four days.

At the public library, I read all the material previously written about the cemetery in the vertical files of the local history room. My favorite article was in the *Coloradoan* (8/16/1959, page 14b), by Mrs. Art (Theresa) Brookman and entitled "Forgotten Old-Timers Rest in Weedy Laporte Cemetery." Then I went to the old newspapers and microfilm to look for burials never mentioned in any articles. My first success was an 1894 obituary about the man buried under the pathetic "C.W. Howell" stone. Newspaper research took hundreds of hours, but slowly my list of names grew.

Wayne Sundberg loaned his copies of early newspapers which weren't available at the library, and I found a few more death notices. (I also learned a good deal of local history, from 1899 to 1911, and was delighted to follow the coming and going of an early minister of the First Christian Church in Fort Collins, Charles William Dean. He is the great-grandfather of my four oldest children.)

Research was frustrating because the place of burial was often carelessly omitted in mortuary records and newspapers. From the 1885 obituary of Ida McNally, one would assume she had been buried near her home at North Park; it was her family who knew she was buried here at Laporte. Deaths of children and Hispanics were often not mentioned at all in newspapers and it was difficult to corroborate information gathered from other sources.

For background, I read Watrous (5) who never mentioned the Laporte cemetery, but wrote about John Provost and other early Laporte families. It should be noted that I use terms such as "squaw" and "half breed" as they were used in Watrous and early newspapers.

Baptism records at St. Joseph's and Holy Family Catholic Churches had information about some children. The old coroner's book in the county clerk's office yielded information about an 1890 suicide. A lot of time was spent tracking down false leads; for each name in this book, there were several others whom I found to be buried elsewhere or did not find at all.

By making innumerable telephone calls, writing letters, knocking on doors and asking an embarrassing number of questions, I located brothers and sisters, sons and daughters, parents, grandchildren, great- and great-great grandchildren of the deceased, and the best information came from them. For one thing, the pervasive poverty and racism of the times emerged from these conversations. Bingham Hill was often chosen because there was no charge for a gravesite. Burials without clergy were common, sometimes because of real or perceived prejudice from some churches.

I was astonished at the clarity of people's memories. Clara Rodgers described the clothes her sisters and brother wore to their graves 77 years earlier; I learned what disease killed them and the bitterness that grew when the family was not allowed in the cemetery to visit the graves after 1942. Eva Martinez remembered a 1913 funeral as if it were yesterday.

I was pleased to find so many keepers of family records. Margaret Isaac has worked on her family's genealogy since 1937 and knew about the Laporte burials of her relatives in the 1870s. Dan Martinez, Adele Treis, Stella Gallegos and Judy Hall are experts on their family trees. Letters came from Kansas and California residents who had records of Laporte burials of people I'd never heard of.

Many relatives of the deceased are mentioned, especially if they are still living near this area, in order to illustrate the continuity of certain families. However, this cemetery investigation was not meant to be genealogy and not everyone is listed. Stories of the descendants of Jennie McGaa Brown, Don Vigil, or Acacio Trujillo would fill three books. Penniless as some of these men and women might have been, they were affluent in the eyes of a population geneticist (such as my husband) who sees success in terms of gene survival.

Has there been community interest? In 1990, it took only three months to raise $2200 needed to buy a set of huge granite stones and have every known buried person's name engraved. In 1996, $800 was quickly gathered to replace the cracked marble tombstone of Alphonse LaRocque. Anonymous donors paid for four small granite stones in early 1998. Boy Scout projects are precious and long-lasting. Yes, people care, and most understand the obligation of remembering the dead. In the 1990s, burials are again taking place, which has created even more community interest.

There are problems. There has been some vandalism and a neighbor who closed off the historic roadway into the cemetery in 1994 has made visits impossible for those who cannot walk the path. The County Parks Department quit mowing because of this lack of access.

4

After ten years, with spurts of thorough and meticulous investigation, even with a timid query on the Internet, one would think I have finally found everyone. I doubt it. I suspect and hope that even more names will be discovered in records and in family Bibles and that others will take up the search for the identities of those buried in the Bingham Hill Cemetery.

John Provost and his Sioux wife, Mary (White Owl), built and lived in this log cabin from 1859 to 1878. Rowland Herring's family occupied the cabin from 1887 until 1910, when it was replaced with a frame mail-order house. (Photo taken circa 1898; loaned by Irving Garbutt of Casper, Wyoming.) Location: 2405 N. Overland Trail.

John Provost and his second wife Virginie, ran the old Laporte Stage Station as a hotel and restaurant from 1879 until his death in 1904. Location: 2601 N. Overland Trail. Both are buried at Grandview Cemetery in Fort Collins.

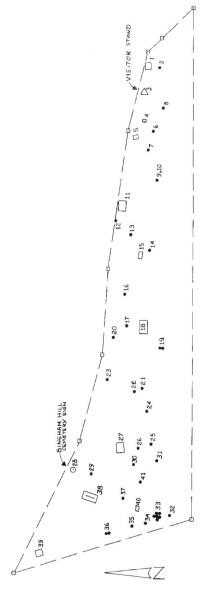

BINGHAM HILL CEMETERY

CEMETERY IS LOCATED IN NORTH½ SECTION 32,
T8N, R69W.

▢ ENCLOSURE FENCE ANGLE POINTS.

——— FENCE.

● GRAVESITE LOCATION WITH KNOWN NAME.

NUMBERS ARE CROSS INDEXED TO KNOWN
GRAVESITES + CEMETERY LANDMARKS.

SURVEYED BY M.R. ELLIOTT USING PLANETABLE
and ALIDADE METHODS, MARCH 1990.

SCALE: 1" = 50 FT., Before Publication

VISITOR STAND

BINGHAM HILL
CEMETERY SIGN

N

6

SURVEYOR'S LEGEND

1. Provost lot
2. Spragg lot
3. Visitor stand
4. DAR marker
5. Jennie Brown with picket fence
6. Alphonse LaRocque
7. C.W. Howell (father)
8. Bill Howell (son)
9. Bill Alcorn
10. Manuelita M. Gonzales
11. Bingham Lot
12. Johnny Thomas
13. Cora Flowers
14. Winifred Farrar
15. Picket fence (4' x 6')
16. A.T.W. & L.D.R.
17. Ida B. Keller (tall obelisk)
18. Picket fence (10' x 12')
19. Sanchez (stone) and Martinez (cross)
20. D.C.A on a rock
21. Baby Garcia, wood cross
22. Queenie Maud Adams
23. Ida May Snuffin
24. Aragon baby
25. Yockey and Pile
26. Yockey
27. Fenced lot (9' x 11')
28. BINGHAM HILL CEMETERY sign
29. Julia Learn
30. L.W.
31. Mrs. Jones
32. L. Holley
33. 6 Robertsons
34. Marble Baby, Mrs. Herrera
35. Don Vigil
36. Acacio Trujillo, Jacobo Trujillo
37. Libbie Garland
38. Memorial Marker
39. Wood storage shed, 8' x 8'
40. Picket fence, (3.5' x 6')
41. Base only; Nellie Land
    marble stone stolen, 1998

North

GUIDE TO THE CEMETERY
AND SOME THINGS TO LOOK FOR

FROM THE POST OFFICE IN LAPORTE, drive south on Overland Trail for 6/10 mile to County Road 50E (more commonly known as Bingham Hill Road). Turn right (west), and drive a little over 1/10 mile. You will pass five houses on the right and cross over two irrigation ditches. Pull off the road by a mailbox with 3605 on its side. There is no parking lot.

You will see a walk-through forest service type gate and a small wood sign on a post: BINGHAM HILL CEMETERY PATH. Follow the path along the west side of the irrigation ditch for about 100 yards to enter the east end of the cemetery. You will pass an apple tree, a survivor from the Herring orchards, and one old cottonwood which measures 23 1/2 feet in circumference. In the summer, there may be mosquitos. Because of cacti in the cemetery and the possibility of irrigation water on the path, do not wear sandals.

In days past, if walking 100 yards was a problem, farmer Roy Juhl would let you drive through his yard to the west end of the cemetery. At present, this is not allowed.

Try to picture the site as it was in the early 1860s when Provost buried his children. Dismiss the huge metal shed west of the cemetery and the irrigation ditches from your mind. Even Bingham Hill Road didn't exist until 1870. No houses were visible except Provost's log home/roadhouse which sat where our house is now – the nearest white house to the northeast – and another log cabin just a few yards below the ditches near Bingham Hill Road, which was possibly Ben Claymore's home. Overland Trail was a dirt road. Travelers on horseback or on foot or in wagons drawn by oxen or horses often stayed to enjoy the hospitality of Provost and Claymore.

To the northwest, the view of the Cache la Poudre River, the foothills and the Bellvue Fold (aka Goat Hill) is especially lovely at sunset. Small, purple iris begin to bloom in late March and the large irises in April and May. Several varieties of wild flowers bloom in the cemetery throughout the spring.

If the cemetery looks less than two acres, you are right. In 1879, two acres were given by Provost and Claymore to be used as a burying place for the dead, but a 1998 survey by Mike Elliott indicates only 1.279 acres are left.

Once in the cemetery, the first prominent gravesite you will notice is the enclosed lot with the oldest headstones in Larimer County. John Provost and his Indian wife buried two children in 1862 and 1866. From their home, they could see the graves on the knoll. Provost names and dates were copied onto granite so the information will be available when the sandstones are no longer legible.

North of the Provost lot are deep cuts taken by two irrigation companies. The closer one is the New Mercer Ditch and the other is the Larimer #2. A strip of land was condemned (June 19, 1883) for the "Fort Collins Water Works Canal" (later Larimer #2 Canal) in order to bring drinking water to Fort Collins. It is unknown exactly when the Mercer was dug, but it was some time before 1880. Several graves in the cemetery were demolished during construction or enlargement of the Mercer ditch and this is mentioned again in the chapter on vandalism.

A visitor stand was built by a Boy Scout; please sign your name in the visitors' book. If no paper or note book is present, it means some rascal stole it again; leave the date, your name, and home town on a piece of your own paper. Between 1987 and 1998, over 10,000 people signed in; over 50,000 people signed in by 2015, and as you do so, you become a part of history. Make comments if you wish, especially if you are related to anyone buried here. Signatures are picked up periodically and kept at our house.

Use the surveyor's sketch and legend at the beginning of this chapter to find each marked stone or structure. As you walk around, refer to "Markers Present in 1998," read each inscription, and then about the person. Some people have little information; others have pages of history.

Next to Provost's lot is a headstone for Abner and Florence Spragg of Bellvue. Near them is a circle of rocks indicating an unknown child's grave. A new bright white marble replica of Alphonse LaRocque's cracked 1877 tombstone was put in place in 1996. LaRocque was one of the first French Canadians who settled along the river. North of LaRocque lies his wife's daughter, Jennie McGaa Brown, one of the most visited grave sites in the cemetery.

Everywhere are small red sandstone markers. Some were set by individuals at the burials of their loved ones and others were placed by some kind souls, probably the Josefsons from Bellvue (2). Whether Josefsons or other men set the stones at unmarked graves, it was an admirable thing to do, for the majority of bodies in the cemetery are accounted for in this way.

Had you visited the cemetery in 1995, you would have seen hundreds of little red survey flags. A dowser had walked the cemetery and detected some 200 graves, most of which had no markers at all! The flags were later pulled as they interfered with mowing.

Nine sandstone markers have names carved by hand: C.W. Howell, J. Thomas, A.T.W., L.D.R., L.W., Jacobo Trujillo, Ma. R. Elvinia Sanchez, L. Holley, and Mrs. Jones. Try to find all these stones. We know the identity of some and think we know who is under others, but still have no clue as to who L. Holley was.

Four new granite markers in the cemetery are for C.W Howell, Bill Howell, Acacio Trujillo, and Mary Inez Pacheco.

Dips in the earth might be coffins that were removed or large coffins which collapsed.

On the north edge of the cemetery, a concrete fence surrounds six graves of Bingham family members. Ten feet west along the ditch bank is the small sandstone marker of 'J. Thomas' under which lie the rather scrambled bones of a red-headed young man.

Here and there is a sandstone block with a triangular hole in the middle. These had been fitted with spikes onto which posts were attached so the posts for fences around graves wouldn't rot in the ground. Unfortunately, fires set by volunteers to burn weeds destroyed most of the posts. You can still see a few burnt stubs. With a metal detector you can find square nails used long ago; these were for fences built around graves since sheep and cattle often grazed in the cemetery.

A few of the generic sandstone markers have half a drill hole on one side. Such holes were drilled in order to place dynamite deep into rock at quarries.

Old-timers in Laporte remember playing as kids in the apple and plum orchards and amongst the gravestones. During the Rowland Herring years, from the 1880s to the 1940s, there were more gravestones, both in the cemetery and between the cemetery and Bingham Hill Road.

There is a high concentration of small children on the west end, near Don Vigil's stone. At least 15 of Vigil's grandbabies were buried near him as were Collamer and Pacheco babies.

South of Vigil are four Robertson stones; next to them are two more unmarked Robertson children and Baby Williams.

To the northwest is the large memorial stone with the names of everyone known buried here at the time it was made – May 12, 1990. North of it is a storage shed that was never used. (See chapter on volunteers.)

A word of advice from an old cemetery watcher: see to it that you have a permanent headstone. It will be a valuable gift to your descendants. Individuals drive here from as far as California to touch Jenny McGaa Brown's grave, and they sure wouldn't know where it is without a headstone. Over 100 years after Barbara Bingham died, family members plant tulips on her grave. People touch their relative's name on the memorial stone. Strangers call and ask where so-and-so's tombstone is and are distressed to learn there isn't one. If it weren't extremely important to find and feel and touch their roots, people wouldn't do it. So get buried in a homemade pine coffin if money is scarce, but spend money on a marker!

Lastly, feel free to adopt a grave and care for it. Pull some weeds, pick up a cigarette butt, plant some flowers, say a prayer, replace a ruined headstone, fix something. Visit often, rest on the benches. Wander around. Don't forget to sign in. If weeds and brush take over again, call your county commissioners and inform them that an important spiritual and historic site needs their support.

MARKERS PRESENT IN 1998

The following headstones are present in 1998. All can be located by following the survey. Listed first are 24 professional markers in approximate chronological order according to dates of death. Following them are nine hand-carved harder-to-find stones. No burial dates are on the homemade stones, but dates for four have been ascertained from other records.

Next listed are the 15 stones and wood markers new in the cemetery since 1985—some are for people who died 100 years ago; others for people who recently were buried there. Three more headstones are on their way from the Veterans Administration.

Last to be documented are two large memorial stones.

Exact spelling, punctuation and capitalization on each headstone has been reprinted here. Notations describe whether each stone is sandstone, marble, or granite, if there is a footstone present and if the stone is broken. There is a photograph of each tombstone in the chapter of photographs.

1860s

On the east end of the cemetery, on the edge of the Mercer ditch, is an enclosure made of large sandstone blocks (8' x 16'; approximately 55 stones, weighing up to 300 lbs. each). A black wrought-iron gate allows entrance. Inside are the **two oldest headstones in Larimer County**.

1. BAZILLE PROVOST Born Feb. 17, 1862. Died Nov. 17, 1862.
2. MARY PROVOST Born June 25, 1854. Died Jan. 22, 1865.
(Both are sandstone; a cross and branches above each name; no footstones.)

A new granite marker, donated by Fort Collins Monument Works, says: REPLICA OF PROVOST INSCRIPTIONS MARY JUNE 25, 1854—JAN. 22, 1865 BAZILLE FEB. 17, 1862—NOV. 17, 1862

1870s (and one 1890)

The next five headstones are in one enclosure (12' x 12') with cement walls. They each have a footstone.

3. JULILA DENNIS BORN May 26th, 1838 DIED. Jan' 21st 1873 IN HEAVEN TO REST (Sandstone has a crack but is upright. Footstone close to headstone, against concrete wall.)

13

4. JOHN E. DENNES. BORN. JAN' 20 1873 DIED. SEPT'13 1873
(Sandstone, also a sandstone footstone.)

5. MARY IDA, DAUGHTER OF L.D. & H. TURNER, DIED APR. 19,
1876 AGED 3yrs. 6ms. 12ds. Gone to the spirit land. (Marble, sleeping
lamb engraved at the top; stone fallen and lower fourth crumbled in
1998. Marble footstone: "M.I.T.")

6. BARBARA A. BINGHAM DIED Sep. 30 1876. AGED 19 YEARS
AND 6 MONTHS. (Etched leaves on sandstone; footstone: B.B.)

7. JOHN W. THARP DIED July 11, 1890, AGED 49 Yrs. 9 Mo's. 24 Dys.
(Marble headstone, piece of rock for footstone.)

8. ALPHONSE LAROCQUE DIED Nov. 15, 1877, AGED 59 YEARS.
(Cross above his name. White marble. Three cracks, lying on ground, in
concrete. Footstone, initialed "A.L." standing 10 feet east of the headstone.
Also a duplicate; see "Stones placed after 1987.")

9. Jennie Brown. Died Feb. 13. 1878. Aged 35 (?) Years.
(Slanted cross above her name which is in lower case letters. Sandstone,
one crack, repaired, standing upright. Footstone. Surrounded by white
picket fence, 5′ x 8′)

1880s and 1890s

10. CORA daughter of T.W. & A. FLOWERS, DIED (?) AGE 5 WEEKS
(Headstone is white, small, broken marble, set in concrete; printing on
west side; unable to read date; marble footstone is unbroken, 4 feet east
of headstone: "C.F.")

11. IDA B. Dau. of A.J. AND S.A. KELLER DIED Mar. 29, 1882, Aged
19 Yrs. 9 Ms. 27 Ds. Not dead but sleepeth (Engraving of an open Bible;
white marble obelisk is over 7 feet tall and considered the most beautiful
in the cemetery. Ornament on top is loose. Footstone leaning against
headstone engraved: "I.B.K.")

12. HERE RESTS A BELOVED WIFE IDA MAY wife of A.C. SNU....
DIED APR. 6, 1884 AGED 22 YEARS Safe in the arms of Jesus
(Clasping hands engraved in marble; "I.M.S" footstone standing 7
feet east of headstone. Stone is for Ida May Snuffin.)

13. QUEENIE MAUD INFANT DAUGHTER OF J.Q. & D.M. ADAMS DIED JUNE 7. 1884. Also: "Safely..?..arms of Jesus" at the bottom. (Marble stone, broken and repaired; Footstone: "Q.M.A.")

14. NELLIE. J. dau. of B.R. & C.E. LAND. DIED June, 16. 1888, AGED 7 Yrs 8 Mos & 20 Ds (Marble; this stone and its base were stolen in 1998; perhaps someone will buy a new one.)

15. EVERET YOCKEY, DIED Sep. 27, 1889; AGED 4 Yrs. 5 M's. 8 D'ys. Too good for earth, God called him home. STARLIN & HOLMES FT. COLLINS (Marble)

16. SARAH WIFE OF DAVID YOCKEY DIED Dec. 28, 1890 AGED 42 Yrs. Gone but not forgotten.
16a. JOSEPHINE A. WIFE OF J. PILE, Dau. of D. & S. YOCKEY. DIED Jan. 5, 1891; AGED 20 years She died as she lived, Trusting in God (Sarah and her adult daughter died 8 days apart; engravings are on opposite sides of one gray marble stone decorated on both sides with flowers and leaves. Also STARLIN & HOLMES, FT. COLLINS)

17. OUR DARLING LIBBIE A. GARLAND DIED Jan. 28, 1890 AGED 17 Yrs. 5 M's. 28 D's. (A beautiful deeply etched hand holds a rose. Marble, broken. On the front: STARLIN & HOLMES)

After 1900

The next four markers are home-made by the brother of the children, but almost professional in appearance. They are of some concrete composition and lie on the far west end of the cemetery.
18. ESTHER ROBERTSON 1904-1911 (plus a cross)
19. GUY D. ROBERTSON 1907-1911 (plus a cross)
20. MARGARET ROBERTSON 1909-1911 (plus a cross)
21. E.A.E. ROBERTSON MOTHER 1853-1916

22. DON VIGIL (Small, granite; there was also a concrete cross with a 13″ silver crucifix attached. Crucifix was on the casket of Ed Vigil's mother, Ramona, and was for all the Vigils buried at Bingham Hill. Concrete crumbled and crucifix was stolen during the summer of 1997; family planning repairs in 1998.)

23. Sleeping baby on a blanket in a sea shell (Marble, several breaks, repaired and upright in 1998; space for a nameplate which is missing. Tombstone is for Crisanta Pacheco Herrera, a midwife.)

24. SPRAGG FLORENCE 1850-1933 ABNER 1847-1923 (A rectangle of marble, set in concrete. Two footstones broken off and stolen around 1990.)

Hand-Carved on Small Red Sandstone Markers
25. HOLLEY. L. L.H. on top of stone. (Southwest corner of cemetery.)

26. J. THOMAS (On ditch edge, 10 feet west of Bingham lot. Sandstone footstone east of headstone.)

27. A.T.W. (East of tall Keller stone; oval of stones around grave.)

28. L.D.R. (Next to A.T.W.)

29. MRS. JONES (Farthest stone straight south of BINGHAM HILL CEMETERY sign; printing on west side; stone shows drill hole for dynamite.)

30. L.W. (Possibly for Lloyd Willis; west of Everet Yockey stone.)

31. C.W. HOWELL (On path before reaching Bingham lot, letters very hard to see; new granite stone placed in 1998.)

32. Ma.R.ELVinia SaNcheZ (Cross above her name; southwest of largest picket fence; footstone with a cross, 6 feet west of headstone.)

33. JACOBO TRUJILLO (Cross—which looks like a kite—and name almost invisible; two stones north of Don Vigil.)

Placed in Cemetery After 1985
34. JULIA LEARN 1895-1985 (Small granite stone near the tall BINGHAM HILL CEMETERY sign; cremains buried.)

35. WINIFRED FARRAR 1885-1891 (Granite, set on concrete; purchased in 1988 by Winifred's niece, Esther Moore; location according to her memory.)

36. MARIA MARTINEZ 3-25-1912 9-17-1913 (Oak cross made in 1990 by Mike Sharpe, father of three Rainbow Riders 4-H members; next to Maria Rosa Sanchez stone.)

37. BABY GIRL GARCIA (Wood cross, placed by her brother in 1990.)

38. INFANT DAUGHTER OF MARTIN AND LOUISE ARAGON MAY 30, 1935 (Granite, set in concrete; placed by Aragons about 1990.)

39. ALPHONSE LAROCQUE DIED Nov. 15, 1877, AGED 59 YEARS (Marble, duplicate of cracked 1877 original, placed in cemetery July 1996. See chapter on volunteers.)

The next four stones are granite, each 12″ x 11″ x 4″, and were placed in the cemetery in April, 1998.

40. CHARLES W. HOWELL 1839 1894 (plus wheat stalk; granite, placed near original stone which says only "C.W. Howell."

41. BILL HOWELL JAN. 30, 1864 DEC. 30, 1939 (Placed at site pointed out by Fred Heustis, who was at his funeral.)

42. ACACIO TRUJILLO JAN. l, 1865 JULY 16, 1924 (Plus cross; placed on west end, near his son, Jacobo Trujillo.)

43. MARY INEZ PACHECO DEC. 24, 1942 JAN. 25, 1943 (Plus cross and flower, placed near Don Vigil.)

44. BELOVED MOTHER MANUELITA M. GONZALES NOV. 10, 1910 JAN. 28, 1993 (Also cross and praying hands, gray granite. East end of cemetery; cremains buried.)

45. Statue of Blessed Virgin for Bill Alcorn (V.A. granite stone will arrive in 1998; cremains buried.)

46. Frances VerStratten JULY 6, 1920 JAN. 5, 1996 (Placed July 1996; cremains buried.)

47. D.C.A. (On a small rock, for Danny Allen; cremains spread on earth.)

48. Not arrived yet. VA marker for Leroy Vigil. Will be placed near Don Vigil. Not arrived yet. VA marker for Cecil Neth.

49. DEDICATED TO THE MEMORY OF DONACIANO VIGIL AND CRISANTA HERRERA ALONG WITH THE GRANDCHILDREN OF DON AND GREAT-GRANDCHILDREN OF CRISANTA 1998. The above inscription on a granite stone was placed by the Vigil family in the cemetery on Memorial Day, 1998. A cement cross with a new crucifix to replace the stolen one was also placed near the grave of Don Vigil.

Following are two memorial stones for everyone in the cemetery:

50. DAR marker, near east entrance: LEST WE FORGET. BINGHAM HILL HISTORIC CEMETERY 1862 RESERVED BY JOHN B. PROVOST AND BEN CLAYMORE (AKA L.B. LESSERT) 1879 DEDICATED IN MEMORY OF ALL THOSE KNOWN AND UNKNOWN BURIED HERE. PLACED HERE BY CACHE LA POUDRE CHAPTER OF THE DAUGHTERS OF THE AMERICAN REVOLUTION THROUGH THE EFFORTS OF ROSE L. BRINKS AND THE AID OF FRIENDS 1987 (3.8' tall, l.2' wide, rose granite, initiated and designed by Josephine Clements.)

51. Large memorial marker, northwest section of cemetery, two light gray granite slabs (each 3.8' x 3'), names on both sides. Left stone begins: OUR LOVE TO THESE PIONEERS AND ANY OTHERS WHO MAY HAVE DIED ALONE, FORGOTTEN, UNLOVED AND UNMOURNED. LORD, GIVE THEM YOUR LASTING PEACE (followed by 62 names). The right-hand stone begins: BLESS THESE CHILDREN AND ANY OTHERS BURIED HERE (followed by 73 names). The stone is landscaped in a 9' x 16' lot. Refer to chapter on volunteers for list of donors.

Additional names which should be on the stone: William Ouderkirk, Crawford Shaffer, Samuel Harrison Clark, Manuelita Gonzales, Frances VerStratten, Danny Allen, Leroy Vigil and Cecil Neth.

Names which should not have been on the stone: Bill Artikurk (misspelled) and Ethel Irene Swinscoe (buried elsewhere).

In addition to the above markers there are five white fenced lots. Three are of pickets (6' x 4', 10' x 12', and 6' x 3.3') and one is of 2 x 4s (11' x 9'). These four surround burial spaces with no tombstones, although old-timers said they had stones in the past. A newly built fifth fence (5' x 8') is of pickets, and surrounds Jennie Brown's stone.

52. BINGHAM HILL CEMETERY SIGN, white with black letters, 10' x 2' about 6' off the ground on 2 posts.

LIST OF PERSONS BURIED
BETWEEN 1862 and 1900
+ indicates a headstone (P) indicates a photograph

1. Bazille Provost +
2. Mary Provost +
3. Janis child
4. Sarah Jane Hand Hardin
5. Susan Isabelle Hardin
6. Crawford Shaffer (P)
7. Julila Spirlock Dennis +
8. John E. Dennes +
9. Mary Ida Turner +
10. Barbara A. Bingham + (P)
11. John W. Tharp +
12. John Thomas + (P)
13. Alphonse LaRocque +
14. Jennie (McGaa) Brown + (P?)
15. John McGaa
16. Cora Flowers +
17. Mildred Pennock
18. James Mattison
19. Ida B. Keller +
20. Fredrick Henry McNally
21. Ida Louise McNally (P)
22. Baby Boy Nugent
23. Ida May Snuffin +
24. Queenie Maud Adams +
25. Hugh McBride, Jr.
26. Willie Curtis
27. Johnny Meyers
28. Tousley Infant
29. Anna Howell Williams + ?
30. Charles W. Howell +
31. Wylie Infant
32. Charles Luther Gordon
33. Nellie J. Land +
34. Everet Yockey +
35. Sarah Yockey +
36. Josephine Yockey Pile +
37. Libbie A. Garland +
38. A.A. Robinson
39. Winifred Farrar +
40. Ida Esther Lasley
41. Collamer Infant
42. Collamer Infant
43. Laura Malaby
44. Charlie Brooks
45. Lester Brooks

46. Thomas Jess Honnold
47. Von Vihl Infant
48. Walter Thomas
49. Samuel Harrison Clark
50. Mrs. Jones +
51. Virginia Murray Wombacher
52. Arthur Edward Wombacher
53. Cora Salisbury
54. Wesley Allen Shipp
55. William Sherman Ouderkirk (P)
56. Mrs. Macklin
57. Milton Lewis
58. Lloyd Raynor + ?
59. Henry P. Blevins
60. Lloyd Willis + ?
61. George Thomas Currey
62. Barkley Relatives

Stones for Unknown People
63. L.D.R. +
64. A.T.W. +
65. L. W. +
66. L. Holley +

Persons buried and later moved
+ indicates a Marker at Grandview
1. Lathrop L. Hills (+ in Highland, Kansas)
2. John R. McBride +
3. Patrick McBride +
4. Mary Jane McKillop McBride +
5. Agnes McBride
6. Elizabeth N. Vandewark +
7. Elizabeth Vandewark +
8. George Franklin Pennock +
9. Elizabeth Ella Pennock +
10. Ida Lesher +
11. Anna Lesher +
12. Maggie Lesher +
13. Herring Infant Girl
14. Cy Crawford (to ?)
15. A.J. Wylie (to Virginia)
16. Elizabeth Flowers +
17. Jacob Flowers +

19

INFORMATION ABOUT PERSONS
BURIED BEFORE 1900

Names and numbers correspond to those listed on the previous page. Persons are arranged chronologically according to date of death except when two or more from one family are involved; then they are placed together.

The following 83 persons have 25 old headstones and three new headstones (placed after 1987) at the Laporte cemetery, five at Grandview Cemetery in Fort Collins and one at Highland, Kansas.

> *+ indicates presence of a headstone in 1998*
> (P) *indicates photo of person is in book*

The following two children are buried in one lot.

1. **Bazille Provost** + Died November 17, 1862 Age 9 months

Bazille was the fourth of nine children born to Jean (John) Baptiste Provost and his Oglala Sioux (or Cheyenne) wife, White Owl, also known as Mary. He was born on February 17, 1862, four years after his parents settled along the Cache la Poudre River; he lived only one summer and died when he was nine months old. His birthplace was likely the log house which his father built around 1859 and in which the family lived until 1878 or 1879.

Cause of death is not known. The knoll south of the house on the 160 acres of land that John Provost had claimed was a lovely and logical place to bury the child. His parents could see his grave from their house, just as I can see it from mine today. As far as we know, Bazille Provost's was the first burial in what is now known as the Bingham Hill Cemetery.

He has a sandstone marker with his name, birth and death dates. A granite replica was placed alongside it in 1988 because the dates were becoming difficult to read.

Bazille Provost has the distinction of having the oldest known gravestone in Larimer County, Colorado.

2. **Mary Provost** + Died January 22, 1865 Age 10 1/2 years

Mary was born June 25, 1854, her parents' oldest child. She was four or five years old when the family came to the Cache la Poudre. At the time of her death, she had several little brothers—Johnny, Billy and

Antoine for sure, and perhaps others, but birth dates for several brothers are uncertain. She was ten years old during the big flood of 1864 when her father made a small fortune ferrying men, horses, and wagons across the Poudre (5) and she died the next winter. Cause of death is not known.

Her burial was described as follows: "The late Eliza Gardener reported in 1936 that her father, Samuel Bingham, made the casket for Mary Provost and that her mother prepared the body for burial. Mary had all her possessions buried with her according to Sioux tradition and her body had to be removed and rearranged several times in order to include everything" (2).

Mary, too, was given a sandstone headstone similar in size and shape to her brother's. A fence of large sandstone blocks was built around the graves, and a wrought-iron gate installed. Years later, the block enclosure was in disarray; ten or more of the heavy blocks were in the New Mercer Ditch. In 1987, we pulled them up and rebuilt the enclosure as best we could, and a volunteer made a new gate.

Digressions are tempting but dangerous. If I don't stick with information regarding only those individuals who are actually buried in the cemetery, this book would never end. The Provost family, however, is an exception. Not only did John Provost start the cemetery with the burial of two of his children in the 1860s (unless it had been an Indian burial ground earlier), and 15 years later donate the site to the community, but he stayed in Laporte until his death in 1904, unlike any of the other French settlers. And whereas neighbor Antoine Janis has a lot written about him, and Ben Claymore's life is covered in a book by Irma Miller (*The Lesserts aka Claymore and Their People*), there simply wasn't much known about John Provost except what is in the biography in Ansel Watrous' 1911 *History of Larimer County*. Nothing was known about Provost's wife and children after they left Laporte.

If the reader is not interested in the Provosts, skip to the next name on the list.

The Provost family history which I uncovered is divided into four parts: (a) their married life in Laporte from 1859 to their separation around 1872, (b) their adult children's lives, (c) John's life after 1878 in Laporte and (d) Mary's life after 1878 on the reservation.

John and Mary Provost in Laporte. Provost was born in Montreal July 4, 1822, and that is about all that is known about his early background.

His mother's name was Mary (4a) but even the Provost Genealogical Society could not, or would not, research his parents or siblings because there were so many Jean Baptiste Provosts in Montreal. Little is known of his youth before he came to Colorado except that he was connected to the Northwestern Fur Company, and was often referred to as one of the "old French trappers."

The Provosts had come from Fort Laramie around 1859 with other French Canadian/Indian couples to found a town which they called Colona, and later, downstream a bit, La Porte. They may have come via Miravalle City, west of Loveland, as Provost is listed there in the 1860 census as "born in Canada, age 36, a trader, three children."

Provost's wife, White Owl, renamed Mary, was born between 1836 and 1839 and was about 15 years younger than he. Her brother sold her to John Provost when she was about 16 (4a). They were married about 1854 in the "Indian style," which means no governmental or church record exists. Yet, some records (4a) indicate they were married "Catholic" in "Casa la puta, Colorado," which means "House of Prostitution," so I don't know if someone had a sense of humor, or what.

John Provost and Ben Claymore each owned half-interest in the 160 acre claim south of the Cache la Poudre River and ran a saloon or roadhouse in a log building with dirt floors. It was the same building the Provost family lived in for 20 years and it remained standing for 50 years, until 1910.

One of Provost's early successful enterprises was to run a ferry during the high water of 1864. That flood caused his lucrative army business in liquor to move downriver but at least he made a lot of money ferrying travelers.

He was one of 142 signers of the "Half-Breed Petition" to the U.S. government in 1867, all of whom were "residents of Dakota Territory in the vicinity of Ft. Laramie, and all of whom were heads or members of Indian families." According to the petition, all the men had come to this country under the auspices of the old Northwestern Fur Company which had gone out of business. Therefore all the signers then had to make their living by "...accommodating the overland travel to the mining regions west. Said families and their half-breed children now number on the Platte and Missouri Rivers more than 2000 souls; that construction of the railroad across the plains has so changed business and travel that all ostensible means of support along the North Platte are destroyed."

They asked for 320 acres each, in a "tract of country to be set apart and to be occupied by themselves, their Indian relatives and friends exclusively," along the Missouri and White Earth Rivers (in northeast Nebraska). Other signers with familiar Laporte names were Ben Clement (L.B. Lessert), T.S. Twiss, Jack Jones (Wm. McGaa), Jack Palmer (Palmier?), and Alp. Larvague (Alphonse LaRocque?). The petition apparently came to nothing, for Provost and Claymore and other signers stayed in Laporte.

A glimpse of their busy life would include running the roadhouse and ferry, growing corn, holding travelers' livestock in corrals on the east side of Overland Trail, and logging. According to Watrous, squaws had a weekly dog feast. For the 20 years John and Mary Provost were here, Laporte was a bustling town, and their eight living children probably thrived. Funerals they attended would have been on Provost's land on the hillside which already held the bodies of Bazille and Mary.

All the normalcy changed after Custer's battle on June 25, 1876. Prior to that date, pressure was building from Washington to take the Black Hills from the Sioux so that gold-seekers would be safe. "Hostiles" (any Indian not on a reservation) were ordered rounded up. After several skirmishes, there was no turning back on either side. Dee Brown's *Bury My Heart at Wounded Knee* is required reading for this phase of history.

After Custer's rout, revenge was the key word. On July 22, General Sherman was given power to assume military control of all reservations in Sioux country and to treat the Indians as prisoners of war. All this turmoil must have filtered down to the peaceful Indian wives and their half-breed children in the Cache la Poudre valley. Settlers were coming faster and faster and prejudice from whites probably increased. The squaws had family ties with reservation Indians and though there was apparently not a specific decree ordering the Indians out of Larimer County, perhaps there simply wasn't anything here for them any more. Husbands left with their wives and children and it seems that all the French/Indian Laporte families, including Claymore, Janis, Palmier, the newly widowed Mary LaRocque and others, left more or less together in 1878. They went first to Red Cloud, the Sioux agency at Fort Robinson, Nebraska, and finally to Pine Ridge, South Dakota.

The personal relationship between John and Mary Provost was apparently not good in the mid-1870s, as they were divorced ("Indian style") around 1872 and she had a child by another man with whom she lived for a year or so (4a). John may have taken that child in, as St. Joseph's records refer to her as Ida Provost. But when the migration of families occurred, Mary left, as did her sons and presumably Ida, and John stayed behind with Lizzie, his only living daughter. He was the only squaw man who did not leave Laporte.

This 1878 exodus explains why there are no continuous French-Canadian/ Indian families living in the area today. Their only reminders are the French names of our town and our river—La Porte and Cache la Poudre.

Henry Moore, then of Winnebago, Nebraska, now of Topeka, Kansas, a great-grandson of John Provost, went to the reservation at Pine Ridge in August 1987, looking for clues to his ancestry. He saw my letter in a file asking about Mary Provost and immediately drove to Laporte. He knew as little about the French side of his family as I knew about the Indian side. The agency never sent any information to me, but because Moore is half-Indian and a descendant, he was able to get copies of many documents and he shared what he found. Much of the following was put together from pages of testimony at probate after the deaths of Mary (Provost) Jumper, Lizzie Provost and Oliver Provost. All the information is fascinating; some of it is not pretty.

The Children. Besides the two buried at Bingham Hill, born in 1854 and 1862, John and Mary Provost had seven other children. Their names and approximate birth dates are: John, Jr., (1855), William (1857), Antoine (1863), Charles (July 28, 1864), Oliver (1865), Louis (1869) and Lizzie (1873). Mary also had a tenth child by another white man around 1876. The last child was usually referred to as Ida Stinking Bear. All the children except Lizzie left Laporte with their mother in 1878, if not sooner.

Dick Baker told me that his father told him that the "Provost boys were mean and the girl ornery and that at least one son was in trouble for horsewhipping someone." As well liked as John Provost was, his children probably weren't the darlings of Laporte, and the community may have breathed a sign of relief when they left.

Serious trouble for the two oldest sons started soon after they arrived at the reservation. On July 24, 1879, William committed suicide because of being shamed in a love affair. Johnny killed the man he thought responsible and in 1881, died in a Michigan prison (8). Details of this tragic affair can be read on page 99 of Watrous' *History of Larimer County*.

Lizzie, Provost's youngest child, apparently stayed in Laporte for a while. A newspaper article (11/8/1883) which listed school students' marks revealed a 96% in writing but a zero in "deportment" for ten-year-old Lizzie Provost. She may have been ornery but was apparently very bright and pretty. Red Feather resident, June Krakel, said her father, John Dexter, remembered a Frenchman (Provost) who had an Indian wife and a very pretty daughter (Lizzie). When he was a teenager Dexter worked for Provost and drove the daughter to town in her father's buggy. Dexter's mother didn't like the idea of his working for a squaw man's family, but jobs were needed. At about 17, Lizzie had a baby who died at 14 days and was buried under the name "Provost" on January 7, 1893, at Grandview Cemetery (7). At some time, Lizzie married William Hall Dixon (Indian style, without clergy or paperwork—also 1990s style), and there is a portrait of them and her father in the local history room of the library. W.H. Dixon in a later marriage became the ancestor of several Fort Collins Dixons. (Debbie Dixon-Dobkins gave a talk about her prolific ancestors at the February 14,1998, meeting of the Pioneer Association in Fort Collins.)

Lizzie's association with Dixon was not just a passing affair; there are several Provost-Dixon family connections revealed in county records. For one thing, Provost's second wife, Virginie, borrowed $800 at 9% interest (3/16/1896) from MaryAnn Dixon, Lizzie's "mother-in-law." A card of thanks in the *Courier* (1/13/1904) to those who aided during the last illness and burial of the late John Provost was signed by Charles Provost, Mrs. Lizzie Dixon, and Wm. Dixon. In his will (10), Provost left his Laporte property to "Lizzie Dixon," and Walter S. Dixon, a brother of William, purchased it from her on October 24, 1904.

After her father's death (1904), Lizzie separated from Dixon and eloped and left town scandalously with Bellvue resident Joseph Pedigo, a married man with several children who were "left in terrible distress" (*Fort Collins Express,* 8/7/1907).

After her brother Oliver's death in 1917, Lizzie Pedigo gave testimony about his heirs. She said that she had been taking care of Oliver's 14-year-old son Alfred for six years and that "I don't want the boy taken from me." Many years later, probate papers at the time of Lizzie's death (1935) state that there was evidence that the decedent never married but co-habited at various times with J.W. Pedigo, a Baker, Ray Mayfield, and a Lawrie (or Lawres), all non-Indian (4a). Her probate papers didn't even mention Dixon! Like Pedigo, Mayfield had a wife—Elizabeth Janis Mayfield. Though Lizzie (also referred to as Beth or Elizabeth) had no children, her papers state "There is evidence that she bore two children, twins, who predeceased her as small babies" (4a). Grandview records for infant burial at Grandview in Lot K-167-39 indicate that a child born December 24, 1892 was buried January 7 and/or January 11, 1893. A possible explanation is that these were the above-mentioned twins who died four days apart.

Antoine went to New York, died 12/30/1938, leaving a widow, Bridget McGrath Provost and children William, Julia (Soams) and Alfred (4a). Louis was a "wild guy," according to Henry Moore. He died March 9, 1924, leaving children Jack, George D. and Julia (or Ruth or Mamie) (4a). Moore had no further information about them.

Oliver lived to his 40s, then had a piteous death like his two older brothers. Most of the information about him came from reservation testimony after his death (4a). He married Minerva (Minnie) Burgess, an actress and Cheyenne Indian from El Reno, Oklahoma, in November 1900, while they were travelling with the 101 Show (a Texas-based show similar to Buffalo Bill's). Children born were Alfred and Lucy and Minnie had two other children previously—Freddie Carr and a Sadie, last name unknown. According to John Provost's obituary in 1904, Oliver did not come to the funeral, and was living in El Reno at the time. Minnie testified that she and Oliver quarreled in 1911, he left her and the children, and she moved to Los Angeles.

Without divorcing Minnie, Oliver married Mollie Trexler Sherrill, a Fort Peck Indian, about September 13, 1916. He killed her and then himself with a razor on February 13, 1917. According to E.D. Mossman of the Fort Peck Agency:

> No children were born of the marriage, but the woman was reported pregnant at the time of her death. Nobody saw these people die, and [but] there was a witness to his attempting murder. He however, chased his wife from the house with a razor in hand and the witness did not follow. Apparently he caught the woman in the yard as she fell over an object imbedded in the snow and [he] cut her throat. Presumably the woman died first as his body was warm when the officials reached the spot, and the woman was already cold. (4a)

Provost's son, Charles Agustus (Count), married Josephine Smith from Pine Ridge. Count was a Sergeant of the Indian Scouts in the Indian Wars, fought in the Battle of Wounded Knee, rode with the Buffalo Bill shows for years, crossed the Atlantic Ocean 14 times, travelled around Rapid City with Denver McGaa and had at least eight children: Hazel Carlow, John Baptist Provost, Mary Moore (the mother of Henry Moore), Charles, Jr., Gertrude Joles, Grace Paralaska Gonsalves, Harold Quincey, Joe and possibly another infant. He also had a step-daughter, Myrtle.

Ida Stinking Bear, also known as Ida Little Killer, had two sons, Harry and James Jumping Bull. She was remembered by some of the Provost great-grandchildren as wearing a long skirt in which she carried a hidden knife as she walked from one relative's home to another. She apparently never learned to write and used her thumbprint as a "signature."

Of Mary Provost's first ten children, then, two died very young, two committed murder, two committed suicide, one died in jail, four sons led fairly normal lives for half-breeds (if crossing the Atlantic 14 times was considered normal), and the lives of the two girls, Lizzie and Ida Stinking Bear, one can only imagine. There surely is material here for a great western novel or movie. No one can deny that they were and continue to be an interesting family.

John Provost in La Porte. Meanwhile, back in quiet Laporte, retreating from his children's coming and going and the three terrible deaths in 1879, 1881 and 1917, retreating backward in time to 1875, there are several jolly references in the diaries of E.N. Garbutt about going over to Provost's for a drink or a game of cards (4c). On January 23, 1878, John married the widow, Virginie Laurin. He was 55, she was 43. Witnesses were Mag and John Palmier, the daughter and son-in-law of Antoine Janis (10). Records at St. Joseph's Church in Fort Collins (1883) list the bride as Virginie Sabourin Provost, born March 2, 1838. Provost left behind his squaw man status and married an accomplished cook who greatly enhanced his reputation. She also dealt in real estate, buying and selling parcels of land in Laporte (10).

By October 1879, just four months after William committed suicide and John, Jr., was arrested for murder, John Provost sold the farm. It had served him well as a roadhouse, saloon and home for some 20 years. Ben Claymore came back from the reservation to sign off on his half-interest in the land.

John and Virginie bought the no-longer-used stage station across the river to the north and they ran it as a hotel, tavern and restaurant for another 20 years. The building is gone but there is a sign at the site, now 2601 N. Overland Trail, where the building once sat.

Fort Collins papers often carried blurbs about John. The *Courier* called him "Laporte's founding father," and "an excellent host in his restaurant and at turkey shoots in Laporte." Following are some of the other articles I found.

10/2/1879: "Mr. Benj. Claymore, an old timer of LaPorte, but now of Red Cloud Agency, was in town on Tuesday giving the right hand of fellowship to an immense number of warm friends and acquaintances. He will remain here until after election." (Timing of Claymore's visit coincides with the October 4, 1879 sale of the Provost/Claymore farm. After 1879, all references to John's place of business is that north of the river; Rowland Herring moved into Provost's old home south of the river.)

4/29/1880: "We are pleased to learn that Uncle John Provost, of Laporte, has concluded to throw open his house this season to the traveling public. Mr. Provost's hotel is situated at the gateway to the mountains on the North Park Road in the little village of LaPorte, four miles and a half west of Collins. Mr. Provost is known from one end of Colorado to the other as a genial, warm hearted gentleman, and all persons favoring him with their patronage may expect right royal treatment."

5/13/1880: "LaPort Hotel (headline) Mr. John B. Provost, one of the 'old timers' of Colorado and a much esteemed gentleman has opened a hotel at LaPorte for the accommodation of the traveling public. Sample room, at all times supplied with choice liquors and cigars. Hitch your horse, stranger, and come in."

6/30/1881: "Uncle John Provost's hotel at LaPorte is growing in popularity every day. No one passes LaPorte without stopping to shake hands with the genial proprietor."

On Christmas Eve, 1883, many Fort Collins residents attended a ball at John Provost's hotel. From Cheryl Miller's *Christmas in Early Fort Collins: 1866-1910* "...the stable connected with the hotel was filled with rigs from here and the surrounding country...many indeed did not get back to Collins until after 5 o'clock."

8/4/1881: "Uncle Jno. B. Provost keeps one of the most pleasant and home-like taverns that can be found along the backbone of the continent from Alaska to Cape Horn, and any one that stops with him once will never fail to stop again."

9/1/1881: "Uncle Jno. Provost is the proprietor of that pleasant resort at LaPorte where he has lived since the earliest settlement of northern Colorado. He was there when town lots in LaPorte were more valuable than lots in Denver and he remembers when the Poudre was nothing but a small creek."

1/31/1884: "It is needless of course to state that the dance at John Provost's last Wed. night was a pleasant affair. How could it be otherwise with 30 jolly young couples gathered to make it such."

Provost was apparently cheerful, but not saintly. *Daily Express,* 3/10/1884: "John Provost pleaded guilty to the charges of having sold liquor on election day and on Sunday, for which he had been indicted, and was fined $30 and costs in each case."

John and Virginie "divorced" (*Express,* 3/19/1885): "We the undersigned have this day severed our marital relations for the mutual benefit of both parties. All debts owing to either party will be paid by Mrs. Virginia Provost and all debts due either party must be paid to her. Signed: John B. Provost and Virginia Provost, Laporte, Colo., March 17, 1885."

They apparently weren't separated long, since their names were soon in the newspapers as a team and her role as a hostess bragged about. In fact, there was a lengthy front-page article in the *Express* on 5/22/1886. Several lines are printed here to illustrate what a Fort Collins editor thought of 1886 Laporte and also in the slim hope that some reader might own one of the souvenir menus mentioned.

FESTIVE GOURMANDS
An Enjoyable Little Dinner Served at Provosts Last Sunday

It was along in the forties that the name of Jean Provost began to get a reputation as being a host worth knowing for it was then that Laporte was swelled with pride at its own importance. It was then an important place indeed, for it was one of the principal stopping places and stage stations between the Missouri and the Elderado. Jean Provost, then as now, kept the little roadside inn that stands there today, and when the big overland stage with its six tired horses and its load of hungry passengers, drew up at the door where Jean was ready to greet them, it was a bustling, busy place. During the rush of overland travel, Laporte was a good sized place, but when by degrees the railroad began to crawl westward, its occupation was gone and it settled down for sleep which for years past it has evidently been enjoying, for surely there is very little to disturb it.

On Sunday last there was a small and select dinner party which will be long remembered by the participants, for it was an exceedingly joyful affair both in the matter of bodily and mental refreshment. It is well known by the knowing ones, and lovers of good things are never long in finding out where good things may be had—that when Madame Provost likes she can get up an excellent dinner.

(The meal had 15 items, seven using guests' names: Consumme a la Bruton, Sauce au Crafts, etc.) Among those present were George Scott

29

of North Park, Frank Brannan of Livermore, Hugh McDonald, Frank Rockford, J.H. Shibley, H.A Crafts and George Bruton. The menus each bore a pen and ink sketch caricature of those present and the inscription: Hotel Provost, Laporte Colorado, May 16, 1886.

What a collector's item one of those menus would be! The 1886 description of Laporte as a has-been town is classic. There are errors— Provost was not running his tavern as early as the 1840's and he had two places of business, not one location—but it is obvious the editor liked Provost. Other articles tell that one son travelled afar and an unnamed brother visited. 12/13/1888: "Antoine Provost and wife are expected home shortly from England." 6/27/1889: "...Antoine was over to Paris to see 'Buffalo Bill,' his old friend." 7/6/1893: "Mr. Provost arrived on Wed. from Troy, N.Y. to make his brother, Uncle John Provost of Laporte, a visit. The two had not met before in 50 years."

Provost's old friend and neighbor, Antoine Janis, died at Pine Ridge on April 10, 1890, but Provost never seemed to run out of energy. 9/16/1890: "John Provost has rented a place on College Avenue and will open a restaurant and boarding house. Mr. Provost is known for setting up good meals." He was about 78 by then.

The last article found before Virginie's and John's deaths was 12/19/1895 and it was about his driving harness being stolen.

Virginie died November 21, 1901, at age 63 or 66, depending on the reference. (Cemetery records say she was 66-8-19; St. Joseph's records indicate she was 63.) According to her obituary, she was born in Chambly, Canada, near Montreal. She'd come here 40 years earlier as the wife of Mons. Laurent. (I was unable to find any information about Mr. Laurent.) She was "well-connected" in that she was the cousin to two bishops in the diocese of St. Hyacinthe, Canada. She was a "great sufferer" and died of cancer. Her funeral service was at St. Joseph's Church and her burial was in Grandview. Provost had paid $30 for a cemetery lot on November 16, five days before she died (7).

Less than a year later, Provost married a third time. In front of witnesses Aaron G. and Mrs. Irene Vanderkarr, he married Mrs. Lizzie White of Pueblo, a widow, on September 29, 1902 (10). He was 79 or 80 at the time.

Provost died at 8:30 o'clock on Monday evening, January 4, 1904, at his home in Laporte, at age 81. According to his lengthy obituary, "John Provost is entitled to the honor of being the first permanent white settler in Larimer County." In part, the obituary states:

But little of a reliable character is known of Uncle John's history previous to his coming to this valley, as he was a reticent man and seldom alluded to things of the past. In 1858, the Cache la Poudre valley was often the temporary home of roving bands of Cheyenne and Sioux Indians with whom Uncle John early made friends, later taking a Sioux woman for a wife to whom several children were born. These with, one exception a daughter, who was with her father in his last hours—with their mother, went to Red Cloud agency more than 20 years ago and were still there the last heard from them.

For years Uncle John kept a road ranch on the south side of the river in the house now occupied by Rowland Herring, later purchasing the house on the north side of the river in the town of Laporte, where he died. In June 1864 at the time of the big flood, when the bottom lands of this valley were all under water and the stream itself was a raging torrent, Uncle John built a ferry boat and until the flood subsided, did a thriving business transferring overland travelers and teams from one side of the river to the other. Overland travel was heavy that year and he made a lot of money with his ferry.

For the past 25 years and more, Mr. Provost has kept the only hotel and road house in Laporte, at which many noted men of the country have, at different times, found refreshments and hospitable entertainment. In the early days Uncle John was well-known and had scores of friends all over the territory. He was genial of manner, kind of heart and charitable to a degree. No one suffering the pangs of hunger was ever turned from his door unsatisfied, whether possessed of money or not. He was one of the landmarks of this county and people of all classes mourn his death. The old pioneers feel his passing with special regret for they knew him much better than those who have become residents in later years.

The funeral of Mr. Provost was conducted at 10 a.m. at his residence in Laporte, and additional services were held at 1 o'clock in the First Presbyterian church in Fort Collins with the Rev. H.S. McCutchen, pastor of the Laporte Presbyterian church, officiating.

Provost's pallbearers were C.W. Ramer of Livermore, T.L. Moore, Louis Blackstock and Robert Miller of Fort Collins, and Rowland Herring and A.T. Gilkinson of Laporte. At this time, Herring already owned the Provost farm. Gilkinson owned land now farmed by Ron Treiber and was the contractor who built the Pleasant Valley Lake and Canal tunnel through Bingham Hill (1600 feet, $27,000) in the winter of 1883-84.

Only one son, Charles Provost of Pineridge, and one daughter, Mrs. Lizzie Dixon of Laporte, were present at the funeral. Those of the family not present were Antoine Provost of Brooklyn, New York; Oliver Provost of El Reno, Oklahoma; Louis, and the mother of the children, from Pineridge, South Dakota.

Provost was buried at Grandview, next to Virginie, who would have preferred, I am sure, to have him buried by the Catholic Church. His first wife might have put him in a tree. Presumably his children, Charles and Lizzie, arranged his funeral; neither his second nor third wives are even mentioned in his obituary.

On January 9, 1928, the *Courier* had three articles of Laporte interest: (a) SARCHET SHOOTING CONFESSED (Attorney Fancher Sarchet was a son-in-law of Rowland Herring), (b) DR. WILKIN DIES AT HOME AT AGE 69 (He was the long-time Laporte physician) and (c) OLD HISTORIC BUILDING IS BURNED DOWN. "The old Provost tavern building and stage station at Laporte burned at about 11 o'clock Sunday night. The Jacobson blacksmith shop adjoining it on the south also burned. . .The Provost tavern and state station was believed to be the **oldest building in Larimer county,** having been purchased by John B. Provost, a squaw man, who conducted a hotel and tavern there for many years."

Today, a sign at 2601 North Overland Trail simply says: THIS IS THE ACTUAL SITE OF THE LOG HOUSE USED AS A STATION HOUSE FOR THE OVERLAND STAGE COMPANY IN 1862.

Indian Mary on the Reservation. What happened to Provost's Indian wife, Mary, after she left Laporte? Who fathered her tenth baby? Her eleventh? The legal documents which Henry Moore brought from the reservation answered some questions. Most of the following is paraphrased from many pages of testimony relevant to the successful breaking of Mary's will in which she'd left everything to only two of her children, Charles and Ida Stinking Bear (4a). Mary's only asset at the time of her death on April 2, 1916, was the half-section (320 acres) patented to her January 17, 1910. She died at the approximate age of 77. Parentheses are mine.

The allottee #3323 (White Owl, Mary Provost, Mary Jumper, Mary Yellow Bear) was born around 1838 and was married four times, first to John B. Provost about 1854 by Indian custom and separated around 1872.

Mary's mother, "Passing Back and Forth," and also called "Walks with Her" or "White Cow," died in 1856; and her father, who died before 1856, was "Medicine Black Tail" or "Holy Black Tail Deer." Both parents are listed as Cheyenne, not Sioux. (According to local Indian historian Larry Newman, if her father were already dead when she was a teenager, that would account for her brother "selling" her to Provost. Brothers took over a father's responsibility.)

At the time of the hearings (1916-17), it was stated that she and John Provost had nine children, of which four survive: Charles, Antoine, Lewis and Lizzie. Oliver was alive at the time of her death but died before the hearings. Those deceased included:

1. John Provost, Jr., a son, died in 1881 at age 26. He was married to Horse Woman or Jennie Shot Close, by whom he had 1 daughter, Suzie Deon, who died at age 41, and with issue of whom Harold Ross and Richard Deon, sons, survive.
2. William Provost, died in 1880, at the age of 23, not married, no issue.
3 and 4. Braxil (Bazille) and Mary Provost, children, died prior to 1870.
5. Oliver Provost, died Feb. 13, 1917, leaving surviving his wife, Minnie, and a son and daughter, Alfred John and Lucy Provost.

By her second husband, an unknown white man (also referred to as "an issue clerk at the Pine Ridge agency"), to whom she was married in Indian custom about 1874, and from whom she was separated the following year, she had one child, Ida Stinking Bear, or Ida Little Killer, a daughter, who survives.

By her third husband, Jumper, who died Oct. 15, 1908, she had one son, Jimmie Jumper, who died about 1880, at the age of 2 1/2 months. Jumper was married twice previously, to Carrie Kills Ahead, and then to Deer Woman, with whom he had a child named Girl or Mrs. Big Leggins.

By her last husband, Yellow Bear, to whom she was married by ceremony Feb. 2, 1914, and who survives—no issue. This marriage was at St. James Church on the White Clay District of the Pine Ridge Reservation; witnesses were Henry Black Elk and Alice Deon.

Since she left her allotment to only Ida Stinking Bear and Charles, several others protested her 1911 will. Frank C. Goings, Chief of Indian Police, protested as guardian of Oliver's children. Her widower, Yellow Bear, disapproved because the will was written before he married her. Ida Stinking Bear (Little Killer) of Oglala, South Dakota, said she had taken care of her mother the last eight years of her life and thought the will should stand as written but whatever Charles wanted was all right with her since he was the older brother. When asked who was the interpreter at the time of the will, Ida says she was blind at the time and didn't know. Charles of Gordon, Nebraska, testified that he didn't think the will should be approved, even though his mother left the estate to only him and Ida. Antoine wrote from Hoboken, New Jersey, that probably his brother Charlie got her intoxicated and had her make the will in his favor.

Louis of Martin, South Dakota, also objected to approval of the will; he said he'd helped his mother at different times and was equally entitled to share in her property. Lizzie (Beth) Pedigo of Vida, Montana, testified that Charles and Ida Stinking Bear didn't assist her mother any more than the rest of the children.

Answers to questions were fascinating. Some of the questions put to Charles, the most "with it" son: Q: When was your mother's death? A: About April 1916. Q: How old was she? A: In the 70s; I do not know her exact age. Q: How many times was she married? A: Twice. (Four is the correct answer). Q: How many children were born of the marriage between your mother and Jumper? A: None that I know of. (There was a son.)

When Mary's husband, Yellow Bear, was questioned, he was just as vague. Q: When did your wife die? A: About two years ago, he didn't know the date. (Yellow Bear is the one who testified that Mary was sold by her brother to Provost when she was about 16 years old.) Q: Did you have a child by the allotee? A: No, too old. He didn't know the number or names of Mary's children by Provost or the name of her son by Jumper (It was Jimmy.) Q: Did she make a will? No. (Right answer was yes.)

Mary's land was eventually sold and a small amount of money divided many ways.

To summarize, Indian Mary had nine children with John Provost, two of whom were buried on the home place in a spot which later became the Laporte or Bingham Hill Cemetery. Mary had two more children, one with an unknown white man, one with Jumper. Her last husband was Yellow Bear.

Henry Moore, great-grandson of the Provosts, invited my family to their family reunion at the Black Hills in August 1988. All Provosts who attended were descendants of only one of John Provost's sons, Charles Agustus (Count) and Josephine Smith from Pine Ridge. Four of Count's children were at the reunion: Charles Ash Provost (Cap) of Fremont, California, named after Charles Ash Bates, a surveyor in charge of land allotments; Harold Quincey Provost of Lakeport, California; Grace Gonsalves of

Crescent City, California; and Gertie Joles of Slidell, Louisiana. Two other surviving children did not attend: Hazel Carlow, of Colorado Springs, who died in April, 1989, and a step-daughter, Myrtle Means of Martin, South Dakota (aunt of Indian activist, Russell Means).

Cap, the head of the family at the time, endeared himself to us not only by graciously welcoming us to his family's reunion but also because he gave my husband an eagle feather and a beaver skin. We were saddened to hear of his death November 23, 1989, of bone cancer.

Doris Compton wrote that her mother, Hazel, the first-born of Count, was the only grandchild to know John Provost. Hazel was born in Cripple Creek and went to South Dakota by wagon. She was five when her grandfather died but she remembered him as having a "real gruff" voice. He scared her at first since he was so loud and boisterous, but fondly remembered him calling her "my little Indian."

My husband and I attended another Provost reunion hosted by Clem Olson and Doris Compton at Grand Ronde, Oregon, in 1990, and on August 5-7, 1994, we held the Provost family reunion here on our farm in Laporte. About 50 Provosts and Lesserts came from across the country to meet on their two grandfathers' first farm. The *Coloradoan* carried a short article with a photo of Grace, Gertie and Quincey. Native American dancers came from Colorado State University and neighbor Audrey Stockton gave rides in a hayrack pulled by her Shires. My husband and I were taken into the tribe; Jim was renamed "Down to Earth Man" and I was "Holy Winged Horse Woman."

People often ask why the Provost lot at the Bingham Hill Cemetery is so big if only two small children are buried in it? When Moore first visited, he thought Oliver had also been buried there—a suicide as a young teenager. Later he learned this was not true. Provost probably built the large enclosure because at the time Bazille died, it was planned for the rest of the family which he presumed would always live in Laporte. He couldn't predict the politics in the future when anti-Indian impetus would send his wife and sons and neighbors away.

3. **Janis Child** Died before 1878 (Possible)

Old-time Laporte resident Frank McConnell said he saw a Janis stone in the Bingham Hill Cemetery when he was young. This may have been a child of Antoine Janis, Provost's neighbor across the river and to the west. I found no written records to verify this but Mrs. Hazel Cuny mentioned in a letter that "there surely must be some Janis's buried at Laporte." Since Janis lived here from about 1859 to 1878 and had 10 or 12 children, it's certainly possible one might have died here, and I trust Frank McConnell's memory.

The next two, a mother and her infant daughter, were listed in the first edition as "probable burials." Since 1994, a wealth of information was sent by Margaret L. Isaac of Denver. Hers was the most valuable response to the 1991 Wil Huett article in **Colorado Country Life Magazine**. *She assured me that her great-grandmother, Sarah Jane Hardin, and her child are definitely buried at the Bingham Hill Cemetery. All the following information came from her; her sources are numerous.*

4. **Sarah Jane Hand Hardin** Died August 25, 1865 Age 36

After Sarah Jane Hardin died, Indian women walked around and around the cabin. "This was their way of showing sorrow," wrote Margaret Isaac.

Sarah Jane Hand was born in Crawford County, Illinois, on July 14, 1829, making her one of the earliest-born people buried in the Laporte cemetery. She was the first child of George Washington Hand who eventually had four wives. Sarah Jane's mother, Mahala Smith, was her father's first cousin.

Sarah Jane married John Hardin on June 22, 1852, and they owned a farm in Harrison County, Missouri. When she contracted tuberculosis, he sold the farm and brought the family to Colorado, where they and their doctor hoped the dry air would restore Sarah Jane's health. In 1864, they moved to Pleasant Valley, north of present-day Bellvue. She became ill and as she grew worse, John moved her to Laporte. She died there and so did their youngest child. John had always befriended the Indians and the squaws comforted him by walking around the cabin at the time of Sarah Jane's death.

Sarah Jane had five children: (1) Louisa Frances, who married Henry Smith and gave birth to John Richard Smith in 1875 near Red Feather Lakes. He was John Hardin's first grandchild and the father of Margaret Isaac, my source of information. (2) George Washington Hardin, who married Emmaline Shipp of Pleasant Valley and ran a cattle ranch operation near Sheridan, Wyoming. They had Byron and Estella, who was engaged to a Pennock, but died in 1906, age 20, of appendicitis. (3) Mary

Jane Hardin, who married Alfred Johnson on December 24, 1878, in Auntie Stone's little hotel at Fort Collins. (4) Amanda Eleanor, who moved to Wyoming in 1884, married Horace Brown, adopted a daughter who had eight children and died, so Amanda raised them; and (5) Susan Isabelle Hardin, who died at five months and was buried near her mother.

According to a story handed down in the family, before they left Missouri, Sarah Jane requested a promise from her young half-sister, Mahalah Hand—and from her husband John—that in the event she did not get well and died, that John would return to Missouri and marry Mahalah.

After the deaths of wife and child, John Hardin took his four living children back to Harrison County, Missouri, and hired his brother-in-law and sister-in-law, Hiram and Caroline Hand, to care for his children. He then freighted for one year from St. Joseph, Missouri, to Denver. After the proper year of mourning, he returned to Missouri and married Mahalah Hand on November 13, 1866, at Bethany. Mahalah was the child of G.W. Hand's second wife, Sarah Shepherd. He intended to return to Colorado soon, but they were delayed by "Indian troubles on the plains," and by the time they did travel by wagon to Colorado in 1869, they brought not only the four living children of Sarah Jane, but also their first-born, Montana Josephine. Also, Mahalah was already pregnant with her second child. They settled in Pleasant Valley, where John had lived before. In May 1871, John Hardin moved his family to the homestead near present day Red Feather Lakes.

John and Mahalah had eight children (Montana Josephine Kilhenny, Martha Emily Perry, Lomira Ann Perry, Matilda Hardin Tompkins, John William, Mark, Allen Roy and Edna Ruth Gibbens), lived on his homestead until their deaths on South Lone Pine Creek and were buried in the Adams Cemetery near Livermore, Colorado, on the Currie Ranch.

In October 1988, while on a "Walking the World" trek through the Canyonlands of Utah, a fellow hiker, Irene Gibbens, then 68, mentioned that she was married to a grandchild of pioneer John Hardin. This is amazing since John Hardin was born in 1826! Hardin's eighth child by his second wife was Edna Ruth, who married Ray Gibbens, and became the parents of John Gibbens, husband of my hiking companion. An amazing stretch of history!

Local descendants of the Hardins include Archie Porter, William Gibbens and John Blair.

5. **Susan Isabelle Hardin** Died August 27, 1865 Age 5 months

She was born on March 30, 1865 in Pleasant Valley and was fondly referred to as "Baby Susan" by her family. Her father, John Hardin, held the baby through the night as she died and, according to Margaret Isaac, he buried her at the side of her mother who had died two days earlier. The immediate cause of both deaths was typhoid fever but Mrs. Isaac had also heard they had consumption (tuberculosis of the lungs).

There was apparently never a marker on the graves, but according to an article by Amanda Hardin Brown in the July 1958 issue of *Colorado Magazine* published by the Colorado State Historical Society, the Hardin graves at Bingham Hill were enclosed by a picket fence. It may be one of the three oldest picket fenced enclosures still in the cemetery.

6. **Crawford L. Shaffer (P)** Died November 10, 1873 Age 24

"Family Bible records of the James and Victoria Ann Barr family, resident in LaPorte during the 1870s, record that her first husband, Crawford L. Shaffer, died at LaPorte on November 10, 1873. He may have been buried in Bingham Hill Cemetery." So writes Raymond Owen of Santa Rosa, California.

Shaffer was born in Allen County, Ohio, on July 23, 1849, and married Victoria Ann Robins on September 3, 1871. Owen doesn't know why Shaffer was at Laporte, what his activities were or why he died so young.

Shaffer's widow gave birth five months after his death, in April, 1874, to Minnie Viola Shaffer in Cloud County, Kansas. Victoria Ann, and presumably her baby and an older child, returned to Laporte and she married James Barr on March 23, 1875. Witnesses were E.N. Garbutt and L.P. Orleans. Barr farmed in Laporte, often in partnership with Thomas Gill. In his 1875 diary (4c), E.N. Garbutt mentioned several times that he helped James Barr plant cabbage.

Raymond Owen has a deed showing Barr bought two lots in Mountain Home Cemetery in June 1874 and probably buried his first wife, Mary (Van Dyke) Barr, there. I went through old lot books at Grandview and compiled a list of about 80 names of those bodies moved to Grandview from Mountain Home; no Barr was mentioned. She may have been one of the ten "unknowns" moved in 1945, or perhaps she is still there.

In the *Courier*, 7/31/1879: "Died, at Ft. Collins, Colo. July 24, 1879, James R., infant son of James and Victoria Barr, aged 13 months."

Though this baby could have been buried in Laporte, near his mother's first husband, it is believed by Owen that he was more likely buried at Mountain Home, near his father's first wife.

The following five persons are buried in the Bingham lot. Ashes of a sixth relative, Frances VerStratten, were added in 1996. She will be discussed in Section III. All six have markers.

The road and cemetery both carry the Bingham name so they are important to local history. Samuel Bingham (b. 1/17/1807) had a first marriage to Anna Hoover (b. 5/4/1811) and together they had Jane, Jacob, Jemima, Elizabeth, Mary Ann, William, John Anderson, Simeon Christopher, James K. Polk and possibly one other child. Anna Hoover Bingham died.

Sarah Crippen (b. 1816 near Knoxville, Tn.) had a first marriage to Levi Dennis (1842) and they had two sons, John and Edward. They moved to Missouri where Levi soon died. The widowed Sarah Dennis married the widowed Samuel Bingham and together they had Jesse G., Matthew, Thomas, Eliza and Barbara.

Sarah's son from her first marriage, John Dennis, married Julila Spirlock in Missouri and several in the family moved west, first to Utah, then to Laporte. The Binghams lived about a mile west of the cemetery where an old silo stands—land owned for years by the Doty and Randleman families and then sold to Ken and Linda Fisher.

John Dennis' wife and child were the first two members of the "Bingham" family to die and be buried here.

Samuel and Sarah Bingham stayed in this area only from 1864 to 1880, then left for Hot Springs, South Dakota. Samuel was buried in Sullivan County, Missouri, May 17, 1883. Sarah was buried in Hot Springs on February 22, 1891, at age 75.

7. **Julila Spirlock Dennis** + Died January 21, 1873 Age 34 years
   Julila was born May 26, 1838 and apparently died in childbirth since she died one day after her son was born.

8. **John E. Dennes** + Died September 13, 1873 Age 8 months
   John was born January 20, 1873 and in spite of the different spelling on the stones, he is the son of Julila. He lived only eight months after his mother's death.

9. **Mary Ida Turner** + Died April 19, 1876 Age 3 years

One of John Dennis's daughters, Sarah, married a Turner and it was one of these relatives who buried little Mary Ida, "dau. of L.D. and H. Turner" in 1876. Her lovely marble headstone was perfect when the picture was taken in 1987; by 1998, a large portion has disintegrated.

10. **Barbara A. Bingham** + (P) Died September 30, 1876 Age 19

Barbara was a sister (younger by one year) of the Eliza Gardner mentioned with Mary Provost's burial. Barbara was to marry George Stearly of Laporte but died of a nosebleed shortly before her wedding (2).

11. **John W. Tharp** + Died July 11, 1890 Age 49 years

John Wesley Tharp was the first husband of Barbara Bingham's sister, Eliza. According to his stone, his age was 49 years, 9 months and 24 days.

From the old coroner's book, now in the Loveland Coroner's office: "July 12, 1890. Upon investigation of the death of J. Wesley Tharp, jurors do say that the deceased caused his death by a cut across the throat said wound was inflected of the deceased himself. Wallie G. Gaugh, Coroner." Excerpts from the newspaper, 7/17/1890:

Our citizens were startled and painfully shocked...that J. W. Tharp, an old and highly respected citizen of Laporte had taken his own life... instrument used was a razor with which he cut his throat...about 10 p.m.... in the yard at the rear of his home in Laporte...he was a great sufferer from cancer of the stomach...growing despondent...Mr. E.N. Garbutt prepared a quieting potion...Mrs. Tharp and Mr. Garbutt found him lying on the grass...in the last agonies of death. He had made 3 gashes across his throat with a razor, severing the wind pipe, but not the jugular vein, and died from strangulation. Mr. Tharp was about 50 years old...a resident of Laporte for upwards of 20 years...leaves wife and 6 children...oldest is 16 and the youngest 3 years old...he served all through the war in an Ohio regiment and was drawing a pension from the government. His remains were interred on Sunday in the Laporte burying ground.

(Note: In June of 1998, bottle collector Mike Holzwarth found an intact bottle labelled "Elixir of opium" while digging in our yard—a home previously owned by Rowl Herring and H.I. Garbutt. Perhaps opium was the "quieting potion" which Ed Garbutt prepared for John Tharp.)

Apparently this suicide occurred near the old Stearly house on Overland Trail across from the Laporte post office.

Tharp's widow, Eliza Ellen, later married William Gardner who was murdered at Owl Canyon in 1904. Many columns of newsprint were devoted to the case. Eliza, born July 13, 1855, died August 5, 1937, at age 82, and was buried at Grandview. Their son, Charlie Tharp, who died February 23, 1964, age 89, was the person who built the concrete wall around the graves in 1959. A street in Laporte is named Tharp after the family.

12. **Johnny Thomas + (P)** Died May 7, 1877 Age about 24

A sandstone marker, found outside the barbed wire fence, on the edge of the Mercer Ditch about ten feet west of the concrete Bingham family lot, bears the scratched notation 'J. THOMAS.' After heavy rains in June, 1988, large chunks of sod fell into the ditch and almost exposed the side of a coffin. Energetic members of the Rainbow Riders 4-H Club decided to move the headstone and body so that both would not eventually slide into the Mercer Ditch. There was some momentary uncertainty about the legality of the process, but one 4-H father was a police officer so the club felt that for this good deed, the law was on their side.

Digging was easy after the rain. The wood casket which narrowed at both ends was rotten and crumbled easily. The first item brought to light on a shovel blade was a skull with brilliant red, curly hair. Most of us thought it was a woman. However, the skeleton was clothed in leather pants and a short leather jacket with wide lapels. "Buckskin Charlie" came to mind, a Laporte person often referred to in the 1875 diary of E.N. Garbutt.

Feet bones were enclosed in brownish wool socks which were still intact. There were no shoes or boots, no beads, jewelry or identification. However, under the head were crumbly greenish paper fragments which after careful examination with a magnifying glass appeared to be a stack of flyers which advertised various teas. There also seemed to be a bit of gauze on the right temple and dried blood in his hair.

Dr. Michael Charney, Colorado State University's world renowned forensics anthropologist, examined some of the bones. The left and right femurs were 46.4 cm and 46 cm in length; the tibia, 36.6 cm. When added, multiplied by 1.3, added to 63.29, and divided by 2.54, Charney came up with a height of 5 feet, 7.5 inches, plus or minus 1.2 inches. J.

Thomas weighed about 135 pounds. His foot, according to sock length, measured an 8 1/2 to 9 size. His knee showed he didn't squat much. His arches were flat. His top central incisors (front teeth) showed "shoveling," indicative of Asian ancestry. (This did not fit with the facial structures, red hair, or the name Thomas. Welsh or English ancestry seemed more likely.) Thoracic vertebrae looked to be of someone who completed growth, that is, over 25 years of age. Grooves on the pubic symphysis were a Group IV, age 24-27.

Because the coffin was so rotten, the 4-H club made no further effort to move it and eventually replaced all J. Thomas' bones where he had originally been buried along with a note of apology and explanation. Students of Dr. Charney helped with the reburial. While the group was reinterring the bones, a man and woman visiting the cemetery saw the activity and instead of asking what was going on, called the Sheriff to report a grave robbing. The deputy who responded bought a copy of *Bingham Hill Cemetery* and said it was certainly his most interesting call of the day. Whereas the 4-H club did not fulfill its original intention of moving the entire coffin and its contents, it was nonetheless a valuable learning experience.

On May 6, 1989, Mark Nelson solidly rebuilt the bank with railroad ties. For this he deserved and was awarded the Eagle Scout badge. Now "J. Thomas" peacefully rests without threat of erosion or more interference. But who was J. Thomas? And when was he buried? For seven years the answer eluded me. Someone had kept his boots, but buried him in buckskin; someone made the effort to scratch J. THOMAS on a stone. He was near the ditch which told me he'd been buried before the 1880s. (*Courier,* 1/29/1880: "It seems to be a certainty that the Mercer ditch will be built and will be equal in capacity to the #2.") I read about a man whose name "might have been Walter Thomas" who was killed in 1894 west of Laporte and he was my best bet until September 24, 1995, when a 120-year-old letter was found (9).

The letter was postmarked "Rochester, N.Y., Jun 20, 1877," and mailed with a 3-cent stamp. It was addressed to E.N. Garbutt, La Porte, Larimer Co., Colorado. The hand-written letter from the father of J. Thomas is printed below in its entirety. The Garbutts, early Laporte residents, also came from Greece, a town near Rochester, New York.

Greece
June 17, 77
Mr. E.N. Garbutt
Dear Sir.

Your kind letter of May 16 is at hand with thanks. We have been busy with our crops and potato bugs is my excuse. Your 2 telegrams I received Monday May 7. I asked your father to write the message. He did so and I took it to Charlots and give it to the operator and it cost me $2.50. I have a witness to prove what I tell you. This is all I know about it. I am sorry you didn't get it.

Your letter of June 1 is at hand and contents every word it is a strong letter you sent me. You are wrong in your thoughts towards me. I have thanked you for what you did for John. We all belive you did your best and were kind to John althrough the time he was with you up to his death and we all thank you again. Your letter has greived me greatly but let it pass. I hope to see you sometime. We are strangers to each other. I never saw you. In my former letter I stated to you my situation in regards to my matters. If John had died at home I could have had plenty of time to meet all the bills (I must have time now). I shall try and send you some money very soon. John whent to Colo. against the wishes of his Father and Mother and Brother and Sister. John was of age and could do has he had a mind to and we helped him all we could. It was outside influence (not ours) that sent him to you. Please put a small board at the Head of his grave with his name on it. You are John's friend. Drop a tear or put a flower on his grave and oblidge your Friend, S. W. Thomas.

P.S. Excuse all mistakes. I can't see good. I have no specks.
S.W.T.

Quite a story! A young man comes west against the wishes of his family. He dies. His father is grieving but has no money to pay for the coffin and possible medical costs related to an illness or injury. I was correct in that it was a very early burial, and also that someone cared for him. How he died, we still don't know; I suspected injury rather than illness because of what looked like blood in his hair, but a letter from Garbutt's sister talks about taking care of John "for so long." Ed Garbutt obviously buried him and did better than put up a board—he put up a stone which is still there today; he may or may not have collected what was owed him. Ed Garbutt constantly worried about money according to his diary entries and letters (4c).

Learning that the Garbutts knew the Thomas family, I re-read the letters from Greece, New York, sent by teenage Nettie Garbutt (future wife of Rowland Herring) to her brother Cameron who was also in Laporte at the same time as his brother Ed. Suddenly a name which had meant nothing before jumped out, not once, but often.

Thurs., May 14, 1874: "**John Thomas** was over last night but did not stay very long he said that he thought it was real lonely here since you went a way." Nov. 22, 1874: **John Thomas** staid here last night him and Fred (her brother) slept in your bedroom." Dec. 21, 1874: "**John** was up here last evening and says he sent you three papurs a few days be fore."

On March 12, 1875, she writes "I see **John Thomas** everie day or two. he was down last night and we had a foil handid game of youchou." (maybe a 4-handed game of something?) On June 23, 1875: "Fred and **Johnie Thomas** halve gone over to Mr Burnses and pa went to wheatland last Friday and has not got back as yet."

On Dec. 26, 1875, "**John Thomas** was over here all day yesturday."

Sometime during the next year, he traveled to Laporte, and the next time he is mentioned is on March 25, 1877: "Father wants to now wheather you halve any potato buges thare or not. Tell **Johnie** that Tom Herrin and Emma Vanderhaden are going to geather no more so he wants to herie up and come home if he will capture Emmie." And in the same letter: "I wish you would come home Cam. Why won't you come? **John** is there for Ned (nickname for Ed Garbutt) and I am so lonely here when Fred and Mollie (the future second Mrs. Rowl Herring) will be gone. Do come home Cam and live to home. It will be pleasanter for us both if it was not for Father I would come out thare and ceep house for you..."

Two months later, the telegram from Ed Garbutt was sent to Mr. Thomas about his son's death. On June 18, 1878, she writes: "You must miss **John** gratley now Cam after halving the care of him so long **Mrs. Thomas** felt verrie badley they all felt verrie bad but I do not think that any of them miss him so much as she."

Did Cam take care of an ill or injured John Thomas? How long did he take care of him? Why is Ed the brother who does the dirty work—inform the parents, ask for money, and so on? Which brother made the coffin and chiseled his name on a stone?

Another finding adds uncertainty. The map of Mountain Home Cemetery lists under Lot #286 the name "John Thomas" and the purchase date 1877! There was a different John Thomas in Fort Collins who was county treasurer from 1894-1896; he died on 2/15/1898 at age 59 and is buried at Grandview. I think it was this man who bought the lot in Mountain Home, and that it is coincidental that it happened to be the same year "our" Johnny Thomas died.

In attempts to find out more about John Thomas, I wrote the library at Rochester, New York, and they responded that they had no obituary for a John Thomas in May of 1877. The Larimer County coroner's book's first entry was December 3, 1881; earlier coroner reports are lost, except for a few in private collections. Local newspapers were of no use. There is microfilm of the *Fort Collins Standard* from March 1874 to November 1874 and of the *Courier* from 1878 to 1880. The missing years are apparently not available anywhere, according to Rheba Massey, because there was once a fire in the newspaper office and all old newspapers were destroyed. Would that some collector have local papers from 1877! Perhaps the mystery of what happened to John Thomas would be solved.

Of all the people buried, John Thomas is the only one whose bones I have held, whose hair I have touched. I often think about this young man and his parents. The many photographs I took of his skull and hair, his leather suit and his socks, may be the only pictures ever taken of him.

13. **Alphonse LaRocque** + Died November 15, 1877 Age 59 years

LaRocque was born in Canada in 1818, making him one of the earliest-born people in the cemetery and the only 1859 settler known to be buried in Laporte. All of the other Frenchmen went to the reservation with their wives in 1878 except John Provost, who was buried at Grandview.

I found nothing about LaRocque from 1818 to 1859, but since he signed the Half-breed Petition of 1867, he must have been associated with the Northwestern Fur Company. He is listed as a "farmer, age 36" in the 1860 census at Miravalle, west of Loveland, but Watrous has Provost and LaRocque already building houses near Laporte by 1859 (5). Hal Sayre, who came to Colorado in 1859, also mentions that "a number of old French trappers were in Colona in the spring of 1860" and he names both John B. Provost and LaRocque. This information came from a Sayre descendent, Hal Collier of New York. John Gray (3) wrote that "On April 10, 1865, citizen 'LaRock [probably old Platte trader and early Laporte settler, Alphonse Larocque] was called on to help weed out government stock from several freighters' herds on Boxelder Creek."

The only wife LaRocque was ever reported to have was Mary, a full-blooded Oglala Sioux. They had one daughter Louisa (Lizzie) and he was the step-father to Jennie (Adams McGaa Brown).

LaRocque once owned the land where Four Winds Stable is now situated (2504 North Shields), according to present owner Carole Throckmorton. From her abstract: Alphonse LaRocque paid $200 for 160 acres on Aug. 1, 1871. After he died, his Indian wife, Mary, sold the land to Tobias Miller. John Lyon, guardian for LaRocque's minor daughter, Louisa, sued and 70 acres was returned to Louisa, the rest going to Miller, and later to the Michauds. Louisa's acreage eventually went to Madame Marie Antoinette Roucolle, and her father and uncle, Pierre and Frank Dastarac. Later 35 acres of that piece of land went to Throckmortons.

LaRocque's widow and daughter left the area with the other Indians on their journey to the reservation in South Dakota. Twenty years later (6/16/1898) the daughter sent a letter to the *Courier* and its contents were discussed in print by the editor: "A letter from Mrs. Lizzie Cuney, at Manderson, Nebr., says her mother is well and hearty, and sends kind regards to all her old white friends in the Cache la Poudre valley. Mrs. Cuney was born here. Her mother is a Sioux woman now very aged. Her father, A. LaRocque, died here many years ago. She also says that Denver MaGaa had recently lost his wife who left a family of seven children." (The writer of the letter, Lizzie, was a half-sister of Jenny Adams McGaa Brown, sharing the same Sioux mother.)

Louisa later married Charles Cuny and had Wilson Joseph Cuny who married Florence Twiss (a granddaughter of Tom Twiss, an Indian agent in the Upper Platte Valley) and they had 12 children, one of whom is Sister Genevieve Cuny, a Catholic nun and frequent visitor to the cemetery.

LaRocque's marble stone had two cracks and was lying on the ground in 1987. A volunteer set it upright. It fell and sustained a third break when it was vandalized in 1988. Then someone set the marble pieces in concrete. The stone settled and became covered with silt every few months. Since funeral director Harold Warren had remarked that Larocque's stone looked like a veteran's marker, I wrote the VA in Washington, D.C. asking if they would make a new marble stone for LaRocque. Not possible, they said, unless I sent his military discharge papers. Instead, I started a fund for replacement and a new identical (except it is three inches, instead of two inches thick) marble stone was set on July 12, 1996. See the chapter on volunteers for lists of donors.

There are references to LaRocque as "Big LaRocque" and visitors to the cemetery might notice that his footstone is ten feet from his headstone. Bill Schneider, the dowser, found a small grave at LaRocque's feet, between a large body and the footstone.

14. **Jennie Adams McGaa Brown + (P ?)** Died February 13, 1878
Age about 35

Jennie has a nice sandstone marker, but a crack makes it impossible to read her age at the time of death.

Jennie's mother was Mary Anpaha (Day), a sister of Chief Anpaha. She was a full-blooded Oglala Sioux, born about 1830 in Wyoming. Many Indian women were given the name "Mary," especially by the Catholic French-Canadians. Mary became the child bride of John Adams, a white trader from Missouri. While living in the Fort Laramie area of Nebraska, Mary gave birth to Jennie in 1843. From Fort Laramie they moved to Fort St. Vrain on the South Platte, then to Cherry Creek, and by the time they moved to the Big Thompson, Mary was the wife of Alphonse LaRocque, a French-Canadian trapper. They had one daughter, Louisa. (According to Hazel McGaa Cuny, "Mary LaRocque had a child born before any of the above dates who belonged to neither Adams nor LaRocque and most likely that child was buried elsewhere.")

By 1859, they moved to the Laporte area where LaRocque died in 1877 and two months later, Jennie committed suicide. Mary LaRocque with her daughter, Louisa, returned to her people at Pine Ridge, South Dakota, where Mary died and was buried.

Jennie was approximately 15 when she married 38-year-old William McGaa, alias "Jack Jones." Their cabin was in Indian Row on Cherry Creek and here Jennie gave birth to their son in March 1859. At the time, he was heralded as being the first predominantly white child to be born in Denver, and was named William Denver McGaa.

As gold seekers caused too much crowding for the free spirits, they moved to Miraville City, west of Loveland. Then they moved to Pleasant Valley (near Laporte), closer to the LaRocques, where they had two more children, John and Jessie. McGaa made many mining claims in Larimer County in the 1860s (10), then disappeared. He apparently died in jail in Denver on December 15, 1867.

Much of the above information on Jennie Brown came from an article by McGaa historian, Zethyl Gates, in the *Loveland Daily Herald* (4/4/1983) and from conversation with her.

"Jennie McGaw and Joseph Brown were joined in marriage at the residence of Benjamin Claymore, August 10, 1868" (10). Ben Claymore was half-owner of the farm we now live on and and so I believe she was married here.

Jennie and Joseph Brown had three children in Laporte—George, Joe and Jenny. According to her relatives, Jennie, the mother, committed suicide about ten years after her wedding, either by drowning in the Poudre River or by poison. She was buried in the Laporte cemetery.

A few months after Jennie died, this interesting *Courier* article (11/30/1878) appeared about her 19-year-old son, Denver McGaa. Note that he is called Denver Brown. "J.A.C. Kissock has sold his little running mare 'Fanny Morgan' to W.D. McGaa. Fanny has a splendid record and if she could have had half a chance she would have beaten all in her class at the State Fair this fall. Consideration $125. Mr. McGaa, better known as Denver Brown, was the first child born in the then embryo city of Denver."

J.A.C. Kissock was mentioned in nearly every early weekly newspaper. The reader might note that this man, an entrepreneur in 1878, is the father of Fort Collins' Raymond Kissock, who was 97 and feeling fine in 1990 when I last talked to him. He died at 101 on 3/6/1994.

Bill Thompson, owner of Laporte Hardware, said that he once met a McGaa in the 1950s. Thompson was working out in the yard of the old Stearly house on Overland Trail which he and his wife own. The man said he was a McGaa and he'd "just come back to town" (Laporte) to look around. This is reminiscent of old newspaper comments, in which the editor would write that Denver McGaa was in Laporte this week; he "just wanted to look around." Thompson's visitor was probably one of Denver McGaa's many sons.

Since the first editions of this book was printed, dozens of interested McGaa and Brown descendants of Jennie have found the cemetery. One of the first to stop by was Edwin Brown of Longmont who arrived on June 28, 1989, with a stack of family records which proved his Indian heritage. At that time, I was unaware that Jennie even had children with Mr. Brown. Edwin informed me that George Brown had nine children, Joe had ten, and Jenny, two. One of George's sons was Joseph who

48

married Eloise Trimble and had Adele, Florence, Joseph, Doris and Edwin. Adele Treis of Kent, Washington, is the family genealogist. Another Brown visitor was Jerry Brown of Denver, a lawyer and educator.

McGaa visitors include Ed McGaa (Eagle Man), a pilot, lecturer, lawyer and author of three books: *Mother Earth Spirituality, Native Wisdom,* and *Rainbow Tribe.* He lives in Minnesota but has given lectures in Fort Collins about building sweat lodges. Visiting from South Dakota were Peri McGaa Strain, Bob and Delores O'Daniel and several other McGaa relatives. Mike Dressen visited from California. There are also several local relatives. Living in Laporte right on a piece of the very land once owned by Antoine Janis is a McGaa great-great grandson, Pete Dressen. He and his sister Priscilla, a veterinarian, are the children of Pat Corrigan, a daughter of Isabel Craven Stair, who was a daughter of Jessie Craven, Jennie McGaa's daughter. Priscilla also has two children, Amber and Alex. The McGaas had their first family reunion in Custer, South Dakota, in August of 1996 and another reunion is planned for 1998. Jennie McGaa Brown would surely be proud of all her descendants.

Zethyl Gates of Loveland has done years of research on the McGaa-Brown family. There is a photograph of a woman who may be Jennie McGaa, but because of the clothing worn, in Zethyl Gates' judgement, it is really a photograph of Jennie's daughter, Jessie.

Jennie Adams McGaa Brown is probably the most famous of the women in the cemetery; at least her name has been in print often because she was the mother of the first baby born in Denver. Her stone had fallen, was overgrown with brush, and for 20 years or more, it was thought to be gone. In 1987, my teenage twin sons, John and Jim, found it while chopping brush. One volunteer epoxied it together and stood it upright, and another built a fence around it. Now her grave is one of the most visited in the cemetery; people come from all over the United States. It is important for people to look for and find their roots. If there is no tombstone, how can one connect?

15. **John McGaa** Died about 1867 Age about 5 years

Knowledge of the existence of this child of Jennie and William McGaa is obscure. In Sacred Heart Church in Boulder, Historian Zethyl Gates found baptismal records written by a priest: "Baptized 3/11/1861, John Denver McGaa, born Ma 17, 1859." But William Denver was born

March 8, 1859. Did the priest make a mistake or did the parents baptize him John but call him William and have another child named John? There is no other known official written record of a John but the family often refers to him.

Hazel McGaa-Cuny, a daughter of William Denver, definitely believes John was born in Colona (Laporte) about 1862 (between William Denver and Jessie), died about 1867 when he was four or five and was buried at Laporte. From Hazel's mother's notes: "John McGaa was 5 years old when he died. Three children were given candy containing ground glass by a Mrs. Provost and two of them died including John. Wm. Denver was also given the candy but he did not eat it."

Adele Brown Treis disagrees and wrote in 1990: "I've heard so many stories of poisonings from that era. I think that was a kind of superstition among the mixed bloods. When there was no explanation for a death it was thought to be caused by 'poison.' The original Wm. McGaa was said to have been 'poisoned' in jail. And a child poisoned by ground glass? I find it hard to believe. How could a Provost woman have been blamed? I believe feuding Indians can make some vicious accusations. In regard to Jennie Brown's 'poisoning' I find it believable that she might have been trying to end a pregnancy. I have never heard any mention of a third McGaa child (John)."

In spite of the uncertainties, little John had his name engraved on the granite memorial. Maybe he was buried and ten years later Larocque was buried at his head with LaRocque's footstone placed to include them both. That would account for the grave dowser finding a small grave at LaRocque's feet.

16. **Cora Flowers** + Died around 1880 Age 5 weeks

Her parents, Thornton Wesley Flowers and Adelaide Obenchain, were married May 1, 1878 (10), so this baby's death was probably close to 1880. The date on the little white, marble headstone cannot be read. Cora was a grandchild of early Bellvue settler, Jacob Flowers, and a first cousin of little Mildred Pennock, who died about the same time.

Cora's family moved to Idaho where her father and brother died violent deaths. Glenn Pennock of Bellvue has the letter from J.C. Fox of Hailey, Idaho, to his grandfather, Charles Pennock, dated Jan. 27, 1910, in which Fox expresses his sorrow at the death of T.W. Flowers and son, Arthur, both of whom died in a snowslide. Laura Jeanne (Tilton) Wunch of Fort Collins, granddaughter of T.W.'s sister, Cora, has a beautiful and unusual "In Memory" card of the two deaths with original photographs of father and son who were ages 56 and 21 at the time of the avalanche. She received it from her Uncle Jasper Tilton who got it from his mother, Cora Flowers Tilton. Mrs. Wunch said that the bodies were not found until the spring thaw.

17. **Mildred Pennock** Died January 29, 1883 Age 11 months

Mildred was born December 22, 1882, the first child of Charles Pennock and Lydia Flowers, a sister of T.W. Flowers. The family was at their railroad tie-camp near the area later named Pennock Pass when Mildred died of membranous croup. Mildred was a first cousin of Cora Flowers.

In April 1890, three more Pennock children—Sardie, Bertha and Florence—died of diphtheria and were buried on the home place at Bellvue. Glenn Pennock said they were later moved to Grandview. Mildred's siblings who lived to adulthood include Arthur, Mary Alice, Charles Eldridge, George and John. (Information from Iola Pennock, Arthur's widow, and her daughter, Lois Johnson.)

There were many little articles in the *Fort Collins Courier* about the Flowers and Pennock families from 1878 to 1887. Reading them gives a glimpse into life in Bellvue.

8/17/1878: 200 of Charlie Pennock's ties went down the river in the flood last night.

8/7/1879: Jacob Flowers Esq. was severely injured from the kick of a fractious horse on Sat. last.

2/2/1882: At Pennock's camp, Patrick O'Brien ruptured a blood vessel in his lung and died. A friend purchased a lot in the cemetery, will put up stone: "Here lies an honest man."

8/3/1882: Chas. E. Pennock is building a fine stone residence in Pleasant Valley. (It cost $1800)

11/11/1882: Jacob Flowers felt an earthquake...shook his house til the timbers cracked.

11/25/1882: 8 foot lioness shot by Jake Flowers—will go to the museum to be stuffed.

1/27/1887: Jacob Flowers was developing a sandstone quarry near Claymore Lake and found a 4 foot vein of coal. Not very good coal, but might find more.

9/8/1887:   Mayor Flowers of Bellvue has just completed a handsome and commodious stone bldg...to be used as store and public hall. (This is the present-day Grange Hall in Bellvue.)

9/22/1887:   The pump house telephone is completed and in operation. Fort Collins has about 3,000 people.

12/22/1887:   Mayor Flowers of Bellvue reports real estate is booming.

18. James Mattison (Madison) Died November 22, 1880 Age: Old

The *Courier*, 11/25/1880, relates that James Mattison was an old gentleman from Laporte who was thrown from his wagon which was being pulled at a rapid rate and hit the corner of a bridge a mile west of Fort Collins, near Kenz Pew's place. His son-in-law, Wm. Hogan, and Tobias Miller took him into town but he died in the wagon. He left an aged widow in destitute circumstances and also a married daughter.

There was another reference to Mattison in a letter dated November 23, 1880, from E.N. Garbutt to fellow Masonic Lodge member, James Barr, Esq, formerly from Laporte, but then living in "Lafyette, Yamhill County, Oregon." Garbutt spells the name differently than the newspaper did and only wrote one sentence about him amongst other Laporte news: "Mr. Madison [shoemaker] was thrown from his wagon yesterday and instantly killed." Raymond Owen of Santa Rosa, California, furnished a copy of this Garbutt letter.

No James Mattison or Madison was found in Mountain Home or Grandview records and thus it can be presumed he was buried at Laporte. Ed Garbutt probably spelled the man's name correctly, but before I read his letter, 'Mattison' had already been blasted on the memorial stone.

19. Ida B. Keller + Died March 29, 1882 Age 19 years

The only information about this young woman comes from her beautiful tall white obelisk. Her parents were A.J. and S.A. Keller, and she is "not dead, but sleepeth." It seems strange that such a magnificent memorial was put up for a girl about whom not one word was written in the March or April 1882 newspapers.

I feel compelled to say something about her or her lovely tombstone, but all I can think of is that one day while walking through our pastures below the cemetery hoping to photograph the one and only elk I've ever seen on our farm, I found two pieces of marble, one plain and one with initials, I.B.K. Why her footstone was so far from where it belonged, I don't know; vandalism never makes sense. A volunteer placed internal rods and hooked the two footstone pieces together and it is now by her headstone.

In the library index files I found one small notice about a "Charlie Keller, a pupil in Room 2" but could not find the article in the 5/12/1881 paper. Perhaps someone will learn more about Ida B. Keller some day.

Her obelisk has been pushed over twice in the past ten years, but fortunately has not cracked, and each time four men were able to lift the heavy column back onto its base.

20. **Fredrick Henry McNally** Died March 29, 1882 Age 12 years

This 12-year-old child was born on Christmas Day in 1869 and died the very same day as Ida B. Keller. *The Weekly Express,* April 6, 1882, merely says: "A son of Mr. McNally living down the river died of inflammatory rheumatism."

His parents were Nicholas and Jemima McNally and he was one of a large family. In February of 1882, Nicholas and his son, Freddie, took a herd of cattle to North Park. Freddie became ill on the trip, died in Laporte on March 29, 1882, and was buried in the Laporte cemetery. Fredrick had a tombstone at one time, according to relatives.

21. **Ida Louise McNally (P)** Died August 11, 1883 Age 16

Ida Louise McNally was born 8/27/1866 and was a sister of Fredrick. Hers is a particularly sad story, not only because the family lost two youngsters a year apart, but because she committed suicide.

Ida Louise's was the only face on the front of my first book; her photograph was haunting. The back of the photo is stamped: "C.T. Wilkins, Artistic Photographer, College Avenue, Fort Collins" and "I have engaged the Sun to Shine for me."

There were several newspaper items about her death. From the *Courier,* 8/23/1883: "Livermore Locals: The sudden death of Miss Ida McNally, a charming and very intelligent lady who was well known in this vicinity, will be a painful surprise to many friends of the afflicted family. Miss McNally had just crossed the boundary dividing childhood from womanhood and was highly esteemed for many beautiful traits of character which so distinguished her. Her bereaved relatives have the sympathy of a wide circle of friends in the Poudre valley."

Also, the same day: "Died. McNally. At her parents' home, on the Canadian, North Park, very suddenly Aug. 11, 1883, Ida L. McNally, beloved daughter of Nicholas and Jemima McNally, aged 15 years, 11 months, and 20 days." This article was followed by a long poem.

A third article: "Canadian Crossing. Our usually quiet community has been considerably stirred up by the occurrence of the past two days. Sat. evening, Aug. 11, Miss McNally died very suddenly at her father's residence. The young lady had been in good health and excellent spirits up to 9 o'clock that evening when she suddenly complained of severe illness and in less than 20 minutes was a corpse. Her remains were buried this Sunday afternoon."

From the *North Park Miner,* Teller, Colorado, 9/6/1883: "From the Canadian, 9/1/1883. "To Editor Minkle. We wish to return our heartfelt thanks to our many kind friends who came to offer all the consolation in their power in our sad bereavement together with their offerings of flowers to deck the remains of our beloved Ida, and the many sympathizing tears they shed shall ever be remembered by her sorrowing parents and relatives. Signed: Nicolas and Jemima McNally."

In spite of an abundance of newspaper notices, two things are noticeably absent—how Ida died and where she was buried. Deaths in the early papers were often described graphically and without mercy, but this family was handled with sensitivity.

Information about Ida came from Frances Bujack; Ida was her grandmother's sister. Ida's parents, Nicholas McNally and Jemima Warren McVeigh, were married in Calumett Island, Lower Canada, August 25, 1851, and they had 11 children—seven in Canada (Francis, Mary, Gertrude, Cornelius, Anna, Nicholas and William) and four in Alcona County, Michigan (Ida, Fredrick, Margaret, and Rachel Eleanor, known as Ella). Their 8th and 9th children were buried in Laporte.

Frances Bujack's mother wrote down stories told by her mother-in-law, Ella. The family came on a boat from Alcona, Michigan, to Bay City, Michigan, and took a train to Fort Collins. Nicholas was a lumberman and worked big crews of men.

They arrived in 1878, first lived at 303 Mathews Street, then on Harmony Road, and in 1879, moved to Pleasant Valley, near Bellvue. Anna married Bob Kerr, and later Margaret married Bob's brother, Will. Mining was booming around Teller City in North Park at that time. Bob Kerr, his wife, and Nicholas went there in 1881; Jemima and the younger children stayed in Pleasant Valley. Nicholas decided to sell out in Pleasant Valley and move to North Park; Fredrick became ill while helping move cattle.

A week after Freddie's death, in April of 1882, the remaining members of the family, Willy, age 13, Margaret, then only 10, Ella, 8, and their parents, made their permanent move to North Park and the journey was sketchily described:

Seven days on the road in 2-seated Dutch buggy...Stopped the first night at Provos in Laporte. 2nd night spent on Dead Man's Hill; 3rd at Tie Siding. Harvey Shup's ranch—2 nights. Before got to Laramie River, it was storming...found a one-room cabin with dirt floor...cabin wasn't locked...a good fire in fireplace and a kettle of beaver tail stew. Stopped and got warm. At Laramie River, met Mr. Pinkam and Billy Brennan and Mrs. Charlie Murphy of the Laramie Plains. One of the horses played out. At Beaver Creek the men walked to Mountain Home to get a stage to take family on. They got a big grey team and hitched it on the buggy, got there April 12, 1882. Anna and Bob Kerr and Will Kerr lived at Teller in 1882 and Ida also lived there one year. Mr. McNally homesteaded a 160-acre ranch and built a one-room log cabin 1/4 mile from present house Bob Kerr built.

Anna McNally Kerr gave birth to a son on November 13, 1882, and named him Fred after her young dead brother. Fred Kerr was the first white boy born in North Park who lived to maturity.

Ida lived with her married sister, Anna, at Teller City, and helped care for the baby. She became pregnant, and being part of a staunch Methodist-Episcopal family, must have felt shamed. She perhaps drank lye, lived several agonizing days, and was possibly taken from North Park to Laporte for medical care. This does not match the article which said she died suddenly. Quickly or slowly, she died 16 days before her 16th birthday and was buried next to her brother in the Laporte Cemetery.

Ida's youngest sister, Ella, married Francis Smith at North Park. Their son, Martin, married Alene Hicks; their daughter, Frances, who married Wally Bujack, furnished the information. Martin had a little box filled with mementos which he'd show to his children. Frances's favorite thing was an unusual locket engraved with a horse's head. It was a treasure previously owned by "young Ida who died of an unhappy love affair." Frances owned it for years before her own death in April of 1996.

Frances said Martin often took her to visit the cemetery where there were two marked headstones for Fred and Ida. On one visit they saw that one headstone was knocked over and broken and Martin put up another. The last time Frances saw the stones was about 1960. In October, 1987, when Frances visited the cemetery with me, she could not remember where they had been, but her father's cousin, Herbert Kerr, said they were in the northeast part of the cemetery.

There are several pages of McNally and Kerr family history in Hazel Gresham's *North Park History.*

22. **Baby Boy Nugent** Died February 3, 1883 Newborn

This child was a son of early Laporte pioneer John Nugent, who helped make Laporte into a "garden basket." The *Courier* (7/15/1886) tells about Nugent's cauliflower, cabbage, peas, beans, beets and radishes, and two "forcing houses" filled with English melons and cucumbers. His granddaughter, Mary McNally, said he also was one of the early growers of rasberries in the Laporte area and that he delivered his vegetables to stores in Laramie and Cheyenne by horses and wagon. The trip took two days there and two days home.

The baby's siblings were Rosalie Landes, George H. (Chick) Nugent, May Garbutt and Elizabeth Runyan. Living in the area are Mary McNally and Jackie Nelson, children of Rose Landes; Virginia Taylor, daughter of George Nugent; and until his death, Walter Garbutt, son of May Garbutt. Walter's grandfather, Fred, was a brother of H.I., E.N. (Ed) and Nettie Garbutt, who married Rowland Herring, who also had a large vegetable farm on the other side of Overland Trail and across the river from the Nugents.

Mary McNally said her mother used to visit the little grave but that she personally does not know where it is. The Mountain Home Cemetery once sold a lot to a J. Nugent, but it is certain little baby Nugent was buried in Laporte.

In "Cemeteries of Larimer County" (2) a "George Nugent, Infant" is mentioned; the child's name might have been George and he might have had a marker at one time.

Of local interest is the fact that six generations of the family have slept in the old log house built by John Nugent by the Poudre River in 1881. McNallys and Nelsons still live in the building.

23. **Ida May Snuffin** + Died April 6, 1884 Age 22 years

Courier, 4/10/1884: "Mrs. A.C. Snuffin died at her home near Laporte, April 6, of consumption. She is spoken of by those who knew her as a very amiable lady and as an affectionate wife and mother. She leaves one child, an infant, and a disconsolate husband to mourn her untimely departure to the spirit world."

Also on 4/10/1884: "We are pained to mention the early death of Mrs. A.C. Snuffin, at 5 o'clock Sunday of consumption. Her funeral services were held at 2 o'clock Monday, Rev. C.H. Stone officiating, after which her remains were interred in the Laporte cemetery. Deceased leaves one child, a husband, father, sister and brother, besides a large circle of other relatives and friends to mourn her death."

A week later: "A. Snuffin has moved from George Stearley's tenement house to one belonging to Thos. Gill."

And on 1/6/1887: "Two unfortunates, named Earl Lapham and Will Snuffin, imbided too freely of something stronger than water on New Year's eve and were run in to undergo the cooling process..."

In 1987, I had found only the first article above and since it did not give place of burial, I put Ida May in the "Probably Buried at Laporte" list. I never connected her with the badly eroded marble headstone with clasped hands and the words "safe in the hands of Jesus" which I guessed was for a young wife of an A.G. SM..., possibly SMITH. I looked up every possible Smith who might have been buried in Laporte and found no one.

In February 1990, old-timer Hazel Kern told me that her mother had a Laporte cousin named Albert Carroll Snuffin, born 2/26/1861 and married 2/1/1882, to a woman whose maiden name, Hazel thought, was Lapham. The young wife had died leaving him with an infant, Edith May, born 2/11/1883. Hazel thought the wife's body might have been shipped to her home in Glenwood, Iowa, for burial. In the middle of the night it came to me that the partially obliterated stone and Ida May Snuffin belonged together. She was not the "beloved wife of A.G. SM..." but of " A.C. SN..." It was one of those "Eureka!" moments. I went back to the newspapers and found the other articles which confirmed that she was buried in Laporte and that the Laphams and the Snuffins were related.

In 1987, the stone was broken; a volunteer epoxied the pieces together. In 1997 the stone again fell into halves possibly from youngsters doing tombstone rubbings. Volunteer Steve Carr drilled holes in the marble and placed rods so once again it is upright.

24. Queenie Maud Adams + Died June 7, 1884 Infant

There was one newspaper reference, 6/12/1884: "Mr. and Mrs. John Q. Adams of Laporte, mourn the loss of their infant child which sad event occurred last Friday. They have the support of the entire community."

In 1990, volunteer Red Jenson built a white wrought iron fence around her little grave and broken marble tombstone.

25. Hugh McBride, Jr. Died July, 1885 Age 18

7/16/1885: "Hugh McBride, Jr., 18, of Laporte was taken ill Sunday afternoon with cholera morbus and died Monday morning. His father is a well known citizen of Laporte." There is no Hugh McBride, junior or senior, buried or reburied, at Grandview, so it is believed this young man was buried at Laporte.

26. Willie Curtis Died August, 1885 Age 2 years

From the 8/27/1885 paper: "Willie Curtis, son of W.A. Curtis, residing 3 miles north of Laporte, age 2 yrs, 4 mo. Victim of cholera infantum."

27. Johnny Meyers Died April 7, 1886 Age 2 years

4/15/1886: "Died. Johnny Meyers, on Apr. 7 of pneumonia, age 2, youngest son of E. M. Meyers of Pleasant Valley."

28. **Tousley infant** Died July, 1887 Age l year

7/28/1887: "Infant daughter of Mr. and Mrs. Tousley, age 1-1/2 at the home of Mr. and Mrs. J.C. Creed of Pleasant Valley. Inflammation of the brain. Mrs. Tousley came here from Iowa to visit her sister." Like the above two children, there is no written word they were buried at Laporte, but none are at Grandview. Her body may have been sent back to Iowa.

There are at least six members of the Howell family buried at Laporte between 1888 and 1940. Daughter and father are listed here and mother, son and grandchildren are listed in the section after 1900.

29. **Anna Howell Williams (+ ?)** May 19, 1888 Age 19

There is a sandstone marker with the initials A.T.W. This may be for Anna Williams.

"On Saturday, May 19, 1888, at the family home, near this city, Mrs. Anna Williams, 18, wife of Eli Williams. The deceased was a daughter of Mr. and Mrs. C.W. Howell and was born and grew to woman's estate in this valley. She leaves a husband, a 10-month old son, father and mother, brother and sister, and a large number of friends to mourn her departure for the spirit land. Her remains were buried on Sunday in the Laporte cemetery."

Anna's baby, Charlie Williams, was raised by his Grandmother Sarah Howell. He is mentioned again in the article covering his grandmother's death.

30. **Charles W. Howell +** Died June 10, 1894 Age 55 years

A small hand-scratched sandstone marker reads—if you look very carefully—C.W. Howell. As I learned more and more about this man I wondered about that pathetic stone. What kind of family did he have? Charles Howell was so well-known, but no one tried very hard to have him remembered. The *Fort Collins Courier,* June 14, 1894, carried this article:

Died. Howell. At his late home, near Laporte, Sunday, June 10, 1894, of cancer. Charles W. Howell, aged about 55 years. The funeral took place at Laporte on Monday, and was very largely attended, Rev. A.S. Phelps of this city conducting the services. The deceased came from Missouri to the Poudre valley in 1864, and has been a resident of Fort Collins and of

Laporte ever since. He was a steady law-abiding and industrious citizen and held the respect and good will of all who knew him. He leaves a wife, one married daughter and a son to mourn an irreparable loss.

There were as many articles about C.W. Howell as there were about Provost. Watrous reported that C.W. Howell paid $7.49 in taxes in 1866, and also, that after an election in 1876 in which only 20 persons voted, he was appointed constable and collector for the year. He was one of 20 grand jurors summoned in 1869. Mr. and Mrs. Chas. Howell are among the many who attended the John Robinson circus in Laporte in 1867, according to Chas. E. Roberts (9).

Other *Courier* articles about this man:

9/17/1878: "Charlie Howell thinks he has produced the 'boss' crop of wheat, so far as quality is concerned, this season and judging from the sample shown us we believe he has. It is of the white Australian variety and the handsomest we ever saw of any kind."

7/3/1879: "Chas. Howell who returned from Estes Park on Wed. says there are a lot of grasshoppers in the park."

3/18/1880: "Mr. and Mrs. C.W. Howell lost a 2-year-old on Friday. The child had been strong and healthy." (This child, as well as another who died in 1882, may have been buried in the Laporte cemetery, but I think not. Lala Nauta of Laporte said she had seen a grave near Howell's stone house north of Laporte, near the tepee rings, in an area now called Kremer's Indian Hills.)

10/28/1880: "Mr. Chas. W. Howell and family left last week to spend the winter in Missouri and Arkansas. Mr. Howell will spend most of the time at Hot Springs, Arkansas under treatment for rheumatism. They go with a team to Bethany, Missouri, Mr. Howell's old home."

1/27/1881: "Mr. Chas W. Howell writes us from Bethany, Missouri, that he reached his father's home in safety after a 37-day trip across the plains. His horses were both sick on the road and he was otherwise delayed by extreme cold weather. He is completely cured from rheumatism. He says he would not give Larimer County for the whole of Missouri. He has experienced nothing but disagreeable cold weather since he left Collins."

3/3/1881: "C.W. Howell is quite anxious to turn his back on the deep mud and return home."

6/15/1882: "A little son of Mr. Howell died very suddenly yesterday."

11/8/1883: "Chas. W. Howell, a former resident of this city but now living in Missouri dropped in from the east Tuesday taking his old friends by surprise."

10/16/1884: "Chas. W. Howell who is nominated for constable on the democratic ticket is known to nearly all the older residents of Fort Collins and is recognized as a strictly honest and capable man....Everybody should vote for Charlie Howell."

5/19/1888: A death notice of Howell's daughter, Anna Williams.

11/1/1888: "Charlie Howell who came here before the Poudre River assumed the magnitude of a rain drop, is running for one of the constables on the democratic ticket in this precinct. Everybody knows Charlie and everybody likes him and we predict a big majority for him on election day."

2/20/1890: "There will be a Washington's anniversary dance Fri. evening, Feb. 21st, at Charlie Howell's residence in Bellvue, to which everybody is invited. Charlie knows how to make them all happy, and he'll do it too, you bet."

8/3/1893: "Charlie Howell brought some vegetables to the newspaper office; they were greatly appreciated."

6/14/1894: His obituary (see above).

6/21/1894: "Mr. M.K. Howell, of Bethany, Missouri, father of the late Charles W. Howell arrived from the east last week, accompanied by his daughter, Mrs. Tucker of Kansas City, and is visiting relatives in this vicinity. Mr. Howell is 83 years old and is a hale and hearty gentleman. He is the brother of Mrs. Phillip Covington."

On October 3, 1997, there were three signatures in the Bingham Hill cemetery: "Alice DeWitt, Great Granddau of C.W. Howell; Debbie Jessee 2nd g.gdau, C.W. Howell; Spencer Jessee, 3rd g.grandson C.W. Howell." I don't know who these people are or where they're from, but how nice of them to stop in! A kind soul brought a new granite marker for C.W. Howell in April of 1998 and placed it by the old one.

31. **Wylie infant** Died January, 1885 Infant

1/15/1885: "The infant son of Frank Wylie of Pleasant Valley died Tues. night of pneumonia."

00. **A.J. Wylie** Died September, 1888

A.J. Wylie was definitely buried in the Bingham Hill Cemetery, and he may still be there. However, the newspaper said his body was being moved in the fall to Virginia, so read about him in the chapter "Buried at Bingham Hill and Moved." He is probably the grandfather of the Wylie infant buried three years earlier.

This is the first time embalming has been mentioned.

32. **Charles Luther Gordon** Died May, 1888 Age 5

5/24/1888: "Charles Luther Gordon, age 5, son of Hicks and Kate Gordon, died at Bellvue of membranous croup. The funeral took place at the Bellvue school."

33. **Nellie J. Land** + Died June 16, 1888 Age 7 years

Nellie's father, Benjamin R. Land, was the road overseer in Bellvue and was prominent in the labor and industrial movement. He owned 160 acres in Pleasant Valley and had "early soil" which produced mature potatoes in June (*Weekly Express,* 1/8/1887). Nellie's mother was C. E. Land, according to the headstone.

From 1888 until 1998—110 years—Nellie Land's perfect, unbroken, small rectangular two-piece marble headstone sat at the west end of the cemetery. Then it was stolen from its base and carried off. If the culprit does not return it, I will probably try to raise money to have a new one made, using photographs as a guide. It is bad enough to die at age seven; how could anyone be so crass as to steal her headstone?

The following three burials are of two cousins, ages four and 20, and the mother of the 20-year-old.

34. **Everet Yockey** + Died September 27, 1889 Age 4 years

His headstone proves he's there, that he was "4 Yrs. 5 M's. 8 D'ys." and that he was "Too Good for Earth, God called him home," but there are no parents' names on the stone and nothing in the newspapers. His stone is similar to and near another Yockey stone so I presumed they were relatives.

In 1987, I called a Jim Yockey who lived on Harmony Road. He thought he had no relatives in the Bingham Hill Cemetery, but when he looked in his family Bible, he found the name Everet, born April 29,

1885, and died September 27, 1889. Yockey did not know how this child fit in his family tree. He said his own father, Charles Henry, was born May 28, 1866 and died in 1945—almost too old to be brother to a child born in 1885. However, I learned later that Charles Henry and Everet were, in fact, brothers—both children of William Henry Yockey.

About 75 Yockeys had a get-together at Red Feather Lakes, northwest of Fort Collins, on July 25, 1996, to place a granite monument for the paternal head of the family, Levi Yockey. Levi was born in New York on August 15, 1814, and had come to Colorado from Ottawa County, Kansas, around 1880. He and his grown son, Jacob, built a two-story log house northeast of Red Feather Lakes near Black Mountain and operated a sawmill. Levi was killed by a horse at age 81 on September 5, 1895, and buried at Red Feather. Levi's great-grandson, David Yockey, from Chico, California, knew the location of the grave because as a young boy he attended the Westlake school at Red Feather and his mother and family had shown him the gravesite. Grave-dowser Bill Schneider confirmed the spot with witching rods. The land is presently owned by Monfort Holdings which gave permission for the headstone to be placed on what was the old Hardin Ranch. The *North 40 News* (9/1996) published a story and photo by Linda Bell about this ceremony.

Betty Amator of Springerville, Arizona, and Carol Yockey of Wellington furnished further family information. Levi Yockey and his wife, Elizabeth (Schlobig), had these children: David Clinton, Edwin, William H., Daniel, Jacob Nathaniel, and Mary E. Levi's son, William, was the father of Everet who died in 1889 and was buried at Bingham Hill. Little Everet's siblings were Charlie, (the above-mentioned Jim Yockey's father), Eva, James, Louise and Fred. David's wife and daughter are also buried at Bingham Hill.

35. **Sarah Yockey +** Died December 28, 1890 Age 42 years

Sarah was the wife of David Yockey according to her headstone. David was one of the six children of Levi. David and his wife, Sarah Elizabeth Bruce, had Julie Ann, Levi Allen, Josephine Alice, Luther Albert, Lorenzo Alfonzo, Expenrince Evelyn and Jarmie Addline.

There was one article in the newspaper, 1/1/1891: "The saddest and most unexpected occurrence that has taken place in this community for some time was the death of Mrs. David Yockey which occurred last Sunday at the family residence near Poudre canyon. Mrs. Yockey had been there but a short time and her death is sincerely mourned by all who knew her. Mr. Yockey and family have the sympathy of the entire neighborhood."

36. **Josephine Pile** + Died January 5, 1891 Age 20 years
She was the daughter of D. and S. Yockey and the wife of J. Pile, according to her tombstone; she died eight days after her mother. Her name and her mother's name are on opposite sides of the same stone which is the only one in the cemetery to have names on both east and west sides. The two Yockey headstones are amongst the prettiest in the cemetery and the only matched pair. They were both made by Starlin & Holmes.

From the newspaper, 1/15/1890: "Mr. Dave Yockey is now mourning the death of his daughter, Mrs. Josie Pyke [sic] which occurred on the 6th. Only one week before had Mr. Yockey buried his wife, and then this blow came, in which all sympathize with him and his family." No cause of death was given for either mother, daughter, or little cousin.

David Yockey left Colorado and died in Kansas in 1920. Most of the family left the area except for Jacob's oldest son, Eli. Eli is the father of Robert Dean Yockey, the deceased husband of Carol (Wright) Yockey of Wellington. Robert Dean and Carol are the parents of Robert Dean Yockey, Jr., from Laporte, Helen Louise Yockey Rumley of Estes Park and Roberta Mae Rumley of Fort Collins. Robert's children are Deanna Allen and Denise Markham. Helen's children are Tammy Elley, Sharon Ferris and Jack Rumley. Roberta's children are Shona Rader and Karen Jimenez. Carol Yockey also has eight great-grandchildren: Courtney and Cayla Allen, Trent Elley, Ashley and Whitney Ferris, Brandyn and Zachery Rader, and Kelsey Jimenez.

Carol Yockey said her husband, Robert Dean Yockey, tried to visit the Bingham Hill cemetery in the 1950s or early 1960s and was rudely refused entrance.

37. **Libbie A. Garland** + Died January 28, 1890 Age 17 years
1/30/1890: "Miss Libbie Garland has been very sick but is now convalescent." Same day: "Died. Garland. At Bellvue, Wed. morning 1/28/1890, of diptheria. Libbie Garland. Age 17 yrs." There was no mention of her parents' names. Her marble tombstone indicates that she was 17 Yrs. 5 M's. 28 D's.

In the 9/18/1890 Courier: "*Since last April there have been 13 deaths among children in Pleasant Valley, 11 of which were caused by diptheria and typhoid fever.*"

Pleasant Valley is the area north of Bellvue and some of the children were probably buried at Laporte, though I found no references of burials between April and September, 1890. Grandview Cemetery opened in Fort Collins in 1887, so perhaps some were taken there.

38. **A.A. Robinson** Died Christmas Eve, 1890 Age 46 years

According to the *Courier*, 12/25/1890, Robinson's dead body was found in the yard near Thomas Rowland's house at Stout. Coroner Gaugh ascertained the cause of death was a clear case of alcoholism. Robinson was "much addicted to drink" and had been "pickled in spirits" for several days before he died. He last worked for Barney Mallon in North Park and was about 46 years old.

Other Stout residents were buried at Laporte and he probably was also. He is not buried at Grandview or at Loveland.

From the Larimer County Pauper Record book, on September 30, 1904, a "Robinson (& children)" was given "Tickets & Cash, $29.15." This may have been the widow of A.A. Robinson.

39. **Winifred Farrar** + Died February 16, 1891 Age 5 years

This little girl was born December 8, 1885. *Courier*, 2/19/1891: "Died. Farrar. On Monday, Febr. 16, 1891, at the family residence near Laporte, of diptheria, Winifred, little daughter of Mr. and Mrs. Reed Farrar, aged 5 years, 2 months, and 8 days."

Her parents were Reed Farrar and Mary Ellen Lee. Winifred was the aunt of Esther Dixon Moore, Hazel Kern, Ellen Allen, Lee Dixon and Gerald Dixon, all of Fort Collins. Information that she was buried in Laporte came from Esther Moore and Ellen Allen.

Times must have been very hard, as in the Larimer County Pauper's Book, it is noted that on May 28, 1902, Reed Farrar was given $5 for groceries.

From the *Courier*, 7/25/1906: "Reed Farrar lost another daughter, Nina E., age 18, due to typhoid fever. She died at St. Joseph's Hospital in Denver and was buried at Grandview."

Hazel Kern said that Winifred's father, Reed, once tried to have his five-year-old daughter's body moved to Grandview but authorities would not allow it because she had died of diphtheria.

In 1988, Winifred's niece, Esther Moore, bought a granite stone for Winifred and had it set in concrete in an area near a picket fence according to her best memory of visiting the grave as a child.

Rolland Moore park was named for Esther Moore's husband. Rolland and Esther Moore had a daughter, LaDonna, who married Kenneth Boulter, and had sons Jeff and Kevin. Jeff has a son, Bret, and Kevin, who is president of the local archeological society, and very interested in history, has a son, Jared Boulter.

40. **Ida Esther Lasley** Died December 11, 1891 Age 16 years

From the *Courier*: "Died Friday, Dec. 11, 1891, at her farm home in Poudre Canyon, of pneumonia. Eldest daughter of Mr. and Mrs. B.M. Lasley. Age 16 years, 7 mos., 13 days. Much genuine sympathy is felt and expressed for the bereaved ones in this their hour of dire affliction. The funeral took place on Saturday last at Bellvue, a large concourse of mourning friends gathering on that sad occasion to assist in the last sad rites and to mingle their tears with those in affliction. Rev. Martin of this city delivered the funeral discourse."

41. and 42. **Collamer Infants** One died about 1891, one earlier

Frank A. Collamer and Achsah Alice Hulse were married May 30, 1878, in Larimer County; two of their 12 children were buried at Laporte. Rosalie Rohrbacker, a Collamer grandchild, said one child's death was brought about by horses which ran away and tipped the wagon in which the pregnant mother was riding. The baby was born prematurely and died. The other was stillborn. Collamer children who lived to adulthood were John, Emma, Mary, Menerva, Frank, Fred, Ruth, Effie, Laura and Arthur. Frank and Fred owned the land on both sides of the river west of Overland Trail where Lion's Park is today. Berniece Collamer Kelly was born on the south side of the river. Some Collamer family history is in *Larimer County History, 1985.*

Many local people knew Art Collamer, who lived at 112 N. U.S. Hwy 287, and sold firewood almost until his death at age 93 on December 17, 1987. He told me that the babies, who were his siblings, were buried "near an Indian who was adopted by a Mexican family." He meant

Donaciano Vigil, which would place the babies at the far west end of the cemetery.

43. **Laura Malaby** Died March 25, 1897 Age 8 weeks
Ross Malaby and Emma Collamer, one of the ten surviving children in the above-mentioned family, were married March 5, 1896. Emma was only 16 or 17 when Laura was born on February 6, 1897. Emma had measles during the pregnancy and the child died as a result.
Later Malaby children were Alma Alice and Ralph. Information came from grandchild Mary Wessels. This family's history is also in *Larimer County History, 1985.*

44. **Charlie Brooks** Died July, 1892 Age 3 years
Charlie's birth was announced 4/25/1889: "Mr. and Mrs. Brooks of Laporte had a 9 lb. son on April 23."
7/14/1892: "Charlie, the four-year-old son of Henry Brooks, who lives a short distance southeast of the city water pumping works, was drowned on Tuesday of last week in the Mercer Ditch. The child was playing along the banks of the ditch near the house and, unobserved by his parents, fell in, death ensuing before his absence was discovered. The grief-stricken parents have the heartfelt sympathy of their numerous friends." (Note: He was only 3 years, 3 months, not 4 years.)
Charlie is the only known person buried at Bingham Hill who died of accidental drowning. The Mercer ditch still runs through the farm which now belongs to Howard Lindholm.

45. **Lester Brooks** Died in the early 1890s Child
Bill Porter of Laporte volunteered the following information. His mother, Della Clifton, came to Laporte from an orphan's home in Colorado Springs as a young girl about ten years old in 1901 and was "adopted" by the William Henry Brooks family which had several boys. They lived on Overland Trail where the Lindholm farm is now (West Co. Rd. 50). She told Bill that the Brooks seemed to lose a son every seven years and that at least two, whose names Porter did not know, were buried at Laporte before 1900. Relatives later wanted to move the bodies to Grandview but since typhoid fever was involved, authorities did not allow it.

Three Brooks youngsters, Dale, Chester, and Benjamin, were buried at Grandview in 1896, 1901, and 1903, respectively. At one time, Mildred Beatty apparently saw Laporte markers, either wood or stone, with the names Lester and Charles Brooke (2). I read of no Brooke family, but Brooks is often mentioned; therefore, I think the markers Beatty saw were for Bill Porter's mother's adopted brothers.

The date of Charles' drowning was printed in the paper; I found nothing else about a Lester but he likely died of typhoid. There are no remains today of any Brooks markers at Bingham Hill Cemetery.

Della went to school with Volney, Ted, Cam, and Lucy Herring. The 1906-1908 newspapers printed several little articles about Mrs. Henry Brooks and her daughter, Della, who visited neighbors, went to town (Fort Collins), bought a piano, and so on.

Della was adopted (though not legally), because when her own mother died, her dad took it so hard he began drinking. When he threatened to kill his mother-in-law, officials took the kids to an orphans' home. In her later years, Della found a sister in Colorado Springs and a brother in Smith Center, Kansas.

Della met and married Frank Porter. Porter was born in Belfast, Ireland, joined the British army when he was 17, spent five years in India, and then became a policeman on the Glasgow, Scotland, police force. He had an Irish buddy, Will Sloan, who came to Laporte, Colorado, because of his cousin, Mrs. Rebecca Falloon. Porter came to visit Sloan, and though he had intended to go on to Canada, he stayed and homesteaded north of Laporte. That was in 1910.

Porter died in 1939 at age 59 due to arthritis in his spine which paralyzed him. Della lived until 1975 and died at age 85. Their son, William Henry Porter, was born February 25, 1918, and was 80 years old the day he related the above information about his mother and father. Billy, as he is affectionately called by most everyone who knows him, still lives northwest of Laporte on the old Shipp homestead, just south of land his father homesteaded. He is calving out 36 cows this spring, feeds sheep, and gets along all right in spite of arthritis. When asked if he was in touch with his mother's adopted brothers, he said the Brooks had moved to Washington State and to Longmont long ago. He had never talked to them about the dead Brooks children.

46. **Thomas Jess Honnold** Died about 1893 Adult male

Thomas Jess Honnold and his wife Susan Annis Honnold lived in a house which no longer exists but once sat on the west slope of Bingham Hill Road, east of the silo. Beehives were in that location in the 1980s and for several years previously. Mrs. Harold (Charlene) Hicks of Fort Collins said several Honnold children were born there, including Tom and Kit.

One day, the family's hogs got out and were running up the ditch bank. Honnold told young Tom to hurry ahead and cut them off. When the youngster, who was about nine years old, looked back, his father was lying on the ground, dead of an apparent heart attack. He was buried in the nearby cemetery.

Young Tom was Charlene's uncle by marriage. She had no other information but Bohlender Funeral records show that young Tom was born 2/19/1884 in Bellvue and was buried at Grandview 7/27/1978 at age 94. The year he was nine would have been 1893.

47. **Von Vihl Infant** Died 1892 or 1893 Newborn

This is one of the burials I learned about because of my penchant for talking about the cemetery. At a back yard party at Willis Smith's house on Vine Drive in 1989, I heard about this baby from Jacqueline Michie, who had learned it from her mother, Rosa Beeson Von Vihl Hoffman, age 92 at the time, and from her aunt, 91-year-old Helen Katherine Nieder, a sister of the Von Vihl baby.

Alfred John Baptiste Von Vihl from Alsace Lorraine married Helen Wolfer in Boulder in 1891 and moved to Laporte. Their first child, a son, had the umbilical cord wrapped around his neck, which caused his death. The baby's uncle, Joseph Von Vihl, made a small coffin and a wood cross for the baby and buried him in Laporte. Other children born to the family were Alfred Joseph (1894), George Charles (1896), Helen Katherine (1899) and Alice Juanita (1903), all born in Laporte. Helen said she used to visit the grave and bring wild flowers but does not now remember where it is.

The baby's brother, George, married Rosa Gertrude Beeson and they had George, Dorothy Kendall and Jacqueline, who married John Michie (County Commissioner 1968-1976) in 1938. The Michies have lived all their married lives on the same farm owned before him by John's father, Adam, and grandfather, Adam Michie, Sr., who purchased it in 1896.

Rosa Beeson Hoffman is also related to the Robertson children (See Robertson.)

48. **Walter Thomas** Died February 5, 1894 Young man

Courier, 2/8/1894: "Laporte News: A young man whose name we hear was Walter Thomas was chopping wood in the foothills just west of here on the 5th and had felled a tree and began to trim the limbs off, when he suddenly jumped up and fell dead without speaking."

One weird story!

Walter Thomas is not at Grandview. I had thought this man might be the red-headed "J. Thomas" which the 4-H Club unearthed, but we later learned that Johnny Thomas was buried in 1877 and has already been discussed at length.

49. **Samuel Harrison Clark** Died July 20, 1895 Age 50

Courier, 8/1/1895: "Pleasant Valley News. July 20. Mr. Samuel Clark, late of Nebraska, breathed his last dying of consumption, aged about 52 years. He leaves a widow and several children to mourn their loss. The family is in a helpless state."

This man's named eluded me and was not in the 1988 or 1990 editions of this book. Upon receipt of a letter of inquiry from Judy Hall of Independence, Kansas, in 1992, I looked once again through 1895 newspapers and found the above death notice.

Mrs. Hall's family records show that Samuel Clark was born January 31, 1845, at Agency, Wapello County, Iowa, that he died at Bellvue on July 20, 1895, and was buried in Laporte on July 21, 1895. He had married Susanna Jane McCleary, born at Grant, Iowa, in 1865 or 1866. They had 13 children: Mame, Kate, Harriet, John, Cyrus, Lillie, William, Charles, Martha, twins Minnie and David, Sophie and Frank. Charles married Virginia Fisher and had Nora and Goldie. Nora married Ralph Hill and they had Charlie, Harold and Cleona. Cleona married Elmer Allen and they had Judy (my informant!), Cathy, Marilyn, Lonny and Dan. Judy has done a great job with family genealogy and if it weren't for her, I would not have known that Mr. Samuel Clark was buried at Laporte.

Clark filed a claim to a homestead on 160 acres of land one mile southeast of Hazard, Nebraska, on December 12, 1883. The 1885 census in Sherman County showed he had 2 mules, 16 head of cattle, 38 swine, and that they had made 300 pounds of butter and raised Indian corn, Irish potatoes and hay.

He apparently had injuries from which he could not recover, and also suffered from TB. Some time in 1894, like so many others, the family came to Colorado with great hopes for a cure. They drove mules pulling a covered wagon up the river about ten miles north of Fort Collins. The eight youngest children at that time were 7, 9, 11, 11, 14, 15, 17 and 19. Sam Clark died within a year after his arrival in Colorado.

After his death the family moved to Lincoln County, Nebraska, where his widow took a claim. She was buried in Garfield, Nebraska, on July 2, 1908.

Mrs. Hall asked to have Samuel Clark's name added to the large memorial stone, but the woman who controls the gate to the cemetery never responded to her request. The Halls plan a 1998 trip to put their own monument up for Samuel Harrison Clark.

50. **Mrs. Jones** + Died August 20, 1895 Adult woman

One particular sandstone marker in the southwest portion of the cemetery is intriguing. Its hand-chiselled name is on the west side of the stone whereas traditionally, at least in this cemetery, names are on the east side. Also, no other stone reads "MRS."

An article in the *Courier* (8/29/1895) is equally odd: "Laporte News. Mrs. Jones, mother of Mrs. Hawley, who lives on W.P. Bosworth's farm, passed away Tuesday forenoon, August 20." The newspaper did not print a first name either, a courtesy usually given to people in their obituaries or death notices. She was apparently only known as "Mrs. Jones."

Erma L. Devers, who wrote several "Hawley" biographies (5) said that the famous early Captain C.C. Hawley was her great-uncle. As we read over one article she had written, we saw that one of the 12 children of C.C. Hawley, Walter L. Hawley, married Maude Jones on June 5, 1886. Our "Mrs. Jones" may have been Maude Hawley's mother.

One Bosworth farm was l/2 mile west of the old Bellvue store and is presently owned by Richard and Sally Brewster; whether that is where the daughter of Mrs. Jones lived is unknown.

51. **Virginia Murray Wombacher** Died May 8, 1897 Age 39 years

The following articles were in the *Fort Collins Courier.*
2/25/1897: "Mr. Wombaker, who lived in Pleasant Valley a year ago but

moved from there to the Harris place, has returned to Bellvue with his family and is occupying the Stimson house. We welcome them back as they are consistent Christian people and we cannot get too many such in any community."

3/4/1897: "Miss Gertie Wombaker, who has had typhoid fever, is slowly recovering." (Gertie recovered, but two months later, her mother was dead.)

5/13/1897) "Mrs. Virginia Wombacher died at Bellvue Saturday. The deceased leaves a husband and eight children to mourn an irreparable loss. The funeral took place Sunday and burial was in Laporte."

5/13/1897: "George Murray was called to the bedside of his dying aunt, Mrs. Virginia Wombacher of Pleasant Valley, last Saturday night and in spite of all the attending physician's efforts she passed away. She was buried in the Laporte cemetery on Sunday afternoon at 4 o'clock, Revs. Bickerstaff and Moore conducting the services."

Richard Funkhouser of Bonner's Ferry, Idaho, had written to Ceil Damschroder, a member of the Larimer County Genealogical Society, asking about his grandmother. Damschroder passed on the inquiry to me, and we found the information that ascertained that Mrs. Wombaker was buried at Laporte.

Later, Carol Funkhouser sent information that Virginia was born June 22, 1858 to James McGrew Murray and Bellmira Hall. She married John Joseph Wombacher on May 6, 1880, and had the following children: Delphine Vivian, Gertie, Leonara, John Murray, Audley Eugene, an unnamed stillborn, Alice Lidora, Raymond Luther, Emma Elizabeth, Alma Viola and Arthur Edward. The newspaper articles didn't mention her cause of death or the birth of her last child. Death was either from typhoid or a bad parturition or both.

52. **Arthur Edward Wombacher** Died September 8, 1897 Age 4 months

Arthur's birth may have precipitated his mother's death; he lived only four months after his mother died. It is presumed by the family that he is buried in Laporte near his mother. There are no markers for them.

53. **Cora Salisbury** Died between 1896 and 1898 Age 5 years

Cora was the daughter of Cassius R. and Hattie Salisbury. Hattie was a sister of Edith Farrell, the mother of Preston Farrell, an old-timer who lived in Laporte for many years and furnished many tidbits of information. Cora was Preston's cousin. Preston's daughters, Dorothea O'Neill and Lois Sharp, still live in Laporte on East Bingham Hill Road.

Cora's relatives first thought she had died in the late 1880s, but Norma Salisbury, widow of this child's younger brother, believed the death was closer to 1896 or 1898. Norma Salisbury, Veda Hoepfer, Leone Thayer, and Lucille B. West are daughters of Frank E. Baxter, a prominent Laporte resident and long-time owner (1905 to 1937) of the Overland Trail store and post office in Laporte (where the West Fort Collins Water District now has an office).

An interesting fact about little Cora is that she was not buried inside the present fenced boundaries of the cemetery but close to the Bingham Hill Road. There had been a fence around her grave for years; old-timer Willie Morgenstern pointed out the area where there were two small fenced areas which both eventually disappeared. Norma Salisbury wrote (2/25/1990): "My husband had an older sister buried at Bingham Hill Cemetery the winter of 1896 or 1898. There was never a marker—just a fence and some chokecherry bushes. When the pig farmer bought it he farmed over the top of it, so I don't know exactly where it was."

Roxxe Wootton of Laporte also remembers seeing the fenced grave while riding in a jeep in the late 1960s. There were apparently several burials between the Salisbury grave on Bingham Hill Road and the present cemetery fence boundary.

54. **Wesley Allen Shipp** Died about 1895 Age about 90

He was known to the family as "Grandpap." According to Shipp genealogy, he lived in Indiana (1830), Illinois (1840) and then Kansas. Apparently his wife died, for he came alone from Solomon, Kansas, around 1868 to live with his son, James Wesley Shipp, who homesteaded along the Poudre River by Bellvue. A short history of James W. Shipp is in *Larimer County History, 1987.* He is the one who found an Indian skeleton in a cave on the north end of the Bellvue Fold.

One day, while fishing the Poudre River, "Grandpap" poked his pole into the sand and walked off. Where he wandered, no one knew, and on his return about a year later, he explained that he had been visiting relatives. (Information from Helen Shipp Bland of Bellvue, a life-long resident of the Pleasant Valley her ancestors helped settle.)

There was apparently once a marker in the Laporte cemetery for a "Walter Shipp, 1810-1895" (2); perhaps it said "Wesley" or "W. Shipp."

James Wesley Shipp, mentioned above, was the father to Henry, Sarah Jane, Lizzie, Charles Allen, George Wesley and William Albert. William Albert had Elsie Mrytle, James Albert, Walter Raymond and Alice Irene. Walter Raymond had William Joseph, Walter Richard, Mary Margaret, Helen Lora and Elsie May. That second-to-last one, Helen, is now Helen Bland, and without her, there wouldn't have been much of a Shipp story in this book.

Newspapers had many little stories about the Shipps, Brooks, Pennocks, Flowers, Provosts, Herrings, Nugents, Gardners and others. Some headliners were the murder of Wm. Gardner in 1904, the death of Sardie Flowers in Idaho in 1906, Lizzie Provost's elopement with Pedigo in 1907 and a Shipp daughter's elopement in 1912.

55. **William Sherman Ouderkirk (P)** Died around 1894 Adult male

This gentleman was first reported by my Laporte neighbors, Harry Dunlap and Jimmy Hyde, to be "Bill Articurk," and that is the way his name was sandblasted (yikes!) onto the memorial. They said he was the first husband of Jimmy Hyde's great-aunt and between the two of them, they made a good stab at how to spell his name.

In March of 1996, Nathelle Stollens of Longmont contacted librarian Rheba Massey who forwarded her name to me. Mrs. Stollens is a granddaughter of William **Ouderkirk**. He was the first husband of Nathelle's grandmother, Louella (Nellie) Myrtle Dunlap Ouderkirk Hurzeler. Louella married Bill Ouderkirk on March 2, 1890, in Nebraska. They had a son, Edward McClure Ouderkirk (1890-1979), who was the father of Nathelle, and a son Elmer who was born April 12, 1893 and who died at six weeks in Nebraska. Ouderkirk was a cowboy-rancher who came to Colorado to live near Louella's brother and father, the Dunlaps.

Mrs. Stollens writes, "Louella's father was James Hamilton Dunlap, who had ten children. Two of her brothers, McClure and David W. Dunlap, married sisters, Fannie and Marie Hurzeler, who had a brother, Emil Hurzeler. They all lived in Fort Collins and that is how Grandma met Emil Hurzeler."

Louella married a second time to Emil Hurzeler on March 18, 1897, in Fort Collins, so Mrs. Stollens believes Grandfather Will, as he was called, died sometime between 1893 and 1896. Mrs. Stollens writes: "The story is that he had typhoid and was just getting so he could eat a little broth. His brother-in-law, Richard Dunlap, brought him a blueberry pie. He said he was going to eat some of it and as soon as he did, he went into convulsions. I understand that typhoid eats little holes in the stomach and intestines and I suppose the acid or seeds is what did the damage. Anyway, he didn't live long. Back in those days lots of people died from doing foolish things. He probably was so hungry for something good to eat that he didn't think of the consequences. It is too bad because he was so young and had a beautiful family and lots to live for. And my brother and I never got to meet and know him."

Mrs. Stollens said her father told her brother that Laporte was where Grandfather Will was buried so she agrees with Harry Dunlap and Jimmy Hyde that Ouderkirk is, in fact, buried at Laporte. Fortunately, she knew how to spell his name.

The Ouderkirk family traces back to Jan Jansen Ouderkirk who came to New York in 1640 when it was still called New Amsterdam. He came from "Ouderkirk on De Amstel" which means "Old Church on the Amstel River" in the Netherlands.

Mrs. Stollens, who is 75 in 1998, and a good genealogist, said that her grandmother didn't talk much about her early life—maybe it was too painful. Luckily, she had a photograph of William Ouderkirk.

Harry Dunlap said that his father, Richard Dunlap, and Ouderkirk had an agreement that the first one who died was supposed to contact the other. Dunlap said his dad never received any messages from the spirit world.

56. **Mrs. Macklin** Died February, 1897 Adult woman

2/4/1897: "Mrs. Macklin of Laporte leaves a husband and 8 children. The family came from Pennsylvania last spring."

This is another woman whose first name wasn't known by the newspaper reporter; also it is a case of presuming she was buried at Laporte since she is not at Grandview.

I called a Mark Macklin of Wellington to ask if he were related to the above Mrs. Macklin. He didn't think so, but he did have a good cemetery story. He graduated with the last class from the Laporte high school (1964) and remembered the cemetery fondly. He and some of his track team would cut off Bingham Hill Road at the cemetery, sit laughing on the ditch bank, then go back to school across the field, thereby having cut in half the coach's orders to run the Bingham Hill-Bellvue loop.

57. **Milton Lewis** Died October, 1897 Young man

In the *Fort Collins Express,* 10/2/1887, under "Bellvue News," Richard Baker found an article which simply said that Lewis was a young man who had been prospecting in the Boulder mines and that he died and was interred in the Laporte cemetery.

58. **Lloyd Raynor** (+ ?) Died February 26, 1899 Age 15 years

3/2/1899. "Died, Sun., Feb. 26, 1899, this city, of consumption, Lloyd Raynor, son of Mrs. John Wallace, aged 15 years. Internment took place on Tuesday, at Laporte."

Lloyd's mother's name was probably Belle L., as a woman by that name is buried next to a John Wallace at Grandview.

A sandstone marker at Bingham Hill has the initials 'L.W.R.' and it might be for Lloyd Raynor.

Local resident Richard Rayner (spelled with an "e" instead of "o") said his family only came here in 1911 so is probably not related. Interestingly, his dad, Olin Rayner, a CSU ag professor, built silos, including the landmark silo on Bingham Hill Road.

There are two Laporte burials which I could find little about, but were mentioned by Ruth Hereim or Mildred Beatty (2) who either saw the headstones at one time or obtained the information from personal interview. They are Henry P. Blevins and Lloyd Willis.

59. **Henry P. Blevins** Died perhaps in 1890s Adult male

He homesteaded 160 acres which included the Bellvue fish hatchery site; I found his name in the grantor/grantee books at the County Clerk's office as early as November 16, 1862. He used a six-year-old black stallion as collateral on a mortgage in 1863. He was on the list of those attending the 1867 Laporte circus (9), bought 160 acres from the United States in 1869, and had other transactions in 1875 and 1876. He was definitely an early settler.

60. **Lloyd Willis** (+ ?) Died perhaps in 1890s Infant

Lloyd Willis was the son of Raymond and Zoe Walters Willis. If Raymond Willis was five years old and remembered the burial of Barbara Bingham in 1876 (2), he'd have to have been born in 1871. I looked up his burial record at Grandview and found he was, in fact, born in 1871 and died at age 90-11-19 on May 15, 1962. When Raymond and Zoe had a child who died, I don't know. Arbitrarily picking age 25 as the father's age would make little Lloyd's death around 1897.

There is an "L.W." sandstone marker, west of Everet Yockey's stone, and perhaps it is for little Lloyd Willis.

From the Pioneer Association Scrapbook in the local history room of the library, I found articles about Raymond Willis. He was a nephew of Louis Blackstock of Bellvue; nephew of Wm. and Perry Bosworth; an authority on the history of Bellvue; a canal rider, then superintendent of the High Line Ditch Company; and his farm was what is now known as the Graves place. He married Zoe Walter of Bellvue on December 19, 1890, and died in May of 1962 at age 90.

61. **George Thomas Currey** Died around 1900 Adult male

Information about this man came from Anna Bryant of Briggsdale who called after her daughter, Myrna Brautigam of Fort Collins, sent a copy of a March 19, 1990, *Coloradoan* article which listed the names going onto the new Bingham Hill Cemetery memorial stone.

Mrs. Bryant said that when her dad, Ralph Currey (born in 1890), was about eight years old, he and his parents lived in the Forks Hotel, which was run by his aunt, Delilah Clark. Ralph Currey pointed to the Bingham Hill Cemetery one day and told his daughter that his grandfather was buried there. Mrs. Bryant believes her great-grandfather was born in Canada and that there was a tombstone at one time.

62. **Barkley Relatives** Died before 1900 Children

Bill Porter of Laporte told a story about a family in the log house which sat below the ditch on Herring's place near Bingham Hill Road, only a few yards from the cemetery, and was at various times probably occupied by Ben Claymore, and definitely occupied by the Victor Apodaca and Ball-Johnson families and by Hikey Harbinson. Anna Mae Grenz of Fort Collins was born in 1924 in the same log cabin, which shortly afterwards was dismantled or burned.

Porter's mother told him that her (adoptive) mother (Mrs. Wm. Henry Brooks) often pointed out the house and said that the "poor relations" of the rich, downtown, hardware store Barkleys had lived there. Some of the children died, probably in an epidemic, and Mrs. Brooks went over to spend the night in order to keep rats from bothering the children's corpses. She stayed until morning when the undertaker came with his team and wagon. Porter was not sure if the family's name was Barkley or not.

Grandview and mortuary records show that two Barkleys, May Isabella, age 15, and Edwin Robert, age 17, died of pneumonia and were buried at Grandview on December 8, 1903. Parents were Edwin Turner and Harriet Ann Barkley. Porter thinks the children his mother spoke of died before 1900 and also were younger. Judging from the size of the Grandview Barkley tombstone, May and Edwin were not the "poor relations."

The Bingham Hill cemetery is just a few yards from where that cabin was, so probably the youngsters which Della Porter spoke about were buried there.

John Baptiste Provost
Donated land for the Laporte cemetery in 1879 after burying two children in 1862 and 1866.

Rowland Herring
Over 100 burials, including one of his infant daughter, took place during his family's stewardship of the land, from 1887-1944.

HEADSTONES FOR UNKNOWN PEOPLE

The end of the 19th century seems an appropriate place to mention the people who have sandstone markers with hand-carved names or initials but about whom I learned little.

63. One stone is marked **L.D.R.** This could be for Lloyd Raynor who died in 1899, or it could be for someone else.

64. **A.T.W.** might be for Anna Williams, Arthur Wombacher, A.J. Wiley, or someone else. The stone is right next to L.D.R., and has a big circle of stones around his/her grave.

65. **L.W.** could be for Lloyd Willis.

Ma.Rosa Elvinia Sanchez, Jacobo Trujillo, J. Thomas, and **Mrs. Jones** have homemade markers but their identities are evident from their names, and they have been written about. Sanchez and Trujillo were buried after 1900. J. Thomas and Mrs. Jones are in Part I.

66. **L. Holley** Date of death, age, and sex unknown

There remains one last totally mysterious person, and that is L. Holley. The stone sits toward the west end of the cemetery with 'HOLLEY. L.' clearly marked on its west side and the initials 'L.H.' on top. Someone wanted to make sure L. Holley was not forgotten.

Many Halleys are mentioned in old newspapers but the stone definitely says "Holley." I called W.D. Holley at Livermore but he is a relative newcomer to the area. I looked in marriage records, microfilm, mortuary records, ran inquiries in "Letters to the Editor" and put the name on the Internet. No response.

Burials in the 1860s and 1870s were nearer the east end of the cemetery, so I don't think Holley's burial was that early, but it could have been anywhere from the 1880s to the 1940s, male or female, child or adult. Another thought is that the stone is for a "Hawley" which sounds the same as "Holley;" it wouldn't be the first time a name was misspelled on a stone. L. HOLLEY is a mystery left for someone else to solve.

PERSONS ONCE BURIED AT BINGHAM HILL BUT MOVED

1. **Lathrop L. Hills (+ Highland, KS.)** Died June 11, 1867 Age 35

   Lathrop L. Hills was killed about six miles east of Cheyenne, June 11, 1867, while with a survey crew locating a route for the Union Pacific Railroad. According to Susan Carlson, in Wyoming Historical Markers at 55 MPH, a marker was placed in 1973 by the Hills family and states in part: "...HILLS WAS RIDING OUT IN FRONT OF THE GROUP WHEN HE WAS ATTACKED BY INDIANS AND KILLED. WITHIN MINUTES HIS MEN DROVE OFF THE INDIANS AND LATER REPORTED THEY FOUND 19 ARROW WOUNDS IN HIS BODY....HILLS' WORK LIVED AFTER HIM. . .THE [FINISHED] RAILROAD REDUCED TRAVEL TIME FROM THE SIX MONTHS REQUIRED BY WAGON TRAIN TO FIVE DAYS FROM OMAHA TO SAN FRANCISCO."

   "This handsome granite marker," Carlson writes, "is hidden south of the post office in Hillsdale." Hillsdale, Wyoming, was named after Lathrop Hills, and the monument is near the ambush site.

   Isaac J. Gibson, an Army guard for the survey team, said he shed many a tear as he helped pull out the arrows with his pliers. The Indians had taken two scalps from Hills' red hair. Hills' body was first buried at the ambush site, then at Laporte.

   At some later date, his body was exhumed and sent by train to Omaha where his father took the body in a wagon to his home in Highland, Kansas, and buried him (9). Hills has the distinction of being the only person buried at Laporte who was (a) killed by Indians, (b) buried three times, (c) had a monument put up in his honor and (d) had a town named after him. His tombstone in Kansas, reads: LATHROP L. HILLS, Division Engineer of the U.P. Railroad, KILLED By the Indians near the present site of Cheyenne, June 12, 1867. Aged 35 y'rs, 8 mo's, 28 d's.

   Four McBrides were buried at Bingham Hill Cemetery in Laporte between 1880 and 1894 and were all moved to Grandview Cemetery on or about February 20, 1897.

2. **John R. McBride (+ G.V.)** Died June 6, 1880 Age 2 years

   Courier, 7/1/1880: "Mr. and Mrs. Thos. McBride of Laporte lost their youngest child, John, Age 3, on Sunday the 20th." (Grandview records and his tombstone say he died June 6, and that he was age 2-9-26.)

3. **Patrick McBride (+ G.V.)** Died July 14, 1880 Age 5 years

Patrick McBride had no newspaper report, but Grandview records plus a white marble tombstone in Lot D-157 tell of this second son's death. He was five years and 15 days old.

Both little brothers' names are engraved on one stone: JOHN R., Born Aug. 10, 1877, Died June 6, 1880 and PATRICK, born June 29, 1875, died July 14, 1880. CHILDREN OF T.R. and M. McBRIDE. This stone for two sons who died a month apart looks like one that might have been moved from Laporte and the timing of other family deaths indicates that it was.

4. **Mary Jane McKillop McBride** Died July 10, 1886 Age 47

Courier, 7/15/1886. "Mrs. Mary Jane McKillop McBride, wife of Thomas R. McBride, born in Airdrie, Scotland, 1/25/1839, died July 10, 1886, at 6:30 a.m. She had been a sufferer for years and death ensued from dropsy of the heart. She leaves a husband and 5 children, 3 sons and 2 daughters. The funeral took place at the residence at 11 o'clock Sunday, July 11, 1886."

As far as I know, she was the only European-born person buried at Laporte. Proof of her burial in Laporte is in the next obituary.

5. **Agnes McBride** Died November, 6, 1894 Age 14 years

Courier, 11/8/1894: "Died. On Tuesday, Nov. 6, 1894, at the home of her sister and guardian, Mrs. Lewis Black, of typhoid fever, Agnes McBride, youngest daughter of Thomas McBride, a former resident of Laporte, age 13 years, 11 mo. Agnes was a bright, kind-hearted active and exceedingly well disposed child and was truly beloved by all who knew her. She was buried on Wed. by the side of her mother in the cemetery at Laporte, Rev. J.F. Coffman conducting the services."

The three McBride children who died had an older sister, Mary R. McBride, who married Lewis H. Black on January 1, 1893. Witnesses were Agnes McBride and H.A. Black. J.F. Coffman, Minister of the Gospel, performed the marriage (10). Agnes was 12 when she signed her sister's marriage certificate and died less than two years later.

On August 4, 1896, only three years after their marriage, Lewis Black died at age 30. In the *Courier,* 8/6/1896, Lewis is described as a farmer with a merry heart and a cheery, happy disposition. "From the time he had to give up work and go to bed, it was less than a week before death intervened, from a rupture of the veriform appendix." He had several brothers and sisters but no children.

Such a painful time for this Mary Black! Her mother, a 41-year-old woman born between Edinburgh and Glasgow buries two young sons far from home in pioneer Laporte in 1880. Six years later, she dies, leaving three more sons and two daughters. The youngest child, five-year-old Agnes, goes to live with her older sister Mary; eight years later, at 14, Agnes dies. Their dad, Thomas B. McBride, by this time is a "former resident of Laporte." Then Mary Black's husband dies.

His young widow purchased 15 grave sites at Grandview, buried her husband, then had the bodies of her mother (Mary Jane) and siblings (John, Patrick and Agnes) exhumed and moved from Laporte in February, 1897 (7). She bought a stone and had it engraved: MARY H. BLACK (her own name), Beloved Wife (of) LEWIS H. BLACK (who) Died August 4, 1896, Aged 30 years. The little boys' tombstone probably was first placed at Laporte by their parents. When the mother died and the Dad left town, no stone ever went up for the mother or Agnes—either in Laporte or at Grandview—or if they did, they were destroyed.

Lewis Black's parents were later buried in the same lot—Philamen P. Black at age 76 on November 1, 1901, and Hannah Black at age 74 on December 26, 1907. There was an obituary for Philamen (he came from New York to Colorado in 1874, had a home and orchard three miles north of town, left an aged wife and 5 children), but none for Hannah.

The Blacks and McBrides have eight empty lots at Grandview. That indicates she and any others in the family left town. What happened to Mary McBride Black? To her three brothers? To all Black's siblings? Did she marry again? To whom? Where is she buried? She is not at Grandview, unless under a different name, and probably not at all, or the available lots would have been used.

(Note: The 'Mary Jane McBride Black' in Grandview records should read 'Mary Jane McKillop McBride,' for the birth and death dates correspond to the mother, not the daughter.)

There are two references to Thomas R. McBride in Watrous. He was dismissed in 1868 from charges of contempt of court in failing to appear when summoned to serve as petit juror, and in 1879, he confirmed a story of Major Whitely about the rescue of "Ute Susan" in 1863.

Thomas McBride was one of Laporte's earliest settlers, but apparently no descendants live in the area today. These details about the McBrides and the Blacks may give clues to a genealogical sleuth who can find some living members of the family and inform them of the value of their eight empty lots at Grandview—over $6,000 at 1998 prices.

6. Elizabeth N. Vandewark Died April l, 1882 Age 30

According to Watrous, Lizzie N. Giles married Elmer E. Vandewark. They came from Beatrice, Nebraska, in 1873 and settled on a farm in Pleasant Valley, near the village of Bellvue. According to her grandson, Richard Baker, she died in childbirth and was buried in the Laporte cemetery.

Baker watched the body being exhumed in the early 1940s. He noticed that the coffin was manufactured, not homemade, and that it had a window of glass on the lid. Baker was amazed to see the rich, brown hair color of his grandmother, who had been buried about 60 years.

7. Elizabeth Vandewark (+ G.V.) Died Sept 12, 1890 Age 8

Elizabeth was the child whose birth caused the death of her mother eight years earlier. She was also exhumed in the 1940s and buried with her mother in one grave at Grandview. There is no notation in Grandview records about the bodies being moved, and only because Richard Baker said so, do we know it to be so.

The daughter has a memorial stone at Grandview but her mother does not, even though the mother died first. Perhaps the mother's stone was damaged or destroyed during its 60 years at Laporte or during the move. Little Elizabeth's stone is in Section I, Lot 46 and says: "ELIZABETH, dau. of E.E. and E.N. VANDEWARK, DIED Sep. 12, 1890, AGED 8 Y'rs. 5 M's. 24 D'ys. Asleep in Jesus."

George Pennock and his wife both died so young!

8. George Franklin Pennock (+ G.V.) Died January 18, 1887 Age 39

Pennock was born May 8, 1847, and came to Colorado in 1864. The *Courier* (1/20/1887) carried a long article about his death:

Death of Frank Pennock

The death of Frank Pennock, of Bellvue, which occurred in this city at 10 o'clock Tuesday evening, is the saddest we have had to chronicle in some time. Mr. Pennock has, for the past year, been suffering from the effects of an abdominal tumor which was causing himself a great deal of pain and his family and friends much uneasiness. Finding he could not live long unless the tumor was removed, as it was constantly increasing in size, he finally decided to take the chance of an operation. The surgeons, after consultation, having but little hope, however, of his recovery, decided to give Mr. Pennock the benefit of whatever chance there might be in his favor by performing the operation and removing the tumor. Nothing but suffering and certain death awaited him unless this was done. By removing the tumor there was a bare possibility of his recovery. He was brought to this city Tuesday, and a tumor weighing about five pounds was removed about two o'clock p.m. The effect of the operation was more than his enfeebled constitution could stand and he gradually grew weaker and weaker, finally passing away at ten o'clock in the morning. His brother, Charles Pennock, and two of his sisters, Mrs. J.M. Tallman and Mrs. M.B. Foster, of Parker, Colo., were in constant attendance at his bedside until the last moment. The remains will be buried at two p.m. today in the Laporte cemetery.

Mr. Pennock was 39 years old and leaves behind a wife and six children to mourn their irreparable loss. He was born in Livingston county, N.Y., and came to Colorado 22 years ago. He served as drummer boy in the 104th New York regiment and was highly esteemed by his comrades. He had very many warm friends in this state who will be deeply pained to hear of his death.

His sisters, Mrs. Tallman and Mrs. Foster, who have been here since Monday, and another sister, Mrs. E.M. Peck, of Colorado Springs, who arrived Wednesday, will remain until after the funeral.

A drummer boy! Frank Pennock and John Tharp are the only two Civil War veterans known to be buried in Laporte. Yet an article in the *Express Courier* by David Watrous in 1941 (sent to me by Mary Gates Emarine) says, "...several civil war veterans ...are buried there." Were there more stones of veterans at one time?

According to Ivan Pennock's family records, Frank's six children were Mary Alice, Ella, William Franklin, Charles Elmer, Anna May and Oliver Porter. Charles Elmer married Elsie Shipp and they had four infants who died (the fourth was mentioned in the *Courier*, 11/13/1907) and presumably were buried on the Pennock farm. They adopted a Bellvue girl, Mildred, and when Elsie was 41, she had Ivan. Ivan had a son Verlin; Verlin and his wife, Carolyn, have Stacy and Kevin.

The stone, once at Laporte, was moved to Grandview to Section F, Lot 75 on 9/23/1958: G.F. PENNOCK DIED Jan. 18, 1887, AGED 39 Y'rs. 8 M's. 10 D'ys.

A book about early Pennock life, *Happy Hardships,* was written by Iola Pennock, who married Arthur E., a son of Charles, who was a brother of George Franklin.

9. **Elizabeth Ella Newlin Pennock (+ G.V.)** Died September 2, 1890
   Age 36

   Mrs. Pennock lived only three years longer than her husband. Presumably she had an obituary, which may have told the cause of her death, but microfilm for the date of her death was not available. She was buried at Laporte.

   Engraved on her husband's stone, opposite side: ELIZABETH E. PENNOCK DIED Sept. 2, 1890; AGED 36 Y'rs. 10 M's. 11 D'ys. STARLIN & HOLMES FT. COLLINS.

   According to Grandview records, O.P. Pennock requested the transfer of their bodies. O.P. was Oliver Porter, their youngest child. Neither my neighbor Glenn Pennock nor Iola Pennock realized Frank and Elizabeth had been moved, nor did a grandson, Ivan, whom I called in Phoenix. Apparently Oliver made the request when he went to the funeral of his cousin, Arthur, Iola's husband, in August 1958. Frank and Elizabeth, who had been buried for 71 and 69 years, respectively, were moved from Laporte in September 1958, and buried in the same grave at Grandview. Their son, O.P., was buried next to them ten years later at age 89 on January 26, 1968.

   Old lot books at Grandview show the names of three more persons who were "Moved From Laporte Cemetery."
10. **Ida Lesher (+ G.V.)** Died 1881
11. **Anna Lesher (+ G.V.)** Died 1888
12. **Maggie Lesher (+ G.V.)** Died 1899

   There were no months of death, ages at death, or when the bodies were moved. One can often learn about family relationships, however, by seeing who is buried nearby. There are six Leshers in Section D, Lot 22: Ida, Anna and Maggie; Mary, wife of Frank Lesher, died January 9, 1902, at age 44-4-28; William A. Lesher, died on October 31, 1904 at age 24-4-28; and finally, Frank Lesher on November 14, 1916, age 65. The three girls, then, probably were children of Frank and Mary Lesher. At the gravesites, barely visible under a pine branch, is a single stone with all six names.

I was determined to learn something more about this family which buried three children in Laporte, then moved their bodies. Lesher was not a Laporte name I was familiar with. With enough research, most questions can be answered, but could I go from one phrase ("Moved from Laporte") and three girls' names to a real story about them? I tried my hardest.

First I asked local old-timers and historians about the name Lesher and was invariably told they were probably relatives of David Barnes Lesher, a local superintendent of schools, after whom Lesher Junior High was named. With the help of Lynn Phillips at Allnut Funeral services, I learned that David Lesher had a daughter, Doris Ann, who died of blood poisoning at age 20 in 1944; a sister, Mabel Gertrude Lesher, died at 89 on December 22, 1977; that he himself died at age 87 on April 15, 1984; Lesher's wife, Florence, died on March 2, 1991; and that Lesher's father was David, his mother was Rose Barnes, and he was born in Denver. So he was not a son of Frank and Mary Lesher. An easier determination could have been made from the fact that he and his family were not buried in the Frank Lesher family plot.

So what Leshers, then, are the family in question? On microfilm I found only one child's death notice. It was in the *Weekly Express,* 2/4/1888: "Annie Lesher, daughter of Mr. and Mrs. Frank Lesher of Dixon Canon, died on Wednesday of pneumonia and was buried Thursday." There was no mention of her age or that she was buried in Laporte.

In the 12/29/1898 *Weekly Courier* under "Stout" news: "Miss Ella Lesher arrived home Christmas evening from Colorado Springs to spend the holidays with her parents." So they lived in Stout and had at least one other child. (Stout was a small town, populated mostly by miners, now under water at the southern end of Horsetooth Reservoir.)

"Frank Lesher was elected overseer for the precinct office at Stout" (11/19/1887). He was apparently well thought of.

A year later he was a happy and industrious man (though he'd lost little Anna in the meantime). "Frank Lesher, the owner of some fine stone quarries in Dixon canon, seven miles west of Ft. Collins, has lately uncovered a valuable deposit of marble, and will take steps to open a marble quarry. The rock is said to be of a fine quality and color. There is a nearly pure white, a red clouded with white, and a white clouded with red. Mr. Lesher will get out some blocks shortly and they will be dressed by Ed Saul of this city" (11/24/1888).

The *Weekly Courier* (9/15/1898) had a story about Frank Lesher, a resident of Stout, who attended the Cheyenne Buffalo Bill Show with sons William, Louis, and Newt. Six years later, in 1904, according to his tombstone, William died at age 24.

There was this item in the *Courier* (1/9/1902): "One of the saddest deaths we have ever been called on to record occurred Wednesday evening, January 8, when Mrs. Frank Lesher of this city, answered the summons of the grim reaper. She died from heart trouble after a very brief illness, leaving a husband and 11 children, the youngest an infant in arms. The eldest daughter, an accomplished young lady, is afflicted with total blindness. We know of no instance more calculated to arouse the deepest sympathy than this one."

Her obituary in the next week's paper stated that she had 14 children of whom 11 survive. The youngest was eight months and the oldest was Miss Ella, a graduate of the Colorado Institute of the Blind. Obituaries provide bounteous and fascinating information. Fourteen children! Bit by bit, information accumulated.

Frank Lesher's own long obituary (11/12/1916) was headlined PIONEER STONEMASON IS CALLED TO HIS REWARD. Lesher had come to Fort Collins in 1879 and was a stonecutter and builder. He furnished the stone for the first building erected by the college and for the Brown Palace in Denver. He also did bridge work. He worked here 31 years, then left in 1910 for Oregon to be with some of his children. He returned six months before his death to be near his son, George, on Mason Street. Surviving was an aged mother, 91, of California, and ten children: Ella Blanchard of San Diego, Louis of Thermopolis, George, Anna Bryant of Pendleton, Oregon, Newton of Chicago, and Myrtle, Hazel and Ray of Portland, and Frank and Emery of Dalles, Oregon.

That answered the question as to why a local family which had 11 surviving children in 1902 did not have anyone living in Fort Collins in 1998. The family had scattered.

In the vertical files in the local history room, Rheba Massey pulled a "Lesher" file. There was one paper in it, a story of a pathetic family with many, many children living at Stout in a shack—poverty-stricken beyond belief. They had yet another new baby and he was born with only one hand; then a pig ate a finger from his good hand. He was blinded in one eye by an explosive; their shack burned down. They moved to another shack by the railroad track in Fort Collins where the little boy sold newspapers.

This "inspirational" story was written by Hugo Evon Frey and although the boy isn't named, it was about none other than Ray Lesher, one of the 14 children of Frank Lesher. The reason it was inspirational is that little Ray grew up to become a well known and highly successful CPA.

I immediately called Ray's daughter, who had sent the article to the library years ago, to inform her I was trying to research her family and also that they had six empty cemetery lots at Grandview, a bit of information I presume was appreciated. She sent me more biographical data, photographs and corrections to Frey's story. She also said they had always kept touch with the local Toliver family.

From information she sent, we learn that Fort Collins' stonemason, Frank Jacob Lesher, was born November 6, 1851, in Tiffin, Ohio. His father was Benjamin Lesher and his mother was Anna Bartmass. He had three sisters and one brother. His wife, and mother of so many children, was Mary Jane, the daughter of Dennis Riordon and Margaret Long. Dennis was born in County Claire and Margaret was born in Tipperary, Ireland. Mary Jane was born in Warsaw, Indiana on August 12, 1857. She had two sisters, Margaret and Katherine and a brother Dennis.

Mary Jane and Frank Lesher were married in 1876. They had 14 children between 1877 and 1899, the first in Tiffin, Ohio, the next 13 in the Fort Collins area, probably at Stout.

Their children and the number of children they had were Ella (who was blind and studied with Helen Keller) (1), Louis (5), George (?), Newton (8), Sarah (2), Myrtle (0), Frank, Jr. (2), Ray (3), Emery John (1), Hazel (2), and Ida, Maggie, Anna and Willie, who died young. Ida and Maggie apparently died as newborns and were buried in Laporte in 1881 and 1899. Anna, however, was ten years old when she died in 1888. The cause of William's death at age 24 is not known.

Ray apparently purchased the headstone for his parents and siblings in the late 1940s and had the three children's bodies brought from Laporte at that time. However, Ray's son, Jack, remembers his father saying he didn't pay for their reburial because the Bureau of Reclamation did. That makes it sound like the children were possibly moved from Stout, not Laporte. Yet Grandview records clearly say, "Moved from Laporte" and I have never heard of a cemetery at Stout. Jack said that his dad said he wasn't even sure if they had the right bodies.

Ray himself, the little boy with one hand and one finger missing from his other hand, and one eye, died at age 92 in Portland, Oregon, July 2, 1961. Ray had three children: Eloise O'Donnell who has two children, Audrey Christine and Michael Craig, four grandchildren and one great-grandchild; Jack, a CPA in Portland, Oregon, who has three children; and Jeri, also of Portland, who has four children.

Considerable information about this important early stonemason is now in the vertical files of the local history room of the public library, and the Lesher family is satisfied to know that their grandfather's important role in the early history of Fort Collins will be remembered by anyone who takes the time to read it.

13. **Herring Baby Girl** Died August 12, 1891 Newborn
(Photo of her father and the log house in which this child was born, see p. 5.)

When Rowland Herring and his wife, Nettie Garbutt Herring, came to Laporte from Greece, New York, in 1887, they had three children, Nellie, 6, Volney, 4, and Cameron, 9 months.

According to a letter Nettie wrote, she and Rowl moved into the "railroad farm" on April 13, 1887 (4b). Here they had Lucy (Judge John Tobin's mother) in 1890 and Ted (owner of Ted's Place) in 1892. And there was an unnamed baby in between the last two.

Doris Atkinson Bice (Nellie and Fancher Sarchet's daughter) had been told by her uncle Cam Herring's widow, Elizabeth, that a Herring baby once was buried at Laporte, but she didn't know any details. Finally, in the library, I found this article (8/20/1891): "Mr. and Mrs. Rowland Herring, of Laporte, are mourning the death of their infant daughter which died Wednesday, August 12, 1891. Mrs. Herring is a sister of E.N. Garbutt of Laporte and Co. Judge H.I. Garbutt of this city. The bereaved parents and friends have the sympathy of all who know them in their affliction."

In the old Grandview lot book, there is a notation that the Herring baby was "premature," that a lot was purchased for $15 by Rowland Herring on June 9, 1893 (the day his dear wife Nettie died at age 35), and that the baby was indeed "removed from Laporte." She lay just two years in Laporte before being moved.

It is interesting that the man who owned the ground that so many persons had used as a burial ground the past 30 years chose to bury his own wife in Grandview and also to move his infant daughter. The baby has no stone at Grandview, but Nettie (his wife of 13 years) and Rowland do; they and the baby are buried together.

Because we live on Herring's farm, I especially search for items of its historical background. Irving Garbutt of Casper, Wyoming, sent a copy of a letter from Rowl Herring to his wife's sister-in-law, who later became his second wife.

> Jan. 13, 1895.
> Dear Mollie.
> I never told you anything about the house yet, have I. It is on the main road. There is as mutch travel on it as there is on the ridg road in Greece. I think the house is asmutch like the old log home as can be. It is part log, part frame. There are five large cottonwood trees in front, river just on the other side of the road. The railroad at the back of the house and a grave yard on the farm, now what do you think of that. don't you wish you had not promised to come out hear and live in a log house.

This letter was amusing to me because 82 years later, in 1977, when Jim Brinks was extolling the virtues of a farm he wanted to buy, he said it had five big cottonwood trees (which were sadly lost in the 1983 flood), a river, a railroad and even a grave yard! The blessing for us was Overland Trail had been straightened about 1976 and the increasing traffic no longer rolled right past the house.

There is no Grandview marker for Rowl's second wife of 34 years, Mollie (Mary) Garbutt Herring, who is buried by her mother and stepfather, the Greens, who also have no marker. Mollie is the one who tired of the dirt floors and the old Provost log cabin and instigated the building of a frame house which Rowl built in 1910. We still live in it today. According to the newspaper, he built the big barn (which is visible from the Overland Trail bridge over the Poudre River) in 1905.

Ann Ryan and Doris Bice sometimes give talks to historical groups based on the letters from Greece, New York, of the teen-aged Nettie Garbutt to her favorite brother, Cam, who had gone west. Nettie must have been one of the sweetest persons who ever lived. She misses her brother so much that the reader aches for her. She takes care of her ill father; apparently her mother is dead. She expresses anger at their brother Fred, who first disgraces the family with a bad debt, then marries Mollie, and later abandons her and two children. Nettie grows up, marries Rowl Herring, moves west, has six babies in all, buries one at Bingham Hill, dies at 35. Reading her letters is heart-rending (4b). Some lines were quoted in the story about Johnny Thomas.

Nettie's son Cam, named after her brother, worked on his Dad's farm for many years; Willis Morgenstern enriched my life with many tales of Rowl and Cam Herring. All three worked hard on this farm. Cam eventually bought a farm on South Overland Trail. He died October 4, 1963 at age 77, leaving a son, Tom, and a granddaughter, Brandi Sue. Nettie's son Ted was in the state legislature, and owned Ted's Place until he died at age 70 in 1963. His son is Dick Herring. Volney had Roberta, Betty, and Jack, all deceased. Nellie married Fancher Sarchet and they had Doris Atkinson Bice and also Clark who is deceased. Doris has children Clark Sarchet Atkinson, Marguerite Wagner, Mary Ellen Laws, and Louanne Johnson. Lucy, mother of Bill and local retired Judge John Tobin, died in May, 1967, at age 77.

14. **Cy Crawford** Date of death unknown Age unknown

"Raymond Willis says there was one case of grave robbing. Years ago a man named Cy Crawford, one of three brothers, had spent the Fourth of July at Livermore. The following day he died of a heart attack. After his burial it was found the grave had been opened and the body removed. The grave robber was never identified." (2)

The article was written in the 1950s and leaves several questions unanswered. Who was Cy Crawford? When did he die? Who stole the body? Why? Where did they take it? Is Raymond Willis to be believed? He's apparently the same Raymond Willis who buried his own child at Bingham Hill, also at some unknown date. (See Lloyd Willis.) Willis was known as an authority on history of Bellvue, but it's too bad someone had not been more specific as to dates and details when writing.

15. **A.J. Wylie** Died September, 1888 Age unknown

9/20/1888. "Bellvue. The death of A.J. Wylie was a very sad affair. He and Mrs. Wylie had just come to Colorado from Virginia to visit their children. He received his injuries Monday evening and died Thursday noon. The body was embalmed and buried at Laporte, but will be sent to his old home this fall. Mrs. Wylie and her children have the sympathy of the entire valley."

He was embalmed—a first for the cemetery.

A.J. Wylie may have been exhumed and sent to Virginia, and it is also possible that he stayed since he had children in Bellvue. To exhume and send a body by train would have been difficult, and often removal and reburial planned at the time of death is never carried out. If a town in Virginia had been named in the article, it might be easy to track him down. Rheba Massey at the library put him on the Internet but there has been no response. Whether or not Mr. A.J. Wylie is here will remain one of the cemetery's mysteries.

There is a home-made stone with the initials 'A.T.W.' It is definitely not 'A.J.W.' Of course, newspapers have been known to make mistakes. The stone could be for him, Anna Williams, Arthur Wombacher or someone else entirely.

Elizabeth and Jacob Flowers may have been buried at Bingham Hill Cemetery and maybe they weren't. They are buried in Grandview now, and records there do not indicate "Moved from Laporte," but then the moving of the two Vandewarks was not noted, either, and I would never have known they were once at Laporte if Richard Baker had not told me he personally saw the bodies moved. Glenn Pennock of Bellvue says the Flowers were once buried in Laporte. Glenn is the son of Eldridge Pennock and grandson of Charles, who married Jacob Flower's daughter, Lydia. Glenn distinctly remembers going to the Laporte cemetery as a child with his grandmother, Lydia, to put flowers on the grave of Mildred, his grandmother's first child. She told him that both her parents had once been buried there.

Because Grandview was a well established cemetery by 1890, and because the Flowers were a prominent family, many of their relatives believe they were probably buried only in Grandview. Yet Lois Johnson says she could not dispute Glenn's memory because he spent a lot of time with his grandparents as a child.

The huge FLOWERS memorial stone in Grandview (Section E, Lot 171) is interesting. On one side: ELIZABETH H. FLOWERS, AUG. 15, 1830 - SEPT. 18, 1890 and JACOB FLOWERS, JULY 4, 1827 - NOV. 15, 1900. On the other side: PENNOCK, LAURA L. (1900-1931) and MAURICE (1897-1945). (Maurice was a grandson of Jacob Flowers; Laura, his wife, died by accidental gunshot.) On the other two sides of the stone are two children's names, CLARK FLOWERS, Dec. 22, 1868 - Nov. 30, 1872, and GEORGE FLOWERS, June 11, 1870 - Nov. 2, 1872. Since Flowers didn't arrive in the area until 1873, those children, ages four and two, are buried elsewhere. Grandview records show them to be "Centotaphs" which means "empty graves."

In the event they were once at Bingham Hill, here are brief stories about them. Most of the information is from Glenn Pennock and Lois Johnson.

16. Elizabeth Meeks Flowers (+ G.V.) Died 9/18/1890 Age 60

Elizabeth Meeks was born around 1830 in Woods county, Virginia, and married Jacob Flowers on January 28, 1853. They lost their two youngest children in 1872 and brought six older children when they came to Colorado in 1873: Thornton Wesley (b. 1854), Sardius (b. 1855), Lydia Catherine (b. 1857), Salvina or Sally (b. 1859), Benjamin Franklin (b. 1861), and Cora (b. 1865).

Apparently they had a "black mammy" for several years as Lydia told her grandson, Glenn Pennock, that it seemed the "Negro woman raised her." A great memory was when the mammy took eight-year-old Lydia to a train to view the body of Abraham Lincoln after his assassination in 1865.

T.W. married Addie Obenchain and had nine children. One, named Cora, was buried at age five weeks at Bingham Hill and her marble stone is still there. T.W. and his son James Arthur Flowers died in an avalanche in Idaho on 1/26/1911. Cora married William Tilton and had three sons, Allan, Jasper and Lester. Lydia married Charles Pennock and their genealogy can be read in *Happy Hardships*.

17. Jacob Flowers (+ G.V.) Died November 15, 1900 Age 74

Jacob Flowers was born July 4, 1827 in Green County, Pennsylvania. He had three steamboats, the *Elk*, the *Malta* and the *Oil City*. At least one was constructed in Florida and somehow taken inland from the Atlantic to the Mississippi. Two ships were lost in a storm on a single night.

The family said Jacob steamed from St. Louis to Kansas City, but not many details are available.

He married and lived in Wyandotte, Kansas, for four years. In 1872, Jacob Flowers and a man named Laidlow came to Colorado looking for a place for a settlement. They decided the Cache la Poudre valley and Pleasant Valley were best, so they returned, organized the Wyandotte Colony and came west. Some families stayed in Greeley and the remainder came to Pleasant Valley in 1873. It is believed the children whose names are on the headstone (Clark and George) died in Kansas or enroute.

Flowers started the town of Bellevue (middle "e" later dropped) and named it for Bellevue, Pennsylvania, or, according to Glenn Pennock, after Bellevue, Idaho. The purpose of the town was to accommodate families of men who worked in the nearby quarries. Flowers owned some quarries himself. He was elected president of the Pleasant Valley Lake and Canal Ditch Company in 1879 and county commissioner in 1881. In the 1890s he helped build the Old Flowers Trail in Rist Canyon (land later owned by Robert, Ralph and Lee McElrath.)

Flowers died quickly. According to Laura Jean Wunch, his great-granddaughter, he ate a hearty meal, complained about his feet being cold, sat down by the stove and died. He was 74.

PERSONS WHO WERE ONCE THOUGHT TO BE BURIED AT BINGHAM HILL BUT AREN'T

1. **Oliver Provost**

   Provost was first thought by Henry Moore, a descendent of Oliver's brother, Charles, to be buried here at about age 13 after committing suicide. He is definitely buried in Montana. (See Provost.)

2. **Samuel** and **Sarah Bingham**

   The 1988 edition of this book suggested that Mr. and Mrs. Bingham might be buried in Laporte. Now it is known that Samuel was buried in Missouri and Sarah in South Dakota. (See Bingham.)

3. **Ethel Irene Swinscoe** Died in 1899 Infant

   Because she lived and died north of Fort Collins, and because I perpetually and wrongly think of Laporte as being north of Fort Collins instead of mostly west, I thought Baby Swinscoe might have been buried here and even had her name engraved on the memorial stone. After reading my book, Dr. Bob Pike said he believed she'd been buried in her family's (the Walter Dixon's) back yard near the Culver Reservoir on North Shields. Esther Moore confirmed this and wrote "....little Ethel Irene was my cousin. Her mother and my father were twins. She was buried in my grandparent's yard. When I was small, I walked across the fields with Grandma to visit the little grave."

4. **Gertrude Mathews** Died 1904

Because her parents were from Laporte, I thought she might have been buried here, but later learned she had been buried in Cheyenne.

5. **Philandra Aurilla Blunk** Died September, 1895

Two *Courier* articles by two correspondents, a week apart, list different burial places for Mrs. Blunk, aka Blunck. One said her remains were laid to rest last Sunday in the Laporte cemetery; the next said she was laid to rest in the Harmony district. Ceil Damschroder had more compelling evidence that she was actually buried at the Harmony Cemetery, southeast of Fort Collins.

6. **Margaret Foidl** Died 1889 Age 44

Until shortly before publication, this woman was listed as a "probable" burial in Bingham Hill. After six years of research, as an afterthought, I wrote a letter to the editor (*Coloradoan,* 2/24/1998) asking if anyone knew her whereabouts. I got a response! Mrs. Foidl is not buried at Laporte, but the story is worth telling, if for no other reason than to encourage researchers that even wrong turns bring good information. The story for me started on June 16, 1992, when Don and Geraldine Hinkle from Yampa, Colorado, stopped at our home. They had been at the Bingham Hill Cemetery looking for, but not finding, the tombstone of a Margaret Foidl. We immediately called Grandview employees who said there was no Foidl in their records. At this point we should have asked one more question, but because we didn't, the Hinkles kept looking and found more details that neither they nor the family of Mrs. Foidl would have learned, had we had an easy answer. So the six years weren't wasted.

The Hinkles gathered their information about Mrs. Foidl from their neighbors, Harry and Ruth Lines (who died in 1963 and 1971, respectively) and from the boss (Richy Richardson, also deceased) of the Cypress coal mine, near Yampa. Mrs. Foidl's daughter (whose name the Hinkles didn't know) often stopped at the Lines' home on her way to visit the Foidl grave. In the 1950s the daughter bought a granite tombstone about 2 1/2 feet long and 16 inches high and had it placed on the country grave to replace a wood cross. Don Hinkle saw this stone.

Mr. and Mrs. Hinkle were told that Mrs. Foidl was 42 or 43 in the late 1880s. On a hot day, she'd been working outside, and possibly suffered from heat stroke. She drank cold buttermilk and died. Her husband used floor boards of the cabin for a coffin and she was buried on their ranch (near Road 27 out of Oak Creek or Road 33 out of Steamboat Springs). Her husband took the children, believed to be one male and one female, to an orphanage in Leadville.

The old Foidl homesite is now called Foidl Canyon and there is still a one-room Foidl school building near where Roads 27 and 33 meet, about 25 miles southwest of Steamboat Springs. According to the *Steamboat Pilot* (12/22/1983) the Foidl Canyon School was named to the National Register of Historic Places on May 9, 1983. The grave was about 1/2 mile southwest of the school.

In the fall of 1962, the Cypress Mine, which strip-mines coal, agreed to move Mrs. Foidl's body for the daughter, who then in her 80s, reportedly lived in Laporte. Hayden resident Bobby Robinson, 87 years old in 1998, was hired to dig up the grave. He recently told the Hinkles that a woman and several "dressed up" men were around; one was Mr. Root from the Steamboat Springs mortuary. Robinson said that they found a rosary, a skull, leg bones and ribs but all the rest was "just crumbles." They gathered the remains, put them in a big pasteboard box and loaded them into a vehicle, which was not a hearse. Robinson remembers nothing about a tombstone, but told Hinkles the body might have gone to Boulder. I called or wrote all six Boulder cemeteries, plus one in Lafayette for good measure (in case the Hinkles mistook Laporte for Lafayette), and no one found records of a Foidl burial. Root Mortuary had no record of moving a body to Laporte.

The story was going to end with the line "Foidl Canyon and Foidl Canyon School remain in Routt County but where Mrs. Margaret Foidl is, nobody knows for sure." But my letter sparked a response from none other than a neighbor, Theresa Brookman, who lives a mile downriver from us. Mrs. Foidl was her grandmother and she is buried at Roselawn Cemetery. I never thought to ask for Roselawn burials separately when I asked if a Foidl were in Grandview. I thought all the city burials were on one list.

Roselawn records do show a Margaret Foidl, born 3/7/1918 and died 9/5/1962, age 44. Totally inaccurate. Had I even thought to ask at Roselawn six years earlier, and heard those dates, the Hinkles and I would have been greatly confused, just as I was in 1998. Brookman said Warren's Funeral Home had handled the funeral and after a call to them, it made more sense. According to Gwen Bohlander, Mrs. Foidl's birth was in 1845 and death in 1889, and she was, in fact, moved in September of 1962. Roselawn recorded the date of her burial as her death date and went back 44 years to calculate a birth date.

One moral of the story is to be suspicious of official records if you're fairly certain they aren't right.

Theresa Brookman went on to say that there were two girls, and maybe three (not a boy and a girl), at the time of their mother's death: Theresa and Margaret, ages ten and five. Their father, Albert Foidl, took them to the House of Good Shepherd, an orphanage in Denver, not Leadville. He visited them two times and never came back.

Theresa Foidl was probably the unmarried daughter who visited the gravesite near Yampa, though it is a puzzle to the family as to how she got there since neither sister learned to drive. Margaret Foidl married Joseph Derfler, and had children Henry, Wilford, Raymond, Theresa, Herman, Katherine and Frank. Theresa Derfler married Arthur Brookman and had Marguerite Kaysbier, Jeane Criswell, Susan La Flan, John, David, and Jim. They also had another daughter, Marilynn Ruth, who died of leukemia at age 16 in 1956.

Everyone in Laporte knows Jim Brookman, if not because of his energetic business acumen, then because of his wife's spectacular flower shop, the French Hen. Theresa's sewing and huge collection of rental costumes were famous for years.

When Margaret Foidl's body was brought down from Yampa, Brookmans had little time to prepare and did not even think of burial at Laporte—but used the lot they owned at Roselawn, next to where Aunt Theresa had been buried (born 5/6/1877, died 11/6/1959). Margaret Derfler (born 8/26/1884, died 3/15/1979), Theresa Brookman's mother, is also buried at Roselawn, so the mother who died after drinking buttermilk and her two little daughters who were taken to an orphanage are all together now.

When Geraldine Hinkle was informed that the body was found, she was greatly relieved and wrote: "What a celebration!. . .we were really pleased to find out at last where she was buried. . .I called Bobby Robinson yesterday [the man who had exhumed the grave in 1962] and he was pleased to find out for sure, too, about Mrs. Foidl. . .please send us the granddaughter's [Theresa Brookman] address so I can write her. . ."

The most significant thing in this story is that there are people who care enough about a pioneer woman who once lived on neighboring land and was buried in 1889, to drive to Laporte to visit her grave! And when they couldn't find it, they prodded me into finding it. That kind of caring is precious.

This concludes the section on people erroneously presumed to be in the Bingham Hill Cemetery, and I will agree with anyone who thinks I am somewhat weird to include it. Has there ever been such a chapter written anywhere, any time, about people *not* in a cemetery? How else, though, would I have met the wonderful Hinkles, had occasion to jabber with the bubbly Dr. Pike, or get scolded by local historian Josephine Clements in a letter to the editor (even though at the time, she didn't know where the Mr. and Mrs. Bingham were buried either)? I explored the Provost family and learned about Oliver's grisly end, met Leslie Moore and other Bingham relatives and also John Brookman, who so kindly drove to my home in a snow storm to edit the Foidl story. Not all the false leads were so intriguing but I thought these deserved to be in the book.

II

CHANGES AT THE TURN OF THE CENTURY

SEVERAL UNRELATED EVENTS took place in northern Larimer County around 1900 that changed the character of the Laporte cemetery. These included the opening of three new cemeteries in Fort Collins, the immigration of many groups of Hispanics and the arrival of morticians.

The Post, Mountain Home and Grandview Cemeteries
   Camp Collins was stationed at Laporte for two years and three months (7/22/ 1862 to 10/22/1864) whereas its lifespan downriver in the area which later became the City of Fort Collins was only one year and ten months (11/14/1864 to 9/22/1866) (3). It wasn't only the devastating 1864 flood that prompted the move, but problems with the Laporte camp being on squatters' properties, and also the bustle, activities and temptations of Laporte in general. For an excellent history of both camps, John Gray's *Cavalry and Coaches* is highly recommended.
   After Camp Collins moved downriver, it established a "post" cemetery, located on the site of the old post office on Oak Street in Fort Collins, and about ten persons were buried there. There is no proof that any soldiers or personnel were buried earlier in the Laporte cemetery, but it is a possibility. Bob Rupp, a fellow member of the "Fort Collins Westerners Posse" (to which anyone historically inclined can belong for $5 yearly dues), while doing research with John Gray for *Cavalry and Coaches* found evidence from "monthly post returns" that 16 people died during the camp's total time in the area—a little more than four years. If "about ten" were buried at the post cemetery, where were the others buried? And if ten died during the Fort Collins period, it seems logical to assume that a comparable number may have died during the earlier, longer Laporte phase of the camp.
   Record keeping was not complete by any means. Rupp has a document ("Letter of the Secretary of War, a report of the inspector of the national cemeteries of the United States, March 12, 1870") which accounts for 106 military burials in Colorado Territory, (Fort Sedgwick, Fort Morgan, Denver City, Fort Lyon and Fort Garland) **but not one single burial is mentioned in Larimer County, either in Laporte or Fort Collins.** That is quite odd.

Rupp thinks that bodies of men who may have died during the Laporte years probably were buried on the military grounds and subsequently lost when the camp flooded. However, on Provost's land (less than a mile from the camp) a cemetery had been established at least as early as 1862, and since Provost was a liquor-selling buddy of the men, it is feasible that a deceased soldier or associate of the camp might have been buried in what was later known as Bingham Hill Cemetery.

The only death at the Laporte camp actually recorded was that of Surgeon Edgerton Perry, suddenly stricken with "black tongue," on April 23, 1863, and buried at Camp Weld near Denver (3) and the only military-looking stone at the Laporte cemetery is that of Alphonse LaRocque. Gray mentions that LaRocque was "called on [by the military] to help weed out government stock from several freighters' herds on Boxelder Creek." However, by time LaRocque died in 1877, the army was long gone. Several of the soldiers had staked claims near Laporte and stayed in the area; perhaps one of them ordered a headstone for LaRocque.

Everything is conjecture. Rupp did considerable research on this subject of whether soldiers were buried in Laporte and has no conclusive answer to that question or why the number of deaths recorded (16) does not coincide with the number of burials in the post's cemetery (about ten).

The fort was completely abandoned by 1867, and whether citizens were then buried in the post's cemetery is not known. A few years passed and the fledgling town (whose name was changed from Camp Collins to Fort Collins in 1869) needed a cemetery of its own. On March 15, 1873, the Larimer Land Improvement Company quit-claimed Block 187, approximately six acres, to the Town of Fort Collins for the uses and purposes of a cemetery (Book E, Page 283, county clerk's office). The area was southeast of town, between present day Laurel Street on the north and Stover Street on the west. It was called Mountain Home Cemetery, platted into 449 lots, and at least 175 citizens bought lots for $30 each. Lots 371-377 and 391-401 were marked "Masonic Ground." Lots 50-103 and 171-195 were marked "Potter's Field." Presumably the rest of the cemetery was for persons who were neither Masons nor paupers.

The city fathers then took a look at the old "post" cemetery located on very desirable high ground, declared it a nuisance and ordered it abandoned. In 1874, six graves were moved. Later when Oak Street was being graded and leveled, the bones of about four more bodies interred in unmarked graves were plowed up, remains were gathered and "properly" buried at Mountain Home.

About a decade later (8/19/1882), long newspaper articles waxed as to the beauty of the new cemetery, except where the "poor and friendless" paupers were buried. Some Laporte and Bellvue residents may have been buried in Fort Collins' Mountain Home Cemetery from 1873 to 1887 but I believe the principal cemetery for that area was still the one on Bingham Hill.

The "new" cemetery in Fort Collins was used less than 15 years! City fathers next decided to place a cemetery far to the west of town (since the city was growing eastward), and once again, bodies were ordered disinterred. Mountain Home, for all its beauty as a cemetery, was to become a "has-been" because Fort Collins needed the space for a park.

The newest cemetery was called "Grand View" for many years but the name eventually changed to Grandview. It opened in late 1887, and as soon as 1888, bodies were moved to it from Mountain Home. Grandview records reflect a move of about 90 bodies, but there must have been some confusion, for not all bodies were moved.

Mountain Home was quickly referred to as the "old" cemetery and there was continual talk about turning it into a park. However, there was that persistent problem of persons still buried. *Fort Collins Morning Express*, 2/2/1907:

> In accordance with the notice made by the committee on streets and alleys the old cemetery south of the city is being vacated preparatory to being turned into a park....it is in position to make a first-class breathing place for that part of the city. The city has ordered that the ground be vacated by the 1st of March, after which time all the bodies remaining in the cemetery will be removed by the city and placed in the Grandview. The graves, many of them, at least, have been left uncared for, most of the headstones have become obliterated, and the grass has grown rank over the graves. Some of the owners of lots there object to the removal of the bodies. **It is within the power of the city, according to the verdict of the city attorney, to condemn any property it sees fit for use as a public park.**

(Many landowners between Fort Collins and Laporte heard those same threatening words in 1979 when the city wanted our land along the Poudre River for a bike trail.)

A year later, 1/2/1908:

> The park committee reported that they will improve the old cemetery at the end of Laurel and has begun work of transforming it into a park. By the coming summer it is hoped to give the old burying

ground the appearance of a park at least. There are a number of bodies still buried in this place but bodies remain which are known and there are negotiations pending between council and relatives of the deceased to have the remains taken up and removed elsewhere.

Alas, there was to be no park. On January 3, 1947, the City of Fort Collins sold Block 187 to Harry G. Worsham Constructors, Inc. for $6,000. On June 4, 1947, Harry G. Worsham divided the land into lots and called it "Eastdale Park Subdivision." Immediately, basements for homes were excavated. Richard Baker was present at some of the excavations and made the following notes: "In July,1947, when Washam [sic] housing project was started several graves were uncovered. One I am fairly certain was the grave of Capt. E. Drake. This was determined by uniform buttons and location of grave. Capt. Drake was one of the officers here at the time Camp Collins was established in 1864. See Watrous. Another body was buried in the same grave [body of man, I believe]. Both in caskets."

Ten bodies (nine unnamed) were exhumed and brought to Grandview en masse in July 1947 (7). As late as the 1950s, Betty Woodworth, writing for the *Coloradoan*, said many families complained that bodies removed from Mountain Home were given just half a lot in the new cemetery. One can see several tombstones very tightly crowded together on the north side of Grandview along Laporte Avenue. It is unclear as to how many bodies were actually moved, whether headstones were moved and bodies weren't, or whether families had to pay for disinterment. It is likely that some bodies remain under the ground today. Whether they haunt any of the dozens of homes above them, I don't know....

Regardless of the city's dubious behavior concerning Mountain Home, Grandview was a success, and by 1900, the majority of adults who died in Bellvue, Laporte and other communities surrounding Fort Collins were buried there. Even the earliest owners of our land who had donated and perpetuated the use of the Laporte cemetery—John Provost and his second wife, Virginie, and Rowland Herring and his wives, Nettie and Mollie—were buried at Grandview.

At this time, burials in Laporte, especially of babies, were done privately and almost secretly. One neighbor of the cemetery, Willie Morgenstern, remembers seeing two men walk to the hill carrying a small pine box, dig a hole with a shovel, bury whoever was in the little coffin, and leave—no prayers, no marker, no nothing. If a clergyman or mortician weren't present perhaps there was a fear of trespassing.

The Laporte cemetery on Bingham Hill Road was probably considered an undesirable and unkempt place as early as 1900. Several families ordered bodies disinterred and moved to Grandview or elsewhere from the 1880s to the 1950s and others wanted to move their loved ones but could not because authorities feared the spread of diseases. Movers and shakers in the community thought its days were over and the Laporte cemetery slipped from society's consciousness.

It is amazing, then, to find almost as many names of persons buried after 1900 (74) as before (83).

Immigration of Hispanics

Around the turn of the century, cheap labor was needed for agriculture and mining enterprises. Newspapers carried ads and articles to lure laborers. In the *Courier*, 6/21/1905: "....there is a need for more workers in the beet and hay fields of the Cache la Poudre valley....40 practical irrigators are needed at $35 a month plus board....scores of good farm workers could find employment at once in this valley and their help is urgently needed right away."

From the *Courier*, 11/4/1907: "....40 laborers, mostly Mexicans, with a sprinkling of Japs, left for Halligan dam, 35 miles northwest in the mountains, where they will engage in wheeling and mixing cement and other common labor. A.L. Tate, the liveryman, is furnishing the labor for this big contract and he will go for more men in a day or two."

Immense rock quarries at Ingleside, nine miles north of Laporte (on land presently owned by Dee Barger), also drew men looking for work. Rock was freighted by horse and wagon until June 1907, when the railroad was extended from Bellvue to Ingleside in order to expedite the transportation of lime rock to the sugar factories. More men were needed at this quarry, and also at Granite Canyon, Wyoming.

The men who came brought wives. They formed communities. An excellent article by Dee Barger about the Ingleside ethnic makeup can be found in *Among These Hills, A History of Livermore, Colorado, 1995,* a publication of the Livermore Woman's Club. Approximately 42 Hispanic families lived in the Ingleside camps and worked the quarry, according to Dan Martinez (4d). He quotes Luisa Garcia Padilla who remembers Ingleside as a community with a one-room Catholic Church served by Joseph P. Trudel, a French-Canadian. The houses were one-room shacks with a pot belly stove, wood plank floors and tar paper roofs. Protruding roof nails were frosted white on cold winter mornings. Water was carried in buckets from a spring or melted from snow. Every family had an outhouse. Into these conditions, babies were born and they often died. On more than one occasion, sleeping parents who kept the baby in bed with them to keep it warm during sub-zero temperatures, rolled on and smothered the infant.

Where did this big influx of families to Bellvue, Laporte and Ingleside come from? One would think they all immigrated from Mexico, since they were called Mexicans by the Anglo population and any time they were mentioned in mortuary records or newspaper articles.

True, a few were from Mexico. The Mexican Revolution in 1910 caused many to seek peace across the river. From the *Courier*, 3/6/1914: "A number of Mexicans testified to the senate foreign relations committee in Washington, D.C., that conditions in the northern part of Mexico are intolerable and their lives are in danger." Angela Tamayo from the state of Jalisco, now living in Cheyenne, Wyoming, was one of thousands who crossed the Rio Grande; she later buried a baby at the cemetery in Laporte.

A few men like Juan Torres and Dem Furones Barrios immigrated from Spain. Torres buried three children at Bingham Hill.

The majority of the Hispanic families, however, came from southern Colorado and New Mexico. Their ancestors arrived in this country long before the American Revolution and they were **Americans**. Most were descendants of Spanish explorers who intermarried with local Indian populations. Several had owned large land grants which were lost for one reason or another, so they migrated north looking for work, opportunity and land. And they found work—hoeing, thinning, weeding, topping and harvesting beets. Besides doing most of the stoop labor for northern Colorado agriculture, they worked on railroad section gangs, road-building gangs, sheep-herding, sheep-shearing, cattle ranching and cowboy jobs (4d).

The Aragon and Martinez families, headed by Jose de Jesus Argon, came in covered wagons in 1904. They have photographs and short histories in the 1987 edition of *History of Larimer County*. In 1906, when he was nearly 60 years old, Donaciano Vigil brought a wife, his recently widowed mother-in-law, two brothers-in-law and eight small children from southern Colorado. These and other families eventually settled near Bellvue and Laporte, raised families, and had sad occasions to use the nearby cemetery. Both Don Vigil himself and his mother-in-law were laid to rest there.

Wherever they came from, when one died, the mortician listed his race as "Mexican," and as likely as not, their names were misspelled. However, bless the morticians, for if it weren't for them and their records, many of the people buried after 1900 may have been forgotten forever.

Morticians

The arrival of morticians in Fort Collins did not affect the character of the Laporte Cemetery population, but the availability of their records certainly made research of the cemetery more complete.

At the time of the earliest burials at Bingham Hill, there were no undertaking services. A casket was made, the dead prepared and laid to rest by family and neighbors. Before the turn of the century, furniture makers built coffins for families who preferred not to do it themselves. According to Darlene McQuire, her grandfather, Edward J. Williams, a blacksmith in Bellvue, also made coffins. Some caskets, especially for children, were homemade, however, through the 1930s and 1940s.

Embalming came into use during the Civil War but was not commonly used in the west for many years. According to records, very few Bingham Hill bodies were embalmed.

H.M. Balmer, the first licensed mortician in Colorado, came to Fort Collins in 1900 and may have purchased one of the established furniture businesses. The *Courier*, 3/8/1905, reported, "H.M. Balmer has just received a new casket wagon of the most up-to-date style. It is a very fine wagon and is a credit to the town..." Later, when motorized vehicles became available, bodies were even more easily transported from outlying areas to Grandview.

Balmer's mortuary was later owned by Mr. and Mrs. Lyle Collins, Everett and Maxine Riddell, Tyler and Edith Hays, and Jack and Elsie Russell. Mike and Susie Reager purchased the business in 1983 and relocated to a new facility on Riverside Drive. They sold the business to Allnut in March 1994, but it still goes by the name of Reager and is under the management of Darren Gunn. "Reager" is the name used in this book for burials from this mortuary, though none were done during the years Mike Reager owned it.

The Goodrich Mortuary had its beginnings when Walter T. Hollowell took over the Frencher Furniture Store and Mortuary in 1902. Hollowell stayed until 1935 when Wesley E. Blythe purchased the business. In 1948, Jack W. Goodrich became his partner and bought the entire business in 1957. In 1984, Jack and Bill Allnut of Greeley took over. In January, 1996, the business relocated to 650 W. Drake Road and is known as Allnut Funeral Services, Drake Road Chapel. Rick Allnut is owner; Paul Telleen, the funeral director.

Most Laporte burials which were aided by mortuaries used Hollowell's; however, when I found a record of a burial in Hollowell records, I placed "Allnut" with the information in this book because that is the name under which the mortuary is known in 1998.

In 1924, Chas. J. Day started a third mortuary. Harold Warren began an apprenticeship with him in 1933. Warren's idol, a soldier uncle, had died of the flu in 1918, and Warren so appreciated the appropriateness of the funeral that he decided to become an undertaker. When Day died in 1941, Warren became manager and executor, and sold the business to Mrs. Milo (Edna B.) Rice. Warren left for the war in 1942, married Dorothy Stegner in September of 1945, was discharged in November of 1945, and bought into the company in 1946. On December 23, 1946, Mrs. Rice died and Warren became owner. In 1960, Milo Bohlender started as an apprentice. In 1968 he bought an interest and in 1980 bought the remaining shares of the Warren-Bohlender Funeral Home.

Harold Warren

Though all the funeral directors aided me in my quest, Harold Warren is the only one I met who personally buried people at Laporte. He remembers handling four or five burials, but I found only two in the records—Florence Spragg in 1933 and a Garcia baby in 1939.

Warren said that the Herrings, who owned the land, were fine people who always said, "Just drive on in," when he gave a courtesy phone call to let them know he was on his way. After the Herring estate sold the land, Warren said he and his clientele were refused entry and burial rights—the hog farmer who then owned the land bluntly said, "No."

When Warren visited the cemetery with a 4-H club in December 1987, he told the youngsters that there were many "county burials" in the 1930s and only $12 was allowed for children. That covered the cost of a tiny casket and box, but not a grave at Grandview, so the free cemetery at Laporte became popular. Usually family and friends excavated the grave site wherever there was room. Warren had never heard that anyone ran into a previous grave or found Indian artifacts while digging.

There were deaths and burials in which no authorities were notified, and therefore, no records are on file anywhere. Times were hard and $5 or $10 was more than some families could afford. One woman told me that Dr. Honstein advised her brother-in-law to wrap his wife's dead premature baby in a blanket and bury it in the back yard of their North Whitcomb

Street home; Warren agreed that back yard burials were common for babies. Often doctors did not know the cause of death and just guessed, according to Warren. Some babies were never seen by a doctor until after death.

Many graves on Bingham Hill have footstones; that practice is no longer allowed at most cemeteries because of upkeep problems. The few depressed areas were caused when a body was removed or when a wooden box placed over a casket gave way. Contrary to a common notion, Warren said most graves are not six feet deep but five feet for an adult and about two feet for a child.

Warren knew so many stories about Father LaJeunesse, Dem Furones, the old doctors and undertakers, and other characters whose paths crossed in one way or another with those buried in the Laporte cemetery; it's too bad he has not written a book.

A sense of compassion emanates from funeral home records. From little notes in the margins, from dismissal or bartering of unpaid bills ("Dear Sir: I am sorry I have nothing to pay you with; would you take my husband's team of horses as payment? They are fine grays."), and from their steadiness in times of crisis, one senses that all the early morticians were decent and sensitive people.

However, one wonders about some of the doctors. In the coroner's book I found these chilling words, "No doctor would come," and in another case, "The brother and father of deceased endeavored all afternoon and evening to have a doctor go to the home to treat deceased, there being no doctor in Fort Collins who would answer the call." The second example was in 1945 and concerned the death of a Hispanic.

All these happenings—a sparkling, new country cemetery west of Fort Collins called Grand View, a rapid influx of Hispanic laborers and their families to the Laporte area, and the arrival of morticians—changed the population of the Bingham Hill Cemetery. A few of the old settlers and their children were still buried there, but the majority of burials after 1900 were the children of newly arrived Hispanics.

Instead of relying only on word of mouth or skimpy newspaper accounts, most deaths after 1900 discussed in this book are accompanied by actual mortuary records which give cause of death, attending-doctor, age at death and some family information. A few baptismal records were also found.

LIST OF PERSONS BURIED BETWEEN
1900 and 1943

+ *indicates a headstone*
(P) *indicates a photograph*

1. Neva Gladys Roberts
2. John Rooney
3. John Rimey
4. Barbara Rosenboom Rimey
5. Arthur F. Jesse
6. James William Whitmire
7. Dolorita Covales
8. Erminia Aragon
9. Rosa Elvinia Sanchez +
10. August Robertson
11. Donald Robertson
12. Esther Robertson +
13. Guy Robertson +
14. Margaret Robertson +
15. Eliza A.E. Robertson + (P)
16. Faustino Chavez
17. Rodolfo Chavez
18. Jose de la luz Cordova
19. Maria Martinez + (P)
20. Baby Boy Williams
21. Roque Armenta
22. Frederico Armenta
23. John L. Armenta
24. Crisanta Pacheco Herrera + (P)
25. Donaciano Vigil + (P)
26. Rosa Gallegos
27. Celestina Videl
28. Josephina Apodaca
29. Jesse Martinez
30. Juanpedro Manifico Trujillo
31. Henry Canchola
32. Jacobo Trujillo + (P)
33. Acacio Trujillo + (P)
34. John Torres
35. Jessie M. Torres
36. Joseph Marvin Torres
37. Abner M. Spragg + (P)
38. Florence H. Spragg + (P)
39. Nameless Travelers
40. Nameless Sheepherder
41. Relative of Jim Vale
42. Baby Trujillo

43. Rodolfo Ulloa
44. Lucia Trujillo (P)
45. Benedicto Trujillo
46. Salina Trujillo
47. Isidro Eduardo Apodaca
48. Cyrilla Apodaca
49. Candido Gallegos
50. Delfino Romero
51. Margaret Vigil
52. Viola Armendarez
53. Baby Aragon +
54. Sam Vigil
55. Federico Donald Vigil
56. Baby Boy Armijo
57. Mary Maxine Vigil
58. Maria de la luz Tamayo (P)
59. Baby Garcia +
60. Fry Infant Girl
61. Fry Infant Girl
62. Sarah C. Howell
63. William Marshall Howell + (P)
64. Unknown Spanish Child
65. Dinkel Baby Boy (P)
66. Mary Inez Pacheco +

INFORMATION ABOUT PERSONS BURIED
BETWEEN 1900 AND 1943

The following persons, buried in Laporte between 1900 and 1943, are arranged in chronological order according to death date, except when two or more are from one immediate family; then family members are listed together.

Spelling of names is often wrong, but they have been copied exactly as spelled in various records. Information which came from mortuary records is so noted—Hollowell Mortuary records are referred to as "Allnut," and Balmer records are called "Reager."

If there is a marker in the cemetery, it is noted with a "+." Of the following 66 persons, 16 have headstones or wood crosses. (Five were placed between 1989 and 1998.) None of the bodies buried after 1900 were transferred to another cemetery.

Several people were instrumental in adding information. Louise Mondragon Aragon's first child was buried in Laporte in 1935, and my compiled names brought back a lot of memories to her. In 1988, Mrs. Lee (Eva) Martinez and her son, Daniel, went over the list, furnished correct spellings of names, and inserted many comments about relationships. These and additional comments made by Daniel in 1998 have all been notated with "D.M." Also, more information was volunteered by several other people in 1998, and all were mentioned in their relative's story.

> + *indicates presence of a headstone in 1998*
> * *indicates a relative of Don Vigil*
> (P) *indicates a photograph*

1. **Neva Gladys Roberts** Died October, 1902 Age 4 months
   Neva was born on June 8, 1902, in Raton, New Mexico, and died in October 1902, at four months of age. Her parents were Solomon Harrison Roberts, born in Lancaster, Wisconsin, and Myrtle Augusta Read, born in Knobnoster, Missouri.

   Neva was the seventh of ten children. The first six were Edith Florence, George, Henry, Haulcie, Harvey and Lala. (Haulcie's wife also had a brother buried at Laporte in 1913, Baby Boy Williams.) The last three children were born in Bellvue: Louie in 1905, Ester Fay (McCormick) in 1912 and James August, who died at birth and was buried at Grandview in 1917. This information is from the records of Louie's son, Dean, who owned the Laporte Plantorium. Dean died suddenly of a heart attack June 21, 1997.

In 1990, Mrs. Esther Roberts Armstrong from Englewood, Colorado, an aunt of Dean Roberts, called with a story about the Roberts family. She was Neva's only surviving sister at the time she called, but has since passed away. She said that the family, originally from Missouri, moved to Pueblo where the father, Solomon Roberts, owned a grocery store. His health was bad and a doctor said he should work outdoors. They moved to Raton where he worked in construction and timber. For the family in the summer, he built a floor, then erected a tent over it. The tent is where Neva Gladys was born on June 8, 1902.

One day a traveler stopped for a noon meal. At that time, Solomon was considering going to Greeley, but the man suggested Fort Collins, as it was near the mountains, a nice farming district and he thought Solomon would like it there. So the family came from Raton in a covered wagon in September 1902. They rented the Blackstock place, northwest of Bellvue, where there was a cherry orchard and a farm. Esther said they rented from Mr. Robertson, president of Poudre Valley Bank. Neva Gladys died there and was buried at Bingham Hill. Louie Roberts, Dean's father, was born on the Blackstock place.

Mrs. Armstrong recalled an incident about 15 years after Neva's death, when she was about four and a half years old. Her pregnant mother had double pneumonia and a doctor advised that a certain medicine was her last chance, but that it would probably "bring the baby." Solomon thought long and hard about it, then decided to let the doctor give the medicine. It broke up the pneumonia, but the baby was born prematurely, lived two hours, and died. He was named James August and buried at Grandview on February 27, 1917 (Reager).

2. **John Rooney** Died March, 1902 Age about 45 years

This man is not at Grandview and he was from Laporte; therefore, it is probable he was buried at Laporte.

Fort Collins Weekly Courier, 3/2/1904: "John Rooney, an inmate of the county hospital, died at 4 o'clock on Monday afternoon of typhoid-pneumonia. Mr. Rooney was brought to the hospital some 5 or 6 days ago from Laporte, suffering from the disease which carried him off despite the care of Mr. and Mrs. Walsh. He was about 45 years of age."

3. **John Rimey** Died March 8, 1905 Age 57

According to the *Weekly Courier,* March 15, 1905: "John Rimey died at his late home three miles west of Bellvue, of consumption, age 57. The deceased came here from Wisconsin about two years ago. He leaves two daughters, one who resided with him and the other in Wisconsin. The funeral will be held this afternoon at his late home and interment will be in the Bellvue cemetery."

From Reager mortuary records: "Person who ordered funeral: Griffith; Cost $40; Died March 8, buried March 9; Cause of death, tuberculosis."

From the Larimer County #1 Paupers Record, "Jany 22, 1905, John Rimey, $45 for Dr. Wilkin, Phy." (Dr. Wilkin was the long-time Laporte physician who lived in the house now occupied by Mrs. Fred Heustis at 2701 North Overland Trail.)

4. **Barbara Rosenboom Rimey** Died September 28, 1910 Age 85

(Allnut) "Barbara Riney, Widow, born in Virginia, 4/11/1827. Died 9/28/1910, 2:30 a.m. Buried 9/30/1910. Age 83-5-17. Cause: paralysis and old age. Father: Mathew Rosenboom, Va. Larimer County paid $25."

Courier, 10/6/1910: "Mrs. Barbara Riney, aged 83, who died at her home in Soldier canon Wed. afternoon, was buried this afternoon in the Laporte cemetery. She was a native of Virginia and has been in Colorado for the past eight years."

Though both newspaper and mortuary spelled her name "Riney," I believe she is the mother of John Rimey who died in 1904, because the dates of their arrival in Colorado coincide. Or, the correct spelling of both names might be "Riney." She is probably the woman who witnessed a murder described in the *Courier* (2/17/1904)—the shooting of William Gardner (second husband of Eliza Bingham) by William Towne at the rock quarry at Owl Canyon. "Mrs. Barbara Rim, a very old lady, testified that she was at the quarry and only about ten feet from Gardner when he was shot. She screamed and begged him not to do it, and she screamed for the men down the road but they did not come."

5. **Arthur F. Jesse** Died January, 1906 Age 49 years

   Courier, 1/3/1906: "Arthur F. Jesse, age 49, a farmer who lived near Laporte, died of consumption. He came with his family in July hoping a change of climate would benefit him, but the disease had taken too strong a hold and he passed away." He is not at Grandview and it can only be assumed he was buried in the Bingham Hill Cemetery in Laporte.

6. **James William Whitmire** Died February, 1906 Age 3 years

   Courier, 2/28/1906: "James William Whitmire, 3 years, 10 days, son of B. Whitmire, and grandson of Peter Macentuch; died at the family home in Bellvue." He was referred to as a lovely child and a poem was printed in his honor. He is not at Grandview.

7. **Dolorita Covales** Died December 1, 1906 Age about 27 years

   Fort Collins Express, 12/5/1906: "Dolorita Covales, a young Mexican woman about 27 years old died of typhoid fever, December 1, and was buried from the Catholic Church. She died at the camp above Bellvue about halfway between that town and the canon. She had come from LaJunta on the 20th of November and was very ill with the disease when she arrived. She was born at Laporte." (It would have been unusual for a Hispanic to be born in Laporte as early as 1879; the newspaper may have meant to say she was "buried" at Laporte.)

8. **Erminia Aragon** Died July 6, 1910 Age 1 year

   (Allnut) "Erminia Aragon, born 2/24/1909, died 7/6/1910, 3:10 p.m., Age 1-4-12. Pneumonia. Dr. C.F. Wilkin. Father: Entimio Aragon, born in Colo., Mother: Ginabua Duran, born in Colo. Burial 7/7/1910. White casket, $15, Chg. to John Baldz, P.O. Box 42, Bellvue, Co."

   Baptism, St. Joseph's: "Erminia Aragon, 3/7/1909. Parents: Entinico Aragon and Genovefa Durand. Sponsors: Johannes Valdez and Anastacita Sanchez. Rev. G. Jos. LaJeunesse."

   (D.M.: Anastacita Sanchez's father was Albino Sanchez; Martin Aragon's mother was Clarita Sanchez-Aragon. Albino and Clarita were brother and sister; therefore, Martin and Anastacia are first cousins.)

   Though the godparents of this child were known, I found no one acquainted with the parents. Erminia Aragon is the first known Hispanic child buried in the cemetery.

9. **Maria Rosa Elvinia Sanchez** + Died August 25, 1910 Age 3 years

(Allnut) "MaRoso Elvinia Sanchez, born Waverly, 3/9/1907, died 8/25/1910, Bellvue, Age 3-5-16. Casket, $18. Funeral 8/27/1910. Pneumonia. Dr. C.F. Wilkin. Father: A.J. Sanchez, born in Colo. Mother: Verzarvel Atencia, born in Colo."

Baptism, St. Joseph's: "Maria Roselbira Sanchez, (Mariam Roselbiram). May 26, 1907. Parents: Albino Sanchez and Bersabel Atencio. Sponsors: Joseph A. Martinez and Sistorante Gardea. Father G.Jos. LaJenesse."

Courier, 9/1/1910: "Rose Elvira Sanchez, aged three and a half, daughter of A.J. Sanchez of Bellvue, died last night of pneumonia. The funeral took place this afternoon, with burial in Grandview Cemetery." (This is an obvious error; she was buried at Bingham Hill and has a homemade stone marking her grave.)

Maria Rosa is only person in this book to have four public records of their existence—a headstone in the cemetery, the mortuary record, her baptism and the newspaper account of her death. Her name is spelled differently in each place.

Information on the next five children is from memories and records of Clara Rodgers and Rosa (Rose) Hoffman of Fort Collins, and from death certificates and other information provided by Betty Jean Spencer of Ogden, Utah.

10. **August Robertson** Died August 12, 1903 Age 2 months

August was born May 2, 1903, at Bellvue, and died August 21, 1903, Age 0-2-19. His parents were Andrew Francis Robertson and Emma Mae Drager Robertson. According to his death certificate, he died of whooping cough.

11. **Donald Robertson** Died March 28, 1911 Age 4 years

Donald was born September 10, 1906, at Laporte, and died March 28, 1911. His parents were Andrew Francis and Emma Mae Drager Robertson. Scarlet fever caused his death. Others in the family who became ill with scarlet fever and survived were Levi William, age 13, Alvis, age 11 (the father of Betty Jean Spencer) and Elesta, age 10. The family had six children in Colorado and two others born in South Jordan, Salt Lake County, Utah.

Long-time Laporte resident Willie Morgenstern had told me of an old abandoned house on the west end of our property near the river. (See aerial photo.) During Prohibition, Cam Herring brewed a little moonshine in it, but Morgenstern didn't know who had lived in it earlier. Clara Rodgers said it was her uncle, Andrew Robertson, and that Donald and his brother, Rudolph, were born there, and that August and Donald might both have died in it. Andrew worked beets for the Herrings, who later, in the 1930s, pulled the house to Overland Trail and sold it and a small piece of land to Rolland Morgenstern. Now its address is 2225 North Overland Trail and the house is owned and occupied by Adele Eastman and her children, Jesse and Alice.

The death of Donald on March 28, 1911, set a chain of sad events in motion. Within a few weeks, three of his cousins were dead, also from scarlet fever. Donald and August are buried in unmarked graves immediately to the east of the three Robertson headstones.

12. **Esther Viola Robertson** + Died May 11, 1911 Age 7 years

Esther was born in Bellvue on December 8, 1904, and died May 11, 1911, at age seven years and five months. Her parents were Samuel Robertson and Maggra (Maggie) Wright Robertson.

13. **Guy Delbert Robertson** + Died May, 1911 Age 3 years, 9 months

Guy was born on August 12, 1907 in Bellvue; the exact date of his death is uncertain, but it was in May, 1911. Parents: Same as above.

14. **Margaret Mattie Beatrice Robertson** + Died June, 1911 Age 2

Margaret was born on October 2, 1909, and died (approximately) June 6, 1911, at one year, eight months. Parents: Same as above.

Although two morticians were in Fort Collins by 1911, there were no mortuary records for these three children. I could find nothing about them in the newspapers, and I expected a headline for the deaths of three children. Was it an accident? An epidemic? All I had to go on was the 1911 date on the tombstones. I asked at least a dozen Laporte and Bellvue elderly people if they had known a Robertson family. My first break came when old-timer Preston Farrell said he remembered a Sam Robertson who worked for George Stearly around 1923 and was known for being proud of a big gold watch he owned. He'd stand on the corner in Laporte, pull it out and say, "Now there's a good watch." But Preston knew nothing about the children.

From that clue (the name "Sam"), in Grandview records, I found a Sam, buried by a Maggie, and using their dates of death, located both obituaries. Sam died at age 75 on May 28, 1948, from burns received when a couch on which he had been sleeping caught fire from a pipe he had been smoking. Maggie died at age 85 in October 1959. The dates sounded right—they were married in 1900—but neither obituary mentioned Esther, Guy or Margaret, and I felt I had reached a dead end.

When Dean Robert's wife, Merilyn, called to relay information about one of Dean's relatives buried in Laporte, she mentioned that one of Dean's cousins had remarked that "Clara Robison's whole family" was buried there. That rang a bell, as there was a Clara "Rogers" listed as a survivor in Maggie's 1959 obituary. The name wasn't in the telephone book, but in the city directory, I found Clara "Rodgers" and information finally became available about the deaths of the three Robertsons who had headstones and also the two cousins who had died earlier.

The deaths of Esther, Guy and Margaret were vividly remembered by Clara Rodgers, their sister, and Rosa Hoffman, their half-sister. Rosa was 11 years old and Clara, eight, at the time of the epidemic.

The three little ones were beautiful children and Clara tearfully remembered how they always walked hand in hand. Esther had a mass of blonde curls which reached to her waist. Guy was the only boy in a house with six girls. Margaret was the family's delight—a bouncy child almost two in May of 1911.

Clara said that Esther became ill first and lived just 24 hours. Dr. Replogle came out from Fort Collins and quarantined the family for scarlet fever. The next day, Guy was feverish and 24 hours later, he was gone. Margaret died a week later. Rose's memory was that Guy died a week after Esther and that Margaret, whom they hoped would recover, died three weeks after Guy. Margaret developed St. Vitus Dance or a similar malady.

Only one neighboring family was not afraid to visit them. After each death, George Bear and his wife brought a homemade coffin lined with white muslin and beautiful, white embroidered pillows. Esther wore a new, pink sateen dress to her grave. Guy was dressed in a red and white checkered shirt and little gray knee pants. Mrs. Bear made a white shroud for Baby Margaret. Rose said she didn't know what people would have done without friends like them. (Bears had children Alvin, George, Beatrice and Ella.) Each coffin carrying its tiny load was driven off in Bear's lumber wagon. Clara remembered watching the wagon leave the yard with flowers on top of the coffin each time.

Morton Young, Fred and Ray Young's brother, preached the services. The four older sisters, Mabel and Rose Beeson and Clara and Letetia Robertson only had sore throats, but none of the family could attend any of the funerals because of the quarantine. Eva Martinez remembered Maggie's grief, especially for Guy, her only son.

Now that I knew the month of deaths, newspaper research was easier and I found these tiny snippets under "Bellvue News" in the *Courier*. Burial place was never mentioned.

(1) May 19, 1911: "Sam Robertson and family have the sympathy of the entire community in the death of their two children, Esther and Guy, from scarlet fever." (2) May 23: "Sam Robertson's children are improving rapidly now." (3) June 9: "Heart-felt sympathy is expressed by all the neighbors for Mr. and Mrs. Robertson as Tuesday's death claimed their baby, little Margaret, by that dread disease, scarlet fever. This is the third little one this disease has claimed from this father and mother in the last three weeks. (4) June 20: "The scarlet fever in Bellvue seems to be over. Mrs. Robertson's folks will be out of quarantine this week."

The next year, on April 16, 1912, Maggie gave birth to another son, Floyd Oliver. When he grew up he made headstones for the brother and sisters he never met. Clara said he purchased blank stones from the monument company near Grandview cemetery for $3 each, carefully and painstakingly chiseled each letter, and placed them in the cemetery. Each year he put black paint in the letters so they could be easily read. One day as he reached down into the tall grass to paint the letters, a rattlesnake struck and just missed his hand.

Robertsons visited the cemetery often until a house was moved between the cemetery and Bingham Hill Road and occupied by a "mean person." (That would have been after 1945 when the Herring estate sold the farm.) The farmer plowed and destroyed many tombstones which stood between the present cemetery and Bingham Hill Road, according to Clara. He put up a big gate so no one could reach the cemetery. Floyd was reassured by the County that people did have access, but then the farmer acquired a guard dog, and the Robertsons finally gave up trying to visit the graves.

Roy Juhl was gracious about letting Clara Rodgers visit the cemetery in 1988. She was 85 at the time, and so grateful to see the graves again and have pictures taken of herself by them. She remembered large white "snowball" bushes in the cemetery and reiterated that gravestones were once all through the field between the cemetery as fenced now and Bingham Hill Road. Clara died at age 93 on October 29, 1996.

Family history. Maggie Wright married John Beeson in Oklahoma and they had Rosa and Mabel Agnes. John died when Rosa was five months old. Maggie then married Sam Robertson in 1900 and eventually settled in Bellvue in the old stone schoolhouse which Robertson remodeled. They had seven more children: twins Letetia and Felicia (Felicia died at three months because of a hole in the roof of her mouth), Clara, Esther, Guy, Margaret and after the youngest three died, Floyd. Floyd, who had one daughter, Juanita, is also dead now but the stones he made are in good shape.

Clara loved her mother but said her father was mean. For instance, he would peel an orange and eat it and then offer the peelings to his children. They had no money for a camera and no photos exist of Esther, Guy or Margaret.

Clara had four children: Neil Charles Smith, who lives in Fowler, Colorado; Delbert Wayne Smith, missing in Korea; and twin daughters who died at birth. Rose married George Von Vihl (whose brother was buried in Laporte around 1892) and they had George, Jacqueline and Dorothy. (See Von Vihl baby.)

15. **Eliza A.E. Robertson** + Died September 8, 1916 Age 62

(Allnut) "Eliza Robertson, born 10/5/1853, Harrison County, Missouri, died Bellvue, 9/8/1916, 4 p.m. Age 62-11-3. Enlargement of heart, Dr. C.F. Wilkin. Parents: Samuel Melton & Elvira Barrett. Funeral 9/10/1916, Church of Christ, Bellvue. Rev. James Bailey."

Her stone was also made by her grandson, Floyd Robertson. She was the mother of Sam and Andrew Robertson and the grandmother of the five dead children. Her full name was Eliza Ann Elizabeth Melton Robertson. Clara remembered that her funeral was very large and that they went to it standing up in their lumber wagon as it had no seats. Clara loaned me the photograph of Eliza with several family members.

Betty Jean Spencer of Ogden, Utah, a granddaughter of Andrew Robertson, recently wrote that E.A.E.'s husband, Levi, is buried in the South Jordan, Salt Lake City, Utah, cemetery along with Andrew and his wife, Emma Drager Robertson, and their remaining children.

Elizabeth Chavez Ambriz of Fort Collins died April 21, 1998, at age 82. She had been born in Bellvue on February 19, 1916, after the deaths of two little brothers listed below. She has one surviving sister, Beatrice Medina, six children, 11 grandchildren, and six great-grandchildren.

16. **Faustino Chavez** Died February 24, 1911 Age 8 years

(Reager) "Faustino Chavez of Bellvue. Born 1/3/1903 in Colo., died 2/24/1911 at Bellview, Age 8-1-21. Meningitis. Dr. Wilkins. Service at residence, 1:30 p.m., 2/25/1911. $35 coffin; $4 burial robe, $1 preserving body. Place of Burial: Laport. Parents: Eulogio Chavez and Cleofus Corrio." Faustino is one of the few persons buried in the Bingham Hill Cemetery who was embalmed.

17. **Rodolpo Chavez** Died December 12, 1913 Age 5 months

(Reager) "Rudolph Chavez, born 6/12/1913, Colo., died 12/12/1913, near Bellvue, Dr. Wilkins, Place of Burial: Laport. Service 2 p.m., 12/13/1913."

Baptism, St. Joseph's: "Rodolfo, 11/15/1913 Parents: Eulogio Chavez and Cleopha Carrio. Sponsors: Moises Medrano and Pedra Carrio."

(Louise Aragon knew the parents of these children.)

(D.M.: Eulogio Chavez, born in 1863, and Cleofas Carrillo were married in 1893 in Pueblo, Colo. Eulogio was a great-uncle to Eva Martinez, Martin Aragon and also Maria Martinez, buried in Laporte in 1913. The godmother's name was Petrocinia, or Petra, Carrillo.)

18. **Jose de la luz Cordova** Died March 13, 1912 Age 5 months

(Allnut) "Joe Cordova, born 9/27/1911, died 3/13,1912, Age 0-5-15 Cause of Death: congenital syphilis. Dr. Curtis Atkinson. Parents: Ed Cordova, Jovita Pino, both born in Colorado. Funeral 3/13/1912. $10 charged to Ed Cordova, works for Harry Widdows, 3 miles south."

Baptism, St. Joseph's: "Jose de la luz, born 9/26/1911, baptized 10/1/1911. Parents: Eduardo Cordova and Jovita Pino. Sponsors: Melecio Jaramillo and Christina Olivas. Rev. G. Jos. LaJeunesse."

(Louise Aragon knew both parents and godparents.)

(D.M.: Melecio Jaramillo was also godfather to J. Telos Martinez, born 12/1/1906. J. Telos is one of seven brothers of Eva and Maria Martinez, who died in 1913.)

19. **Maria Martinez + (P)** Died September 17, 1913 Age 1 year
(Allnut) "Maria Martinez, born 4/20/1912 in Bellvue, died 9/17/1913, 12:30 a.m., Age 1-4-27. Summer complaint, enteritis. Parents: J.V. Martinez, born in Costillo County, Colo. and Cleofes Aragon, born in N.M. Cost $15."

Baptism, St. Joseph's: "Born 3/25/1912 (correct date), Baptized 4/14/1912. Parents: Valerio Martinez and Cleopha Aragon. Sponsors: Librado and Sophia Martinez."

Maria may have been born with a heart murmur as she was always small and pale, according to her older sister, Eva Martinez, who attended this funeral when she was eight years old. Eva furnished a photo taken at the cemetery of the baby, its parents and godmother, Sophia Martinez. A wooden cross at the grave can be seen in the photograph.

Maria Cleofas Aragon, the mother of Eva and Maria, was born in Crestone, Huerfano County, Colorado (not in New Mexico as mortuary records indicate), on 9/21/1878, and died in Fort Collins on 11/22/1965. Their father, Jose Valerio Martinez, was born in San Pablo, Colorado, 1/30/1868 and died 8/31/1940 in Fort Collins. They came to Larimer County in 1903. Other children in the family besides Eva and Maria were Abel, Ben, Telos, Irvin, Nora, Joe and David Robert Martin, who died at 79 on July 31, 1997. (The boys all changed their last name to Martin.)

Godparents Librado and Sophia were brother and sister from a different Martinez family. Eva married Librado "Lee" in 1924. Lee Martinez Park in Fort Collins, dedicated in 1985, was named in his honor. Lee and Eva had ten children: Alonzo (killed in WW II), Daniel, Santana Moore, Matilda Maxwell, Evangeline Mondragon, Gloria Maxwell, Anthony, Joseph (died of bronchial pneumonia 12/2/1940), Philip and Robert.

When Eva Martinez died at age 94 on October 7, 1997, Holy Family Church was filled with friends and descendants, who numbered 34 grandchildren, 73 great-grandchildren and 13 great-great-grandchildren.

20. **Baby Boy Williams** Died October 13, 1913 Age 1 day
This baby was born and died on the same day. His parents were

Edward Joshua Williams and Sarah Bethel Cox. He was one of 12 children; two others were buried in 1895 and 1896 in Trinidad, Colorado. This information came from Darlene McQuire and her mother, Florence Williams, who married Haulcie Roberts in 1921. The dead baby is Florence's brother.

When Clara Rodgers visited the cemetery in 1988, she mentioned that her father, Sam Robertson, helped bury the Williams baby just north of her sister Margaret's grave.

There is no headstone, but about 30 years ago, Florence placed a bottle with information about the baby in the ground at the location of the grave. While the Rainbow Rider's 4-H Club was cleaning one day, they unearthed a jar containing a note. It was taken to Dean Roberts, who opened the rusty lid, read the note, rewrote and replaced it. The jar was later reburied in the same place.

The next three brothers died within a two month period.

21. **Roque Armenta** Died October 22, 1914 Age 9 years

(Allnut) "Roqqe Armento, born Johnstown, Colo. 5/29/1905, died Lee's Lake, 10/22/1914, 4 a.m. of typhoid fever. Age 9-4-23. Dr. C. F. Wilkin. Funeral 10/23/1914. Parents: Charles R. Armento and Genivieve Sanchez of Bellvue, both born in Colo."

Walt Little of Fort Collins remembered "Rocky's" funeral; he said old man Aragon (Martin Aragon's father, Christopher) took the coffin to the cemetery with his team and spring wagon and that several people followed on foot. Little also thought that a Willie Armenta died in 1913 and was buried at Laporte. I found no records of a Willie, only Rocky, Fred and John—all buried in 1914.

A later baby of Carolo Armenta and Genoveva Sanchez was baptized Petrum Rockum (Pedro Roqqe) on July 16, 1916 at St. Joseph's. Sponsors: Benjamin (Bendito) and Lucia Aragon, who were brother and sister.

22. **Frederico Armenta** Died December 1, 1914 Age 6 years

(Reager) "Fred Armento of Bellvue, born 1/1/1908 in Colo., died 12/1/1914, 2 p.m. Age 6-11-0. Dr. Wilkin. Buried 12/2/1914 at Bellview. Parents: Charles Armento & Mary Sanches, born in Colo. Coffin $16. Funeral service in Bellview." (There was a note about why there was no payment—the baby's father was in the penitentiary.)

Baptism, St. Joseph's: Frederico Armenta, born 2/6/1909, baptized 4/4/1909. Parents: Carolo Armenta and Genovefa Sanchez. Sponsors: Atonnius Apodaca and Adelaida Aragon. Rev. LaJeunesse.

(D.M.: Antonio Apodaca and Adelaida Aragon were married June 1, 1906, in St. Joseph's Catholic Church. Antonio died 1965 in Ely, Nevada. Adelaida was born 8/1/1886 in Huerfano County and died 8/22/1949 in Ely, Nevada. Adelaida was a daughter of Jose de Jesus Aragon and Agustina Lucero Aragon.)

23. **John L. Armenta** Died December 23, 1914 Age 3 years

(Reager) "John L. Armento, born 2/6/1910 in Colo., died 12/23/1914, Age 3-10-17, Dr. Wilkins, Service and Burial: 12/24/1914 at Laport. Chg. $13 coffin, $2.50 burial robe: $15.50, paid."

(These three brothers, ages 9, 6 and 3, died within two months, probably all of typhoid; the third burial was on Christmas Eve, 1914.)

Louise Aragon lived on the 300 block of Cherry Street as a child and Armentas lived across the tracks. She remembered that Charlie Armenta went to prison. Genoveva Sanchez, the mother of the three boys, was Martin Aragon's aunt, a sister to his mother, Clarita. The dead brothers had a sister who lived, Mary.

The following two were members of an extended family who lived at Doty's. Doty's, later known as the Dow Randleman place, and now owned by Ken and Linda Fisher, is on the west side of Bingham Hill and recognized by its large silo. About 1/4 mile east of the main house and silo, near the irrigation ditch, was a small tenant house. (See Honnold.) How many in the family worked for Doty's is not known, but living in the house were Crisanta Herrera, her son-in-law, Don Vigil, Vigil's wife and several children, and Crisanta's sons, Juan and Manuel Herrera.

Juan (John) and Manuel respected their brother-in-law, Don Vigil. Since he was oldest, he would make the decisions that concerned the family. Don, in turn, respected his mother-in-law, though they were about the same age.

24. **Crisanta Herrera + * (P)** Died January 17, 1916 Age 70

(Allnut) "Christiana Herrera, widow, born 1/29/1846 in N.M., died at D.D. Doty's near Bellvue, 7 p.m., 1/17/1916. Age 69-11-18. Buried 11:30 a.m. No service. No clergy. Parents: M. Pacheco and Louise Valdez, both of N.M. $35, charged to John Herrera." Stella Gallegos found this obituary which is full of errors and misspelled words in the *Courier* (1/18/1916):

MEXICAN WOMAN DIES ON BELLVUE RANCH. On the Doty ranch at Bellvue, Mrs. Chritiana Hererera died last night following an attak of grippe. The woman was 70 years old and unable to withstand the shock of the grippe which has attacked so many people in this vicinity this winter. The deceased was the mother of Juan Hererera, who is employed by Doty. She was born in Mexico. The remains will be buried at the little cemetery not far from Bingham hill.

Family information came from Dora Vigil and her daughters, Lorraine Vigil and Tina Gallegos; Sadie Gallegos; Stella Gallegos; and Cecilia Beecher and her mother, Carmen Grass. For one thing, the marble headstone, a baby lying in a sea shell, belongs to Mrs. Herrera, who was more commonly called Grandma Pacheco. She had spent a lifetime helping with baby deliveries and was known for her skill with breech births. She often accompanied Dr. Wilkin of Laporte on difficult deliveries. The headstone was a perfect choice for her, and it does not belong to some "unknown baby" as was sometimes reported in old newspaper and magazine articles about the cemetery.

Crisanta Pacheco was born January 29, 1846, in New Mexico (not Mexico, as the newspaper reported). Her father was Martinez Pacheco and her mother was Louisa Valdez. She married Casimiro Herrera and they had ten children between 1865 and 1885: Vicenta, Jesus, Manuel (a bachelor who homesteaded in Rist Canyon and who died of stomach cancer in 1952), Antonia, Ramona (who married Don Vigil and had ten children), Juan Andres, Juan Francisco, Cecilia (who was a singer and also a midwife), Maria Paula and last, Juan Reyes (who is referred to as "John" throughout the rest of this story) who paid for his mother's funeral, was the father of Stella Gallegos, uncle of Sadie Gallegos and died of a heart attack in 1969. Dr. James Wise signed his death certificate.

Crisanta's husband, Casimiro Herrera, was born near Taos, New Mexico, in 1838, died at age 65 in Englewood, Colorado, on September 9, 1903, and was buried in Pueblo.

The family, living in the little house on Bingham Hill in the teens and '20s was a lively one, and most of the stories of orneriness revolve around Crisanta's grandson, Ed. Ed once scared his grandma by shaking a rattlesnake's rattle while she was praying the rosary. Another time he pushed his Uncle John, who was sitting on a fence looking at newborn pigs. Don had to jump in and help John out before the sow attacked him. Ed ran away for a day but came home when he got hungry. His dad was mad but Uncle John said not to spank him because he said he acted the same when he was young.

Grandma Pacheco would often accompany the older daughters of Don and Ramona to the dances. In fact, it was the only way they could go. However, she had a romantic nature and would often let the girls meet young men and receive letters from them. Sometimes Ed would tattle on the girls—then they and Grandma got into trouble.

Crisanta Herrera is the first of nearly 20 Vigil relatives to be buried at Laporte and she has many living local descendants. Her son John, for instance, is the father of Stella Gallegos who recently celebrated her 55th wedding anniversary on April 4, 1998. (Stella's children are Johnny, Ruth Oritz, Roberta Irvine, Brenda Gallegos and Leroy Santistevan; and she has nine grandchildren and 13 great-grandchildren.) Other relatives are mentioned under Donaciano Vigil.

There is one professional photograph of Herrera and her son-in-law, Don Vigil, in Alaska in the home of Betty Tullos, a daughter of Bill Vigil. Apparently his wife, Ramona, was shy about having her picture taken so Crisanta posed with her son-in-law, Don. Lorraine and Dora Vigil loaned a snapshot of the portrait for this book.

25. Donaciano Vigil + * (P) Died October 17, 1918 Age about 76

(Allnut) "Don Vigil, born in N.M., birth date unknown. Died near Bellvue, 10/17/1918, age 76, Farmer. Father: Unknown. Mother: Pacifica Ban. Cause of death: Typhoid fever. Service 10/18/1918 by Rev. G. Joseph LaJeunesse at family residence. Cost $63 ($50 casket, $10 hearse delivered to Bellvue, $3 burial robe)."

This man with the little gravestone had a long but undocumented history and he left many descendants. His first name was Donaciano; his adopted surname was Vigil. Apparently he talked little about his past; his children thought he was a pure-blooded Indian (maybe) and had been "adopted" by a Vigil family. What Vigil family adopted him and under what circumstances is unknown. He may have been born in Taos, New Mexico, and his father may have been killed in an Indian raid.

From the photograph loaned by Dora and Lorraine Vigil, one can see his proud look. Eva Martinez remembered him as tall and thin and kind. Some relatives think he was Spanish or French; others believe he was Spanish, French and Indian. Funeral records call him "Mexican" and list his mother as Pacifica Ban, a name Vigil first mentioned on his deathbed. Pacifica has variously been guessed to be Irish, Indian or Spanish. Donaciano's ancestry will probably remain a mystery, though recent family delving has found his mother may have been a "saloon girl" and that he might have had a half-brother.

Other bits of information about Vigil are that he was a rodeo rider around Walsenberg and Trinidad, a deputy sheriff at Taos and a refinery worker and homesteader around Pueblo. It is thought he owned a ranch and race horses at Gardner, Colorado. When he was young, he had a wife named Polonia, whom he married in Santa Fe and loved dearly. She was a small woman and he would pick her up and set her in the buggy or wagon. She apparently died in childbirth a few months after marriage and he was heart-broken. He eventually went to Colorado.

He met Ramona Herrera in the Walsenburg area. Her parents saw Don riding by in a horse and buggy and thought he had money. Ramona was only about 13 when they married and Don was between 45 and 50. Ramona once told Lorraine Vigil's grandmother, Nicolasa (Dora Vigil's mother), that she didn't love him at first, but that after she started having babies, Don was so good and kind; furthermore, he promised to take care of her mother, Crisanta, and her family.

Don and Ramona had eight children near Walsenberg: Magdalena, Lillie, Grace, Marina, Lee, Ed, Tobe and Julia. When the family moved to the Bellvue area in 1906, he also brought his recently widowed mother-in-law and her sons. In Bellvue, they had Bill and Annie. Relatives used to tease Annie because she was born the same day their mare had a foal.

Whether they lived all their Bellvue years at Doty's on Bingham Hill isn't known, but they were there when his mother-in-law, Crisanta Pacheco Herrera, died in 1916, and at least through the time he died. It must have been a full house with all his children and his mother- and brothers-in-law. Don was apparently strict with the girls and insisted on meeting the boyfriends who called. Yet he was often gone sheepherding nine months at a time so left their moral protection to Grandma Pacheco.

Vigil may have been haying or working sheep in North Park in 1918 when he became ill with typhoid fever. Florence Vigil, a daughter-in-law, said he was brought down to Bellvue by Frank and Art Collamer in their stage. He was buried near his mother-in-law at Bingham Hill. There was no obituary in the newspaper.

One daughter, Magdalena (Minnie) married Andy Trujillo and they buried a child, Juanpedro, in Laporte, just two months after Don Vigil died. Minnie's only daughter, Angel, also buried a baby in 1936 in Laporte. (See Armijo.) Grace married Juan Torres, an immigrant from Spain, and they had several children, three of whom were buried at Bingham Hill. (See Torres.) One of Grace's daughters, Mary Vigil, also buried a daughter. (See Maxine Vigil.)

Lillie married Porfirio (Hap) Apodaca and buried two children, and maybe as many as seven, at Bingham Hill. (See Apodaca.) Tobe married Mary Trujillo; they buried two children. (See Freddie and Sammie Vigil.) Tobe was the father of Sadie Gallegos.

Ed married Dora Ortega and they also buried a baby. (See Margaret Vigil.) They also had Frank, Gloria Valdez, Tina Gallegos and Lorraine Vigil, who helped so much with this story. (Tina's children are Art, Jerry and Rudy Gallegos, successful businessmen in Fort Collins. Gloria had Elaine and Joanna, who is the mother of Anna Marie. Frank owns a paint business in Colorado Springs and is the father of Tonya, Frank, Tim, Dora and Chris.)

Lee and Marina died young—Lee in a quarry explosion and Marina, who homesteaded land in Rist Canyon, of dropsy. Julia married the Greek, Jim Vangel, also known as Jim Banjo, and lived at the store at Ingleside. They had no children but she had a second marriage to a Davies, in which she adopted his two children.

Bill married Florence Krickbaum and they had Bill, Glen, Leroy (d. 7/4/1997), Paul, Dale, Cliff, Betty, Dorothy, Ilene and Edith. Leroy was the father of Chris, who was lost April 30, 1978, on Grey Rock Mountain when he was nine years old. In spite of a massive search, he was never found.

Annie Mondragon of Hemet, California, the last living child of Don and Ramona Vigil, died April 20, 1998. She had told me that she was seven when her father died. She married one of Louise Aragon's brothers, Telesforo, and their children are Gene, Daniel, Richard, Ramona and Bob (deceased).

At least 16 grandchildren and great-grandchildren of Don Vigil are buried near him, but his wife, Ramona, was buried at Grandview, because some "they" said she couldn't be buried in Laporte. Ramona was a heavy-set woman who collapsed with a heart attack over the kitchen stove while she was cooking an egg for her son, Ed. She was buried on April 20, 1927, at age 52 (Reager). Her death certificate has "acute dilation of heart" as cause of death.

According to dates in mortuary records, Vigil was 33 years older than his wife and fathered babies until he was about 70. On Grace's birth certificate, however, Vigil's age was written as 50, and Ramona's as 25, only a 25-year difference.

The cremains of his grandson, Leroy Vigil, will be buried near Don's grave in the spring or summer of 1998. (See Leroy Vigil.)

26. **Rosa Gallegos** Died March 6, 1916 Age 6 days

(Allnut) "Rosa Gallegos from N.W. of Ft. Collins, born 2/29/1916, died 3/6/1916, 4:30 a.m., premature birth. Age 0-0-6. Dr. Wilkin. Father: Philip Gallegos, works for J.W. Dealy. Mother: Anastacita Barela, born in Colo. Coffin, $10."

Baptism, St. Joseph's: "Rosa Margarita, 3/5/1916. Parents: Philiberto Gallegos and Anastasia Barela. Sponsors: Benjamin and Lucia Aragon. Fr. LaJeunesse." (Anastasia Barela was the aunt to Louise Aragon's son-in-law, Frank Barela.)

(D.M.: Philiberto Gallegos was a brother of Tircia Gallegos Padilla of Bellvue. Tircia and Manuel Abedon Padilla raised a family of 17 children in Bellvue on the Harvey H. Griffin farm. Anastacita Barela was born 4/27/1894, a daughter of Francisco Barela and Maria Adelaida Martinez Barela. Adelaida, Jose Valerio Martinez and Lucan Martinez were brothers and sister; Jose Valerio was the father of Eva Martinez.)

27. **Celestina Videl** Died March 16, 1916 Age 1 year

(Reager) "Celestina Videl of Willow Street, Ft. Collins, Age: 1-4-20. born 10/26/1914, died 3/16/1916. Parents: Dorotes Videl, born in Mexico and Celestina Chavez, born Colorado. Cost $25."

(D.M.: They also had Tony, Beatrice and Virginia.)

28. **Josephina Apodaca** Died March 21, 1916 Age 1 day

(Allnut) "Josephine Apodaca, born and died 3/21/1916, 10:20 p.m. W.T. Hollowell, Coroner. Place of Birth: Back of Herring's, log house. Place of Death: Back of Herring's, log house. Measles. Parents: Victor

Apodaca and Tomasita Cordova. White pique casket, $15." (This log house sat below the ditches near Bingham Hill Road, a few yards from the cemetery.)

Another Josephina Apodaca had been born 9/12/1912 and baptized 10/13/1912. Sponsors: Rejis Trujillo and Ursula Benavides. Apparently she died and the second Josephina was born and died in 1916. The first Josephina might also be in the Laporte cemetery.

(D.M.: Apodaca children who lived include Melecio [Mel], Jose [Joe], Alvina, Presiliano [Pries] and Porfirio [Percy]. Pries' widow is Mae Tafoya Apodaca and she lives on Grant Street.)

29. **Jesse Martinez** * Died April 5, 1917 Age 4 days

(Allnut) "Son of Julius Martinez, 310 Willow St., works for Street company. Born 4/1/1917, lived 4 days, died 4/5/1917. Cause of death: Convulsions. Burial: 4/7/1917. Parents: Julius Martinez and Sucindina Pachio, both born in Colo. $10."

30. **Juan Pedro Manifico Trujillo** * Died Dec. 5, 1918 Age 2 months

(Allnut) "Juanpedro Manifesto Trujillo, born 9/17/1918, died 12/5/1918, 4 a.m., near Bellvue. Age: 0-2-19. Dr. Wilkin. Parents: Andres Trujillo, Madalena Vigil. Coffin, $15. Burial 12/6/1918."

Baptism, St. Joseph's: "Juan Pedro Manifico [Joannem Petrum Magnificum] Trujillo, baptized 9/17/1918. Parents: Andrea Trujillo, Magdalena Vigil. Sponsors: Victor Apadaca, Thomacita Cordova. Rev. G. Jos. LaJeunesse."

This child with the magnificent name, born one month before his Grandfather Vigil died, lived less than three months. Minnie was Sadie Gallegos' favorite aunt and she often told Sadie the story of how little Pedro died. Minnie's only other child was Angel Armijo, who also buried a baby at Bingham Hill in 1936.

31. **Henry Canchola** Died May 28, 1919 Age 6 months

(Allnut) "Henry Canhola, born 11/29/1918, died 5/28/1919, Age 6 mo., Pneumonia, Dr. C.F. Wilkin. Parents: Joe Canhola and Carmen Serna, both from Mexico. Homemade casket furnished. Chg. $5."

This Canchola family lived at Ingleside and the father might be the gun-fighting Ignacio Canchola headlined in 12/4/1914: "Outside of Shack Looks As Though Mexican War In Progress." Canchola had two bullets in his shoulder and a gun stock had been broken over his head, but he refused to be taken from Ingleside to the county hospital.

After reading the 1990 edition of this book, Celia Trujillo Silva de Campos, her husband, Rudy, and sister, Florinda Kangeter, all of Colorado Springs, visited us in Laporte and brought photographs and poignant stories connected with the deaths of father and son, Acacio and Jacobo Trujillo. Campos, a granddaughter of Acacio Trujillo and niece of Jacobo, has done extensive traveling to find old records and did the final editing of the next two stories.

32. **Jacobo Trujillo + (P)** Died 7/15/1920 Age 15 years

(Allnut) "Jacobo Trujillo of Bellvue. Age: 15-7-11. Born Rouse, Colo., 12/4/1904; died, Bellvue, 7/15/1920, 9 p.m.; cause: pulmonary tuberculosis. Dr. R.W. Morrish. Silver gray casket, $90. Did not direct this funeral. Think no services were held. Parents: Acacio Trujillo and Selestina Baca, both born in Colo." (*Note:* Rouse is too small to be on Colorado maps, but it is ten miles south of Walsenburg. Larimer County Magistrate, Janet Rodriquez, was born there.)

According to Campos, when Jacobo was about 14, and his sister, Beatriz, was about ten, Jacobo's mother, Celestina, took their baby, Evelinda, and ran off with another man, leaving Jacobo and Beatriz with their father, Acacio.

In the summer of 1920, the family was living in a one-room cabin, not much more than a shack, in the mountains west of Bellvue where Acacio did timber work. When Beatriz related the story to her own children years later, she said she didn't even know Jacobo, her beloved big brother, was sick; she had never heard that he had TB. One day, he just died. According to mortician's records, he died at 9 p.m. It was improper to leave a body alone, so early the next morning, when Acacio took a team of horses to get a wagon to bring the body to Laporte, he left eleven-year-old Beatriz to watch the body. She looked at Jacobo on the bed and knew he was dead, but wanted to talk to him. She went outside and as she sat on the step waiting for her dad, the wind made sad whispering sounds in the pine trees. All the rest of her life, whenever Beatriz heard the sound of wind in pine trees, it brought sad memories of having lost her only brother who cared for her.

Jacobo was buried in the Laporte cemetery in a fine coffin; four years later his father died.

33. Acacio Trujillo + (P) Died 7/16/1924 Age 59 years

(Allnut) "Acacio Trujillo. Farm Laborer. Born 1/1/1865 at LaVeta, Colo., died 7/16/1924, 12:45 pm Age: 59-6-15. Widowed. Cause: Apoplexy. Dr. E. I. Raymond. Funeral, 8 a.m., 7/18/24. Catholic, Rev. Pedro Trudel. Parents: Policarpa Trujillo and Gtifanito Cruz both from N.M. Charge to Andrew Trujillo, works for Alex Baker." (For some reason, there is no record of his burial from Holy Family Church where Father Trudel ministered.)

To correct the mortuary's spelling, Trujillo's mother was Estefana, not "Gtifanito," and his father was Hepolito, not "Policarpa." Acacio may have died of a stroke (apoplexy), but the family thought he had fluid around his heart. Also, according to Campos, he was not a widower.

Several people helped with this rather tangled genealogy: Lorraine Vigil and her cousin, Angel Armijo, Celia Campos, Nora Castellanos and Stella Gallegos (Acacio's first wife was her mother's aunt).

Jose Acacio Trujillo married his first wife, Rufina Pacheco, in St. Mary's Catholic Church in Walsenburg on August 21, 1886. Rufina's parents were Rafael Pacheco and Leonar Garcia Pacheco. Acacio and Rufina had four children: Jose Eufemio, Crespina Candida, Jose David and Juan Andres (Andy). Only Eufemio and Andy grew to adulthood, and both buried children at Bingham Hill. None of the informants knew what happened to Rufina.

Acacio then married Celestina Baca who had a ten-year-old daughter, Floripa, from another union. Acacio and Celestina had Jacobo in 1904, Beatriz in 1908 and Evelinda in 1916. When the children were young, Celestina left with another man, Jesus Ortiz. Therefore, when Acacio died, he was not widowed as reported to the mortician; his wife had just left him.

After Jacobo's death, Acacio sent Beatriz to her mother in Minatare, Nebraska. There are three Mexican nationals in this story who were undoubtedly the bane of Acacio's life. The three men were cousins. Acacio's step-daughter, Floripa, had married one, Urbano Roman, and they had gone to Minatare. Acacio's wife, Celestina, ran off with the second, Jesus Ortiz, and also went to Minatare. When Beatriz arrived, the third cousin, Serafin Silva, got the 12-year-old girl pregnant. When Acacio found out, he was very angry at both Celestina and Serafin and left for Minatare. He took the couple to the justice of the peace and saw that they were married. He returned to Colorado and Beatriz never saw her father again.

When Celestina heard Acacio was on his way to Minatare, because she apparently owed him money, she and Jesus rapidly left for Ohio, and Beatriz never saw her mother again, either. Celestina stayed in Ohio, died there in the summer of 1927 and was buried in Bowling Green.

Beatriz stayed loyal to her 27-year-old husband and between 1921 and 1941, she and Serafin Silva had ten children, three who died at birth—Herlinda, Juanita and Roberto—and seven who lived—Celia (source of information), Enrique, Serafin Jr., Ramon, Victoria, Florinda and Enedina. These seven children had a total of 25 children, none of whom live in the Fort Collins area.

Evelinda, Celia's (half-) aunt, lived with their family on and off but finally disappeared, never to be heard from after 1937. It is believed that she died in Denver.

Andy Trujillo, Jacobo's older half-brother, is the son who took care of his father Acacio's burial. He was married to Minnie (Magdalena), one of the ten children of Don Vigil, who had been buried six years before Acacio, also at Bingham Hill. Andy did farm labor and worked for the pickle factory in Fort Collins and was killed by a truck at age 45 in 1938. He is the father of Angel Armijo who has the distinction of having two grandfathers buried in Laporte—Don Vigil and Acacio Trujillo. Eufemio, the other living child from Acacio's first wife, married Vitalia Archuleta and had Lucia, Benedicto and Salina (all buried at Bingham Hill in 1927, 1929 and 1930). They also had Cora (1927), Nora (1932) and Joe (1946). Cora, the mother of Joe Dominguez Jr. and Sam Trujillo, died when Sam was five years old. (Sam works for the Fort Collins Water Department and has Amy, Sonya, Aaron and Sam, Jr.)

Nora married Joe Castellanos and has Eugene, Diane and Barbara Wilson, three grandchildren and two great-grandchildren. Sam's kids also call Nora "Grandma" as she raised Sam from the time he was eight years old. Nora donated the photo of her sister, Lucia, buried at Laporte.

Sarah C. Howell died 12/5/1921 and belongs here chronologically but she is listed next to her son, Bill, who died in 1939.

The following are three infant grandsons of Don Vigil, children of his daughter, Grace, and Juan Torres.

34. **John Torres** * Died March 19, 1922 Age 5 days

(Reager) "John Torres, born 3/15/1922, died 3/19/1922 in Laport. Funeral 2 p.m., March 20, 1922. $10. Parents: John Torres, born in Spain and Grace Vigil, born in Colo. Service 2 p.m., Place of Burial: Laport."

35. **Jessie M. Torres** * Died Sept. 23, 1924 Age 7 days

(Reager) "Jessie M. Torres, born 9/16/1924, died 9/23/1924, buried 4 p.m. 9/23/1924, Bellvue. Goods ordered by Mrs. Harrison, bill charged to Larimer County."

36. **Joseph Marvin Torres** * Died 4/15/1927 Age 10 days

(Allnut) "Joseph Marvin Torres, Bellvue, born 4/5/1927, died 4/15/1927, 4 p.m. Broncho pneumonia. Burial 4/16/1927, afternoon, no service. $15 charged to Larimer Co. Furnished casket and box but did not attend funeral."

When Cleo Furones Holsinger of Fort Collins was about seven years old, she went home with her friend, Gladys Torres, and watched the new baby nursing its mother. A few days later, another little friend, Mildred Spaulding, told Cleo that the baby had died. Her mother took care of the baby after its death. Mildred said the dead baby was lying on the sewing machine and it scared her.

Juan Torres, father of the above three children, came from Spain when he was about 16 years old with his friend (and perhaps cousin) Demetrio (Dem) Furones Barrios. Furones became a foreman at the Ingleside Quarry where Torres lost a hand in an explosion. Men who took Torres to the hospital said he yelled only once when his mangled hand was cut off and that he went home from the hospital the same day. He wore a hook afterwards.

When Cecilia Beecher was about two years old, she went for long walks with Torres down the railroad tracks, from Watson Lake where her grandfather lived, to Graves Dairy. She just barely remembers a big man holding her little hand.

Torres children who lived include: Steve, Sye, Emma, Mary, Alex, Manuel, Gladys, Ray and Dora—they were all friends of Louise Aragon. Juan Torres was buried at Grandview 5/1/1939 by Father Juan Fullana. Many remember going to his "Velorio" or wake.

37. **Abner M. Spragg + (P)** Died October 24, 1923 Age 76

(Allnut) "Abner M. Spragg, born North New Brunswick, Canada, on 3/17/1847; died Bellvue, 10/24/1923, 9:30 p.m., age 76-6-17. Cause: acute dilation of heart. Farmer. Dr. J.D. Carey. Parents: Wm. Sprague and Jane Burnett, both born in Canada. Burial: 10/20/1923. Rev. J.A. Ellis of the Bellvue Mission Church officiated. $183.75 charged to Jessie Brubaker (his daughter), Admrx."

Mr. and Mrs. Spragg are the only married couple in the cemetery who were buried next to each other and have a headstone.

38. **Florence H. Spragg + (P)** Died November 4, 1933 Age 83

(Warren-Bohlender) "Florence H. Spragg, born 9/23/1880, died 11/4/1933. Age 53-1-11. Funeral 11/7/1933. Cause: Carcinoma of the face. Dr. Little. Parents: Norman Bassett and Hazel Hale of Pennsylvania."

(Note: Her birthdate and age are wrong. Her obituary and stone both indicate she was born 9/23/1850 and was 83-1-11 at time of death. Also, the newspaper spelled her name wrong.)

In the *Fort Collins Express-Courier,* 11/5/1933:

MRS. SPRAGUE, 83, DIES AT BELLVUE HOME SATURDAY.

Mrs. Florence Bassett Sprague, 83, mother of Mrs. C.O.(Jessie) Brubaker and Mrs. Dan Shunn of Bellvue, died at her home in Bellvue at 9 o'clock Saturday morning following an illness of nearly a year. Old age was given as a cause of her death.

Mrs. Sprague was born Sept. 23, 1850 in Ill. She came to Bellvue about 12 years ago from Nebr. Mr. Sprague is buried at the cemetery near Laporte. While living in Bellvue Mrs. Sprague attended the Pilgrim Holiness church and did much work in the Cache la Poudre union of Women's Christian Temperance Union as long as her health would permit.

She was the mother of 12 children, five of whom survive her. Besides the two daughters living in Bellvue, Mrs. (Ivis) Atkinson of White River, S.D., Mrs. Bertha Dillon of La Junta, and Mrs. Agnes Herron of Encampment, Wyo., survive as do 27 grandchildren and 12 great-grandchildren. Miss Florence Dillon, a granddaughter of La Junta, came two weeks ago to be with Mrs. Sprague through her illness."

Mrs. Mabel Burns said she went to this funeral; it was during the first winter in which the Burns came down from North Park for their children's schooling. Mrs. Norman (Marie) Brubaker remembered Mrs.

Spragg as a very nice little lady who was blind. Also, she stated that at one time family members wanted to move their bodies.

Mrs. Paul (Ruth) Brubaker of Riverton, Wyoming, was able to furnish a photograph of Mr. and Mrs. Spragg and a little more information. She is married to Paul Brubaker, a grandson of Florence, and the last of the of Jessie's children. (Their children are Clara Rose, William and Richard.) She wrote that Florence Spragg had lost most of her eyesight as a child, yet was able to write some family history for a granddaughter in Oregon. Ruth had a chance to see it once, and noted that the handwriting was amazingly good.

Local descendants of the Spraggs are Norman and Marie Schelt Brubaker and their children (and grandchildren): Norma Gertson (Randy Staley, JoLynn Staley, David Gertson); Joan Edwards (Eddie); Karen Bryner (Rodney, Gregory, Jean Ann, Wendy and Sandra); and Dennis (Jennifer, Kristen and Jeff). Flora Shunn's children are Dorothy Watters, Minnie Ahlbrandt and Vernon, all deceased.

Kate Moon from Encampment, Wyoming, said that Jot Herron, Agnes's husband, was with the Buffalo Bill Wild West Show, and the story most often repeated about him in Encampment was that he could stand on the floor, jump and kick the ceiling and come down on his feet.

The next three entries are vague concerning the dates but probably happened in the 1920s.

39. Nameless Travelers

Ed Vigil told his family that when they lived on Bingham Hill Road (where the beehives were on Dow Randleman's, now Ken Fisher's farm), old or ill travelers often stopped for the night and sometimes they died. Vigils helped bury them at the cemetery and a jar containing wild flowers and written identification was always buried with them.

(That house, occupied by the Honnolds in the 1890s, and in which Mrs. Herrera later died, was torched by students during College Days in the mid 1950s. Later, in a trailer at the same site, an old man named Pete Fulmer [Stuttering Pete] lived and watched cattle which belonged to Brights from Livermore.)

40. Nameless Sheepherder

Berniece Collamer Kelly lived with her family along the Poudre River, west of Herring's barn, on property which flooded in 1923 and now belongs to the Colorado Division of Wildlife. When she was about five years old, around 1920, an old sheepherder stopped to spend the night in his wagon. He was dead the next morning. She believes the unidentified man was buried at Bingham Hill.

The sheriff told Mr. Fred Collamer that he could have the sheepwagon. Berniece said that inside was a little black, Negro doll. She had never seen anything like it before and she kept and treasured it for years. Berniece said that besides sheepherders, gypsies camped every summer along the Poudre River by their house.

41. **Relative of Jim Vale**

Duayne Canfield of Laporte said that Jim Vale, who married Lily Garrett, told him that someone in his family was buried at Laporte. Thomas Melville Young, also of Laporte, remembered that in the 1920s, a Vale relative was killed by lightning at North Park. This might be the same person.

42. **Baby Trujillo** Died October 31, 1923 Age 1 day

(Reager) "Baby Truzillo, Mexican, Residence 7 mi. north, born and died, 10/31/1923. Premature. Dr. Brown. Funeral 4 p.m. 11/1/1923, Burial Laport. Cost $10. Pd. $8. Parents: Tony Truzillo, Lena Padilla, both born in Colo."

(Louise Aragon knew both parents; Trujillos had two more children, Frances and John.)

(D.M.: Tony Trujillo was a brother to Macario [Mack] Trujillo who married Martin Aragon's sister, Lucia.)

43. **Rodolfo Ulloa** Died June 28, 1924 Age 2 months

(Reager) "Rodoldo Ulloa, born 4/23/1924, died 6/28/1924 Age: 0-2-5 Parents: Anatosio Ulloa and Antonia Alakarie, both born in Mexico. Dr. Brown. Place of Burial: Bellvue, 6/29/1924. $8."

Baptism, St. Joseph's: "Rodolfo Ulloa, 6/21/1924, Parents: Eustacio Ulloa and Anastacia Aleala. Sponsors: Julian Martinez and Secunda Maestas. Rev. G. Jos. LaJeunesse."

(Louise Aragon knew the godparents.)

(D.M.: Correct spelling: Rodolfo and Anastacio. Julian's wife was Secundina Pacheco.)

The father of the next three children, Jose Eufemio, was a brother to Andy Trujillo who married Magdalena (Minnie) Vigil. The children were cousins to Juan Pedro Manifico Trujillo.

44. **Lucia Trujillo** * (P) Died May 13, 1927 Age 1 year

(Allnut) "Lucila Trujillo, Age: 1-3-27, daughter of Joseph Trujillo, P.O. Box 260, Ft. Collins [born in LaVeta, Colo.] works for Clara Brown, and Veta Archuleta, born in N.M. Baby died 5/13/1927, 1 a.m., Dr. V.E. Cram, bronchial pneumonia. Services Rev. J.P. Trudel at the Spanish Catholic Church, 1:30, 5/14/1927. Lambskin coffin, $12."

A photograph of Lucia was donated by her sister, Nora Castellanos.

45. **Benedicto Trujillo** * Died May 3, 1929 Age 2 months

(Allnut) "Benedicto Trujillo, born 3/2/1929, died 5/3/1929, 5 p.m. [No cause of death given.] Dr. J.D. Carey. Funeral 5/4/1929, 10 a.m., Spanish Catholic Church, Rev. J.P. Trudel. White lambskin coffin, $12.50 plus $5 for sedan."

Baptism, Holy Family: "4/14/1929, Fr. J.P. Trudel. Parents: Infermio Trujillo and Vitalie Archuleta. Sponsors: Andres Trujillo and Magdalena Vigil."

Death Records, Holy Family: "Enterada en Laporte el dia 5 de mayo."

46. **Salina Trujillo** * Died November 11, 1930 Age 2 months

(Reager) "Salina Trujillo, born 8/22/1930, died 11/11/1930. Age 2-0-9, 8 miles S.E., Chg. Ray Pitcher, Zigler Place. Dr. Carey; Spanish Church, Fr. Trudel, 11/13/1930. Age 2-0-9. Parents: Joe Trujillo, b. Colo., Vetalu Archuletta, b. N.M. $4."

*The next two are grandchildren of Don Vigil. **There may be seven babies in the family buried in Laporte, not just the two listed.***

47. **Isidro Eduardo Apodaca** * Died August 31, 1927 Age 3 months

(Reager) "E. Edward Apodaca, born 5/15/1927, died 8/31/1927. Age 3 mo. Funeral 9/1/1927. Dr. Honstein. Chg. $12. Parents: Percy Apodaca and Lillie Vigil, both born in Colo."

Baptism, Holy Family: "Isidro Eduardo Apodaca, May 20, 1927, Father J. P. Trudel. Parents: Porfirio Apodaca and Ligia V. de Apodaca. Sponsors: Jose Dolores and Refugio M. Cordova."

(D.M.: The godparents are the parents of Marie Cordova who married Deziderio Lucero of 400 Hickory Street; "Dezi" is now deceased.)

48. **Cyrilla Apodaca** * Died September 24, 1928 Age 2 months
(Reager) "Sally Apodaca, born 7/7/1928, died 9/24/1928. Age: 0-2-17. Dr. Cram. Place of death: Jungles. Parents: Porfirio Apodaca and Ligia V. de Apodaca."

Baptism, Holy Family: "Cyrilla Apodaca, born 7/7/1928, baptized 7/10/1928. Parents: Porfirio Apodaca and Ligia V. de Apodaca. Sponsor: Agueda Vigil."

(D.M.: Agueda Vigil married Gabriel Vigil; they resided on the 400 block of N. Loomis.)

According to Fort Collins native (b. 1938) and historian Don Woeber, the Jungles was an area thick with cottonwood trees near lst and 2nd Streets. Many towns throughout the country had an area near a railroad track and a river called "The Jungles" by hobos. According to 1907 newspapers, the Fort Collins Jungles was a place of vicious murder and mayhem. By 1915, when Hispanics moved there, it had calmed down, though there were frequent arrests for gambling, bootlegging and gunfights.

Florence LaBadie of Fort Collins is the sister of the above two children. Her mother was Lillie, or Eligia. Florence was born in 1921 and they did not live in the Jungles, but along the river on North College, a separate area.

Of Cyrilla's death, Florence has only the faintest dream-like memories. The baby was taken to a doctor in Denver but died on the way home. Pennies were placed on her little eyes so they would stay closed. Florence doesn't remember Isidro at all.

Lillie had nine children. Florence is the oldest; only she and Carl survived. She believes the other five, including a set of stillborn twins, might also be buried at Bingham Hill. Lilly died of pneumonia at age 37 on October 17, 1933, when Florence was 12 and Carl was only eight.

Florence's father, Porfirio (Percy or Hap) Apodaca was about nine years old in 1905 when his parents (Victor and Tomasita) came from Pueblo. They all lived in the log house on the Herring place and picked apples and worked sugar beets. Tomasita was light-skinned and Cam

Herring affectionately nicknamed her "the Russian." Florence said they also worked for Jimmy and Louise Hyde, who were vegetable and fruit producers in Laporte.

Florence herself had 15 children: Lillian, John, James, Judy, Patricia, Martha, Emily, Victoria, Josephine, Kathy, Nellie, Santos, Porfirio, Carmen and Mary Ellen.

49. **Candido Gallegos** Died December 24, 1931 Age 2 months

(Reager) "Candidio Gallegos, 313 Cherry St. Born 10/17/1931, died 12/24/1931. Age: 0-2-7. Pneumonia. Dr. Miller. Buried 9 a.m., 12/26/1931, Fr. Trudel. Parents: Candidio Gallegos and Alviretia Gurrle, both born in N.M."

Moses Gallegos of Fort Collins is a nephew of Candido Gallegos and Alvinita Gurule. Correct spellings were given by his wife, Mary Romero Gallegos, whose parents, Tomas and Claudia Serrano Romero, were residents of Ingleside.

According to Nora Castellanos (Alvinita Gurule, Candido's mother, was her husband's aunt), living siblings of Candido are Teresa, Paul, Jim, Roland, Pete, Carol and Clarence. Two died: Sam and Margaret.

50. **Delfino Romero** Died April 24, 1932 Age 7 days

(Allnut) "Delfin Romero, 238 N. Meldrum. Born 4/17/1932, died 4/24/1932. Age: 7 days. [No cause of death given.] Parents: Delfin Romero and Louisa Mares. Funeral 4/26/1932. $5."

(Delphine Garcia of Fort Collins said the family now lives in California and that they had another child who was killed in an auto accident. The father died in late 1987.)

(D.M.: The father of the baby, Delfino, was a brother of Juan, Telesfor, Alvino Romero and Trinidad Romero Mosqueda. Juan Romero married Martha, a sister of Lee Martinez. Telesforo, who ushered at Holy Family Church was a well-groomed, handsome man, who died a paraplegic at the Veterans Memorial Hospital in Denver. Trinidad married Casildo Mosqueda and was the mother of Steve Mosqueda, a painter at CSU for over 20 years. Steve's children are Steve, Laura, Jerrie and Reuben.)

51. **Margaret Vigil** * Died November 5, 1932 Age 1 day

Margaret was a child of Ed Vigil (son of Donaciano Vigil) and Dora

Ortega. She was a full-term baby who was born at home but lived only a few hours. She had been a breech birth and had the umbilical cord around her neck. The doctor told Ed to put the baby in a cardboard box and bury her at Laporte. Grace Torres, Ed's sister, helped bury the baby.

An older child was Ernestine (Tina) Gallegos, and younger than Margaret were Mary, Solomon, Gloria (d. of diabetes at age 53 on June 15, 1989), Jim, Frank and Lorraine.

Ed Vigil, who died in January 1987, was close to his father, Don, and greatly responsible for keeping his memory alive. Lorraine said that Don's great love of hunting was also instilled by Ed into many of the grandchildren.

Ed and Dora have 15 grandchildren, 24 great-grandchildren and two great-great-grandchildren. Tina and her husband, Ed Gallegos (d. 3/5/1993) own Gallegos Sanitation. Their children, Jerry, Arthur, and Rudy are the parents of nine grandchildren. Gloria had two daughters, Elaine Quintana and Joanna Valdez who has a daughter, Anna Marie.

52. **Viola Armendarez** * Died April 24, 1933 Age 9 days
(Reager) Viola Armendarez, born 4/15/1933, died 4/24/1933. Age 9 days. Dr. Honstein. Parents: Jes Armendarez and Emma Torrez, Funeral 9 a.m., 4/26/1933, Fr. Trudell. Chg. to County."

Emma was a daughter of Juan Torres and Grace Vigil, so this child was a grandchild of Juan Torres and great-grandchild of Don Vigil.

The baby was baptized by Mrs. Ed (Dora) Vigil, who went to the funeral at Bingham Hill.

53. **Baby Aragon** + Died May 31, 1935 Age 1 day
(Allnut) "Baby Aragon, born and died 5/31/1935. Parents: Martin Aragon, born in Bellvue and Louise Mondragon, born in Ft. Collins. Dr. Honstein. Funeral 6/1/1935, 4 p.m., Father Trudel. $21."

This first child of the Aragons was born with a skull deformity. Louise never saw the little girl and was still in the hospital when the baby was buried. Martin made a coffin out of native lumber and he and two brothers-in-law, Leonard and Telesforo Mondragon, buried the infant in the Bingham Hill Cemetery.

Louise was the child of Francisco Mondragon and Nicolasa Apodaca. Her father was born in the San Luis valley, married in Walsenberg, and came here in 1905. He and his wife also had Natividad, Mary, Telesforo,

Leonard, Alfred, Richard, Valoise and Martha. Francisco worked at the Halligan Dam and later on the Holy Family convent. Telesforo married Annie Vigil, the youngest daughter of Don and Ramona Vigil.

Martin's parents, Christopher Joseph Aragon and Clara Sanchez, came by covered wagon caravan to this area in 1903. Clara's father had a land grant (signed by President Wilson) near Espanola, New Mexico, but gringo squatters eventually took over, and the family lost it. The family became very successful in Larimer County. The children were Ben, Everett, Timothy, Sam, Lucy, Gabriel, Jesse, Martin and Isabel.

The four oldest boys owned five steam engines for thrashing and also a great deal of well-drilling equipment. These businesses plus four farms were lost in the Crash of 1929.

Martin, the youngest son, remembers going to St. Joseph's Church from the Trilby area with his parents in a two-seated buggy. In 1952, Martin started the Aragon Iron and Metal Corporation on Highway 287. He and Louise Aragon have three living children, Edward, David and Priscilla Barela, ten grandchildren and 11 great-grandchildren.

54. **Sam Vigil** * Died February 5, 1920 Age 5 months

(Allnut) "Sam Vigil, born in Laporte 8/30/1919, died near Bellvue, 2/5/1920, 7 a.m. Age: 0-5-5. Parents: Tobe Vigil & Mary Turriji, both born in Colo. Dr. C.W. Wilkin, Chg. to Mrs. Torrez. Buried at Grandview; this funeral was not directed."

Sam was Tobe's first child. The "Mrs. Torres" who paid the bill was Grace Torres, Tobe's sister. Sadie Gallegos did not know where this child was buried, but Grandview has no record of him. With his grandfather and great-grandmother being buried in Laporte, it seems likely he was buried near them. The farthest west picket fence in the cemetery might be the one which Tobe built for his children.

Tobe's other children were Archie, Eva, Sadie (source of information), Edward, Bertha, Pete (died July 1995), Julia, Mary Ellen (died December 19, 1994) and Freddie who died in 1937 and was buried in Laporte. Those who lived to adulthood had about 35 children, according to Sadie.

Sadie Gallegos herself has eight children: Toby, David, Dolores, Nancy, Danny, Freddie, Robert and Tammy. She also has 20 grandchildren and nine great-grandchildren.

55. **Federico Donald Vigil** * Died August 6, 1937 Age l year

(Reager) "Fred D. Vigil, born 4/25/1936, died 8/6/1937. Age: 1-3-11. Died: Hospital. Dr. Gleason, Funeral 8/9/1937. Services, Laporte cemetery. Parents: Tobe Vigil and Mary Trujillo. $10."

Baptism, Holy Family: "Federico Donald Vigil, Aug. 8, 1936. Parents: Tobies Vigil and Maria Trujillo. Sponsor: Francisca Ocosta."

This child's death is well remembered by Freddie's big sister, Sadie Gallegos, who was 11 years old in 1937. The cause of death, according to the family's belief, was "Ojo Malo" or "Evil Eye."

Fred's mother, Mary Antoniette Trujillo, believed, as did many of her friends and neighbors, that a baby could become ill if looked at, but not touched, by an admirer. Sadie didn't remember who looked at Freddie, but someone did, as his eyes sank in and he became very ill and dehydrated. Antonia broke an egg into a bowl and set it by the baby's head. Sadie said she will never forget seeing a perfect image of an eye form in the yolk—a sure sign of "Evil Eye."

To cure babies with "Ojo," either the person who caused it or a person named Johnny, Jenny or someone with a J name, could ingest salt and pass the salt into the sick baby's mouth. Either Antonia didn't choose the cure or perhaps she didn't know how to cure "Ojo," because Fred became sicker.

Tobe had delivered each of his ten children but was gone a lot, often looking for work in Wyoming, and he was not at home when Fred became ill. They lived on the river bottom near Vern's Place west of Laporte at a place called Willow Nook. They had no car and in desperation, Antonia walked, carrying Fred to the hospital on Lemay Street, a distance of over ten miles.

People with communicable diseases were isolated in a small building behind the hospital called the Pest House (later used as the Thrift Shop) and that is where Fred died. When babies died of dehydration, it was usually called "summer complaint" but I noticed that no "Cause of death" was written on Fred's records.

Sadie said she can still see Freddie's little face and curly hair when he was lying in his tiny white coffin. He had been her "little pet" and she cried her heart out as she marched up the hill to the cemetery. It wasn't just the loss of Freddie that hurt so much. Sadie's sisters often made her take care of Freddie when she didn't want to, and to get even with them, she would pinch him. Sadie still feels guilty about this—60 years later.

56. **Baby Andrew Armijo** * Died July, 1936 Age l day

Parents of this child are George Armijo and Angel Trujillo, daughter of Andy and Minnie Trujillo. Angel is the sister of Juan Pedro Manifico who died in 1918. The parents had chosen the name Andrew for the baby who was born four months prematurely and died the day he was born. Angel said her aunt, Grace Torres, took charge and buried little Andrew in a shoe box.

Angel and George, who also had Helen, Joe and George, live in Cheyenne, Wyoming.

57. **Mary Maxine Vigil** * Died November 3, 1937 Age 2 months

(Reager) "Mary Maxine Vigil, born 9/2/1937, died 11/3/1937, 402 Pine St., Ft. Collins, Age: 0-2-1. Pneumonia. Dr. Taylor. Funeral 9 a.m., Holy Family, Fr. Johns. $12.25. Parents: Salome Vigil and Mary Torres."

Mary Torres was a daughter of Juan Torres and Grace Vigil. Her husband, Sam Vigil (not related to Don Vigil), owned Sam's Place, now called El Burrito, still on 404 Linden Street. They had another daughter, also named Maxine, and other children, one of whom died of leukemia.

(D.M.: The priest was Father Juan Fullana, not Fr. Johns.)

58. **Maria L. Tamayo (P)** Died February 25, 1938 Age 2 months

(Reager) "Marie L. Tamayo; race: Spanish; residence: Engelside. Born Wyoming 12/5/1937, died Laporte 2/25/1938, Age: 0-2-20. Parents: Joe Tamayo and Allino Londaros, both born in Mexico. Funeral 2/28/1938, 9 a.m. Service at Engelside. Interment Belliview by family. Cost: $10."

Baptism records at Holy Family indicated that another baby born to these parents 12/6/1946 was baptized 2/23/1947, and named Marie de la luz. Her parents were "Jose Tamoyo & Ongela Landeros. Sponsors were Pablo and Eulalia Bustos."

I called Paul Bustos who said he was Angela's cousin and that she lived in Cheyenne. She had an unlisted phone number but a mortician there helped me locate the family.

Antonio Tamayo confirmed that Maria was his sister and that she was buried in the Bellvue (Laporte) cemetery. She was one of a set of twins and ill from the time she was born. She died on the trip as the family moved from the quarries at Granite Canyon to Ingleside. Her twin sister, Ramona Hansen, lives in Casper, Wyoming, and has six girls and a boy.

Maria Tamayo Esquibel from Cheyenne, the second Maria, furnished a photo of the first Maria on the day of her burial and the following information.

Maria L. Tamayo was the beloved daughter of Joseph M. Tamayo from the state of Michoacan, Mexico, and Angela Landeros from La Primavera, Mexico, in the state of Jalisco. Joseph came to the United States in 1919 at the age of 16. His father, Tomas, and twin brother, Frank, came with him but returned to Mexico during the years of Prohibition (around 1930). Besides working in the rock quarries, Mr. Tamayo worked for a rancher north of Fort Collins, Victor Andkons (?) of Laredo, Texas. Joseph Tamayo died in Cheyenne on December 7, 1967.

Angela Landeros came to the United States in 1919 as well. She and her brother Fidencio travelled in a makeshift boat across the Rio Grande with her father, Alejo Landeros. Alejo's wife had died of smallpox in 1917. His mother helped him with the children for a few years after she arrived to the states, but she died and after that, Alejo was alone in raising his children. Both children, Angela and Fidencio, presently reside in Cheyenne. Angela became a naturalized citizen in 1978.

Other children besides Maria (who was baptized at St. Mary's Cathedral in Cheyenne) born to Joseph M. Tamayo and Angela Landeros are Wallace, Ramona Hansen (Maria's twin), Antonio, Helen Pino, Dolores Esquibel, John, Mary Esquibel (the second Maria de la luz), Carmen Greenwood, Steve, Teresa Baca, Josephine Tamayo, Bruce (died at birth) and Joseph Thomas.

59. **Baby Garcia** Died December 20, 1939 Age 1 day

(Warren-Bohlender) "Baby Garcia, born and died 10/20/1939, Larimer County Hospital. Parents: John Garcia, born in Texas, and Bertha (Bersabel) Jiron, born in Colo. 226 Willow St. Catholic. Dr. Platz. Funeral 10 a.m., Sunday, 10/22/1939. Burial, Laporte. $3."

John Garcia of Laporte was two years old when this baby died. He said his father and Harold Warren buried her alone, according to what he remembers being told. Other children in the family are Patricia Ann (d. 5/1/1944), Della Martinez, Frank, Mary, John, Tony and Patrick. John married Viola Barela and they have Claude and Marie.

Frank Garcia, principal of a school in Los Alamos, New Mexico, brother of Baby Garcia, visited the cemetery in March 1990, and put up a wood cross for this child.

There was one other known husband/wife buried at Bingham Hill (the Spraggs) but Charles W. Howell was the only person buried at Bingham Hill who also had his wife, a married daughter, a son and great-grandchildren also buried there. His was also probably the most "inbred" family, in that he himself married a cousin and his son married a niece's daughter. C.W. Howell and his daughter's burials were covered in Part I.

The next four persons listed are C.W. Howell's wife, two baby great-granddaughters and his adult son. C.W. Howell married Sarah C. Howell, a cousin, in Missouri, and they had at least five children: two small sons who died in 1880 and 1882; Annie, who had one child (bachelor Charlie Andrew Williams), died at 18, and was buried in 1888; Mary (born 7/26/1853) who married Emmet Harris (11/23/1880) and had 12 children (Sarah, Charley, Annie, Effie, William, Jessie, Cora, Callie, David, John, Almeda and Bessie); and Bill, who married Ivy Pratt, his niece's daughter, and had three children. Brother and sister, Bill and Mary, were somewhat deaf.

Mary Harris's oldest daughter, Sarah, married William Fry, and one of their daughters, Lily Fry Hout of Bellvue and her Aunt Bessie Asbury (who is 91 years old in 1998) of Delta, Colorado, furnished some of the family history.

60 and 61. Fry Infant Twin Girls Died about 1908 Newborns

Sarah, a granddaughter of C.W. and Sarah Howell, and her husband, William Fry, had premature twin daughters who were buried at Bingham Hill. Their sister, Lily Hout, believes Dr. Replogle delivered them. (He is the same doctor who quarantined the Robertson family in 1911.)

Another locally well-known brother of the Fry babies was Floyd, who owned the Columbine Lodge in the Poudre Canyon until his death. His grandson, Scott Fry, was raised by his grandmother, Glendolyn (Glenny) Burgess Fry Whitlock, and now lives in Loveland.

62. Sarah C. Howell Died December 5, 1921 Age 85 years

(Reager) "Widow. Residence: Fork of road to Bellvue and Livermore. Born 2/22/1836, died 12/5/1921. Age: 85-10-13. Born in Missouri. Parents: William Howell & May Slaton, both from Mo. Funeral at residence, 10 a.m., 12/7/1921, Burial at Laport. Dr. Wilkins. Billed $77; $35 paid by Larimer County. Clergyman: Bellvue minister."

Sarah lived 27 years longer than her husband, W.C. Howell, who died in 1894 and 33 years longer than her daughter, Annie. She died in the family home in Bellvue in which her great-granddaughter, Lily Hout, now lives (4620 W. Co. Rd. 52E) Lily was about ten at the time of Sarah's death but doesn't remember anything about the burial at Laporte.

Bill Porter of Laporte said Sarah "homesteaded" what is now known as the Kremer Ranch. She lived in a stone house near a spring, east of Highway 287 near the "Indian rings." She was a tall, athletic woman who would walk into Laporte (about six miles) carrying butter and eggs to sell or trade at Baxter's store; she was also ornery and often left cattle gates open. (This land, whose owners include Richard and Alford Maxfield, Kremers, Ferguson, Ted Yelek and Si Halliburton, has recently been sold off in 40-acre lots and is called Kremer's Indian Hills.) Lala Nauta thought some Howell buried a child near the old stone house as she once saw a little grave there. This would fit with the newspaper clippings about C.W. Howell—he lost two small sons in 1880 and 1882; on the other hand, Billy Porter heard they'd died along the way from Missouri.

When Annie died, Sarah raised her grandson, Charlie Williams. As a youngster, he pulled a pair of scissors down from a hook and blinded himself in one eye. An article in the *Courier*, 12/25/1907, said "Charlie Williams, who is recovering from a severe attack of typhoid was able to be out driving and called on his grandmother, Mrs. Howell, last Tuesday." Lily Hout remembers this Charlie as an ornery cuss. He tried to throw a cat from an upstairs window once and instead he and the cat both fell out. He stayed with Lily's parents a long time and worked on threshing crews. He went to Florida and was on his way home when he got sick and no one ever heard what happened to him.

63. **William Marshall Howell** + (**P**) Died 12/30/1939 Age 75

(Reager) "William Marshall Howell, resident of Bellevue, Age 75-11-0; born in Mo. 1/30/1864, died 11:30 a.m., 12/30/1939 at Bellevue; cardiac failure, flu. O.W. Miller, Coroner. Retired cook. Resident of Colo., 74 years. Parents: Chas. W. Howell and Sarah Howell, both born in Mo. Wife: Ivy. Funeral Wed. 1/3/1949, 2:30 p.m., Drawing Room, Clergyman Franklin Moore; Internment: Laporte; Cost $100. Pd. by Larimer Co.

Express-Courier, 1/2/1940: "Balmer and Collins Mortuary. Howell, William M., of Bellvue. Services Drawing Room, Wed., 2:30. Interment, Laporte."

WILLIAM HOWELL, 75, IS DEAD AT BELLVUE

William Howell, 75, a resident of the Laporte vicinity since he was one year old, died at his home at Bellvue Saturday at 11:30 a.m. He had been ill two weeks with influenza and developed pneumonia Friday night. His family was at the bedside at the time of his death.

Mr. Howell was born in Missouri January 30, 1864. He and his family moved to a farming site near Laporte a year later.

One of his last occupations was that of a cook on a railroad dining car. For the last several years he has been unable to work because of failing health.

Whole Family Ill. Mr. Howell is survived by his wife, Mrs. Ivy Howell, a sister, Mrs. Mary Harris, two daughters, Wilma Cathryn Howell and Margaret Ann Howell, and a son, Billy Howell, Jr., all of Bellvue. The entire family is reported to be suffering from influenza.

Five people recalled Bill Howell to me. Fred Heustis of Laporte remembered that his brother-in-law, Cam Herring, was all dressed up in a suit one day and said he was "going up to help plant old Bill Howell." Cam may have been a pallbearer. Heustis showed me where the grave was and said that it was cold that day, and they didn't dig it very deep. Vic Tamlin told me that he and three others, including Dick Falloon and Hiram Foster, dug the grave for Bill Howell on Jan. 3, 1940, and the ground was very hard. Georgia Maxfield remembered when "old Billy Howell" died. She said her father-in-law, Richard Maxfield, let Howell live in their log house south of Ted's Place where he did some chores for rent. Bill Porter also remembered that Bill lived about 1/4 mile south of Ted's place on land belonging to Alford Maxfield and that he married when he was quite old and that the children were small when he died.

Bill Howell was Lily Hout's great-uncle. She said he was a colorful character who wore a big hat. He loved to fish and could always come home with a line of fish. He purchased one of the first hearing aids and it had a thick wire that came out of his ear to a big battery in his shirt pocket.

Bill's widow, Ivy (who was a daughter of his niece, Effie Harris Pratt), later married Ronald Calvin Heath. They lived by the lake near the cement plant north of Laporte and then moved to Cheyenne. Ivy's father was from Vermont; her mother was Effie Harris Pratt. With the help of Heath relatives and Evaline Hendricks Lamle, Ivy's sister from Nebraska, we located the three Howell children, all of whom were born when Howell was in his 70s.

Bill Howell of Gainsville, Florida, said he was about four and in bed with his father who got up to go to the bathroom and fell over dead. He was supposed to have a tintype of his father but didn't know where it was.

145

Margaret Potts from Lebanon, Illinois, said she didn't remember the funeral but that her mother told her she tried to get into the casket as she thought her dad was sleeping. Margaret's birth certificate (May 20, 1936), shows her dad to be 74 when she was born which would have made him closer to 78 at his death if the certificate is accurate. She can only recall one instance of her father and that was sitting on his lap; Grandmother Pratt stood at the kitchen table kneading bread. She remembered hearing about the "Unknown Spanish child" and also about Billy Porter.

Cathy Stowe of Abilene, Texas, wrote about remembering her Aunt Lili Hout, the Vigil family and the Herring place. None of the three children had a photograph of their dad, so when one was found in an old newspaper, I sent copies to the three children in 1998, eight years after our last correspondence. Two letters were returned; the third didn't answer.

Howell was the last adult (full body) burial in Laporte. It is incredible to think of the history he lived through. He was in Laporte when Mary Provost died in 1866. He would have known Provost, Claymore, Bingham, LaRocque, Jennie McGaa Brown and Rowl Herring. It is sad that some historian didn't visit before 1939 to record his recollections of these early people.

Bill never received the publicity his father (Charles W. Howell) did, but there were these two articles: "The editor returns thanks to Billie Howell for a jar of splendid white clover honey made by his busy workers. Billie never forgets the newspapers and when he has anything particularly nice he is sure to whack up with them" (8/20/1896); and "Wm. Howell of Laporte has moved into the back of the stone mill and expects to work a part of Jake Flowers' place this coming year" (11/19/1896).

There was one undated feature article and photograph of Bill Howell in the Richard Baker scrapbooks. He tells the story of a neighbor who stole $135, was chased by a posse, captured and stuffed into a hole in the ice in the Poudre River and drowned. He also recounts crossing the plains in 1865 and joining a band of 150 wagons at Ft. Kearney.

A hard-to-read sandstone marker (C.W. Howell) belonging to Bill's father is west and south of Provost's lot. In 1998, small granite markers were placed for both Howells, father and son. There are no markers for Sarah Howell, her daughter Annie, or the twin babies. (Unless the stone marked A.T.W. is for Annie Williams.)

64. **Unknown Spanish Child** Died between 1936 and 1940

Helen Bland and her sister, Mary Margaret Colard, remember that their mother (Laura Ebert Shipp) took in a Spanish woman with a very sick child. Shipps lived on the Porter place, which was north of Vern's Cafe and later became the Rothe Quarter Horse Ranch. The lady with the baby was either walking along the road or she was a Bellvue woman. They do not remember if she had a husband, only that she was too poor to have services after the baby died. Their father, Walter Shipp, a minister with the Church of Christ, buried the child at Bingham Hill. Both Helen and Mary Margaret went to the funeral but neither remembers the mother's or child's name.

65. **Dinkel Baby Boy (P)** Died May 6, 1942 Stillborn

When the *Coloradoan* (3/19/1990) published a list of people buried at Bingham Hill, Mrs. Alex M. (Mary) Dinkel, then 85, called to tell about the death of her son on May 6, 1942. He was her 10th child, born in a house in Windsor used as a hospital. He was full-term but had died a day or two before birth and was therefore not baptized.

Ernest Bogard and Alex (died 10/26/1989) built a little coffin and buried the baby while Mary was still in the hospital. Bogard said they buried the baby along the fence line on Bingham Hill Road where other babies were buried.

The Dinkel baby was not given a name but his living siblings include Peggy Winter, Edwin, Hubert, Elvira David, Marie Crites, Elizabeth Delehoy, Dolores Clark, Melvin, Cleo, Robert and Richard. At the time of her death in July, 1990, Mrs. Dinkel had 48 grandchildren, 70 great-grandchildren and four great-great grandchildren.

So many local people are connected to the Laporte cemetery!

66. **Mary Inez Pacheco +** Died January 25, 1943 Age 1 month

Maria Pacheco was the last child buried in the cemetery before a gate was installed along the entrance road and slammed shut.

(Allnut) "Mary Pacheco, born Dec. 24, 1942, Ft. Collins, died Granite Canon, Wyoming, 1/25/1943. Age 0-1-1. Dr. Honstein, pneumonia. Parents: Joe Pacheco, Clara Marquez, both born in La Veta. Burial, 1/26/1943. Noted: Father brought baby here in car. Casket $21, pd. cash, 1/26/1943." Cecilia Beecher remembered this child's death since her family also worked at Granite Canyon.

Clara and Joe (Greg) Pacheco, who now live on Loomis Street, said that Mary Inez was already dead when they drove her to Fort Collins. Friends and relatives pitched in to pay for the coffin and Greg and his brother-in-law, Joe Solano, buried her near the foot of Don Vigil's grave.

Clara said she had the same dream many times after the baby was buried—that the little white dress on her dead baby was backwards and Clara was always trying to turn it around for her. Clara, Ida and Ida's husband, Ron Gonzales, placed flowers on nearly every grave at Bingham Hill every year between 1987 and 1995, but now that the cemetery's driving access is closed, they stopped. Clara can't walk well enough to go up the path.

Pachecos put a wood cross by the baby's grave in 1989; later they laid a plaque with a picture of St. Agnes. Both soon became weather-beaten and in 1998, a small permanent granite headstone was placed for the baby.

Ida Gonzales shared this interesting family history. Martina Trujillo was a sister of Acacio Trujillo, previously written about. Martina married Cayetano Montoya and they had Andreita, Crisanta, Ramona, Jacobo, Jose Onesimo and Sara Lena. Sara Lena Montoya married Edras Marquez, and they had Sidelia, Lucas, Stella, Clara, Bertha, Louie and Phil. Clara is the mother of the little baby, Maria Inez, who was buried at Bingham Hill. Edras died in October, 1926. Sara Lena then married Edra's half-brother, Gabriel Marquez and had Annie and Martha.

For the other half of the family. Acacio Trujillo was married to Rufina Pacheco. It is believed her parents' names were Rafael Pacheco and Leonar Garcia Pacheco. Besides Rufina, they had Jose Gregorio and Abram. Jose Gregorio married Librada Maestas and had Ramon, Maria, Eufemia, Gertrude and Dolores. Librada died. He then married Sabina Martinez and had Louis, Lois, Juan and Jose Gregorio, Jr. Second wife Sabina died at age 39 giving birth to a baby girl, Monica, who also died. Mother and baby died December 25, 1919, and her husband, Jose Gregorio, Sr., died four days later at age 79.

Older half-brother Ramon came from Montana with horse and buggy to Fort Collins to pick up the three youngest children—Jose Gregorio was only four, Juan was seven and Lois was 13. Ramon did not return to Montana but went to work in the mine at Ingleside; he raised the children and never married. Juan and his older half-brother Louis later got into trouble with the law. Little Jose Gregorio grew up, went to school in Wellington and married Clara Marquez.

We're back to the beginning of the story, as Clara and Greg Pacheco are the parents of Maria Inez, the subject of the story. Pachecos lost two other children, Rita and John, who were buried at Grandview. They also have four living children (Rudy, Manuel, Delores Lopez and Ida Gonzales), 16 grandchildren and 24 great-grandchildren.

Mary Inez Pacheco was the last known baby burial in a continuous stretch of cemetery use from 1862 to 1943. Wood Hill bought the farm from the Herring estate June 3, 1944, and sold off 22 acres (the land between the cemetery and Bingham Hill Road) on May 6, 1946. There was no longer access to the cemetery, either to bury or to visit.

Three of the six daughters of Donaciano and Ramona Vigil: Magdalena (Minnie) who married Andy Trujillo; Grace, who married Juan Torres; Eliga (Lillie) who married Porfirio (Hap) Apodaca. All three women buried children in the Bingham Hill Cemetery between 1918 and 1928.

III.

After January 1943, there were no more foil-body burials in the Bingham Hill Cemetery. For the first time in its history, antagonistic landowners prevented burials or even visits. Although there were apparently reassurances from the county that access would be allowed, no one in the county or community pursued preserving the historic right-of-way. A new owner in 1962 allowed cemetery visitors and volunteers who stopped at his house to ask permission—a reasonable arrangement which was never abused. He understood the inherent obligation that goes along with owning land which blocks a cemetery. In 1992, another person took control of the land, and the situation in 1998 is that a walking path is open, but driving to the cemetery is prohibited. That has not prevented recent burials; it simply requires that the body be cremated, or small enough to be carried up the path.

LIST OF PERSONS BURIED
BETWEEN 1985 and 1998

+ indicates a headstone
(P) indicates a photograph

1. Julia Barde Learn + (P)
2. William James Alcorn + (P)
3. Danny Cecil Allen(+ Hiawatha, Kansas) (P)
4. Cecil Neth + (P)
5. HopeDean
6. Manuelita Gonzales + (P)
7. Frances Ellen VerStratten + (P)
8. Leroy Vigil + (P)

INFORMATION ABOUT PERSONS BURIED
BETWEEN 1987 and 1998

Five sets of cremains and one miscarried fetus have recently been buried in the Bingham Hill Cemetery. Cremains are "cremated remains", that is, the ashes and small bone fragments left after a body is heated to about 1600 degrees Fahrenheit for about two hours. The cremains of an adult weigh 8-10 pounds and have the volume of a large coffee can. A fetus is an incompletely developed baby. The ashes of two of these individuals will be buried in 1998 after their memorial stones arrive from the Veterans Administration.

+ indicates presence of a headstone in 1998
* indicates a relative of Don Vigil
(P) indicates a photograph

1. **Julia Barde Learn+ (P)** Died October 17, 1985 Age 90 years
   Julia Barde was born on March 23, 1895, in Guthrie, Oklahoma, to Anna and Frederick Barde. Goodrich Funeral Home (now Allnut) handled the burial. She may have converted to Catholicism shortly before her death as she was buried from John XXIII Catholic parish with three priests officiating: Richard Ling, Tom McCormick and Ron Weissbeck. A social worker planned to scatter Julia's ashes near her little tar papered home on 9th Street (Lemay), north of Vine, but I knew the dwelling was scheduled to be demolished and thought burial at Bingham Hill would be more appropriate since she loved visiting our farm. Several months after her death, her ashes were buried at Laporte.
   The *Coloradoan* (10/18/1985) printed an obituary and John Pfeiffenberger wrote about Julia in the *Triangle Review* (10/3/1985). Her father was a newspaper editor and Julia was a young ballet star. She met many prominent people including Theodore Roosevelt, Will Rogers, William Taft and Sitting Bull. She married Clarence Learn in 1917; he taught at Colorado A & M until his death of influenza on September 24, 1935. There were few survivor benefits at that time and Julia lived an austere life. She had a brief marriage to a Mr. Cox about whom she had nothing good to say. Her daughter, Margaret Learn, was crippled and visited from California only rarely; she died before Julia did. Julia's son,

151

Bob, of El Cajon, California, was not close to his mother, did not come to her funeral and never responded to letters written to him about his mother's death.

Julia had very poor eyesight but insisted on baking several fruit cakes at Christmas time which she delivered to employees of Steele's Market and City Drug and to other friends in downtown businesses she frequented. No one who knew her will forget her, especially the cute curtsy she'd give upon leaving a room.

2. **William James Alcorn+ (P)** Died May 19, 1989 Age 39 years

Bill Alcorn died in the Fort Collins home which he shared with his wife, Judith A. Dunegan Alcorn, and her son, Tim. His certificate of death was signed by Timothy Wirt, M.D. His funeral at the Reager Mortuary was a small, private affair. A member of the American Legion played taps; those attending were his widow and stepson, and his divorced parents, Richard W. Alcorn and Helen Learn Alcorn.

Bill was born June 26, 1949, at home in Clairton, Pennsysvlania—literally at home—as his mother didn't make it to the hospital. He was the fifth of five children, the others being Richard, Joseph, Theresa Jones and Bernice Smith. His mother said he was a happy child who loved to play "Army," and was a whiz on the Gettysburg battle. He was always interested in animals and the outdoors. He took a correspondence course from the North American School of Conservation and spent the summer at the Shoshone National Forest when he was 16 years old. He applied for a slash line or clean up crew position at Yellowstone, but instead, joined the U.S. Army on June 27, 1967, as soon as he turned 18. He left for Vietnam on January 3, 1969, and returned a year later.

After the war, Bill continued to love the outdoors and also enjoyed hunting. He worked for the Bureau of Mines in Pennsylvania and later for the Forest Service in Colorado.

He married Judy Dunegan on August 12, 1978, and was a good step-father to her son. Judy said he was very easy going—a peaceful man. In 1983, when he was a student in the Forestry Department at Colorado State University, he had a seizure in a classroom. Headaches and tunnel vision led to a diagnosis of a tumor in his brain.

In the fall of 1987, Bill and his mother, Helen Alcorn, who was visiting from Clairton, Pennsylvania, drove out to see the Bingham Hill

Cemetery. They had read an article in the *Coloradoan* calling for volunteers and had come to look around. Bill volunteered to cut brush, but because of the developing tumor, he was unable to help. It was believed by his family that his cancer came from being exposed to Agent Orange in Vietnam. He died less than two years later.

Bill's cremains were buried at Bingham Hill in February of 1994. Paperwork has been completed and he will have a veteran's stone at his grave before the end of 1998. At present, Bill's gravesite is graced with a statue of the Blessed Mother and the American flag.

3. **Danny Cecil Allen(+ rock) (P)** Died September 5, 1991 Age 38
   (This tribute was written by Louise Allen, Danny's mother.)

   Danny C. Allen was born March 13,1953, in Denver, Colorado, the son of Cecil Charles Allen (deceased May 6, 1974) and Louise Lugenbeel Allen. He had one adopted half-sister, nine years older, Barbara Scott, now of Norfolk, Virginia.

   Danny was a happy child, easy to raise and never a problem. When young, he loved books and his hunger for learning continued through his life. He especially loved music. At six, he began piano lessons, then studied drums, clarinet and voice, but piano was his top priority.

   Danny was gentle and sensitive—always for the underdog. He worked in a nursing home while in high school and became very upset if he thought a person was being mistreated. People in general loved him. He received a scholarship from Berthoud High in 1971 and studied one year at the University of Northern Colorado. He went to Cabrillo College in California and received a degree of Associate in Arts.

   As a musician he worked in various bands on the Front Range and in ski resorts. One band was called the "Bear and Whale," and another, the "Terminators." The last bands he worked with entertained U.S. troops in Asia in 1989 and in Iceland and Europe in 1991.

   Danny's problem with alcohol began when he was in college and became worse over the years. After being in a treatment center he got along better for several months, attending many AA meetings and helping others whenever he was called upon. His tour to Europe was a big downfall, for when they got to Germany, he followed the crowd and took that fateful drink, which no recovering alcoholic dare do. He admitted afterwards that he should not have gone on that tour, that he had fallen off the wagon, but he told his mother he was all right. He wasn't, however, and his long battle with alcohol ended on that terrible Thursday night of September 5, 1991, at about 6:15, when a gunshot to his head took him from those who loved him so deeply. The agonizing loss of Danny remains year after year, always with the word "Why?"

His funeral service was given by Pastor Gordon Peterson from Loveland; there was standing room only at the Reager funeral parlor.

He had married Elizabeth Lappart on October 13, 1984, in a garden wedding at his mother's home. Danny, Elizabeth and her two sons, Brian and Chris, thus became a family. On or about December 7, 1991, Danny's widow scattered his ashes in the Bingham Hill Cemetery and some time later carved his initials on a rock which she placed at the site. Elizabeth is remarried to Jeff Knutson, and has a young daughter, Jessie, born May 30, 1996.

There is a granite marker in remembrance of Danny in the family plot in Hiawatha, Kansas, and also a brick on the Memory Wall at Larimer County Hospice which has been engraved: "Beloved Son, Danny C. Allen, 1953-1991."

One of the many letters Mrs. Allen received after the funeral describes the impression young Danny made on others. Following is part of several pages written by a high school friend, Karl E. Scott, who related when he, Danny and Mr. Nickels, their band teacher at Berthoud, "jammed" one Sunday afternoon. His words give a glimpse of Danny's musical genius.

> Dan played for 1 hr. 45 minutes non stop without any sheet music in front of him. It was then that I realized just how gifted he really was. Within Dan was a sea of sound that only he could let flow thru his soul and out his fingers....he covered all boundaries from classical to pop to rock, to spiritual, to honky-tonk, and is the only keyboard player that I've heard or heard of that could out of the clear blue sky play music never written or heard by mankind before....

4. **Cecil B. Neth + (P)** Died October I, 1992 Age 67

(Parts excerpted from his obituary in the *Coloradoan*)

Cecil B. Neth, 67, of Fort Collins, died Thursday, Oct. 1, 1992, at home. A funeral service was held at the First Presbyterian Church.

Cecil Berle Neth was born Oct. 30, 1924, in Bismarck, North Dakota, the only child of Iva Mack and Harold Berle "Fuzzy" Neth, and the stepson of Dot Neth. He grew up in California and graduated from the Huntington Beach High school where he distinguished himself as editor of the yearbook and as a member of the school newspaper staff, the tennis team and the Latin Club. He also was the originator of the school war bond drive.

Neth left the University of California at Berkeley to join the Air Cadets and served as a bombardier with the 34th Bomb Group of the 8th Air Force during World War II. He received the Distinguished Flying Cross.

He was married for seven years to Mary Pieper, and they had one daughter, Shelley, who has three children, Dylan and Dayna Scheie and Jesse Neth.

During the Korean War, he was recalled to service and sent to Germany where he worked on the *Stars and Stripes*. He subsequently worked as a correspondent for the *Paris Herald Tribune* and *The London Daily Telegraph*.

While working as editor of the *Overseas Family and Weekly* in Germany, he interviewed and promptly fell in love with Jane Cords, a young schoolteacher who was traveling across Europe on a motorscooter with her best friend. A story he wrote about the adventurous duo was the beginning of a romance that would last the rest of his life. Cecil and Jane were married on Valentine's Day, 1960, and during the next 14 years, they had five children: Hal, Caitlin, Cara, Marcy and Alexander.

Cecil received a bachelor's degree in journalism in 1969 from Northern Illinois University. Cecil moved from the *Wheaton Journal* in Wheaton, Illinois, to the *Chicago Sun-Times* where he worked on the financial page, as a suburban editor, an editorial writer and, finally, as the editor of the editorial page.

Cecil taught editing and reporting in the Department of Technical Journalism at CSU for seven years and was named the department's Professor of the Year in 1981 and also received Sigma Delta Chi's statewide Journalism Educator of the Year award.

He returned to the *Sun Times* in 1984 as an editorial writer. He was diagnosed with amyotrophic lateral sclerosis (also called Lou Gehrig's Disease) in 1985 but continued to write editorials from his home in Fort Collins. During this period he won several awards for editorial excellence.

After his retirement in 1987, he worked on letters and completed a book, *ALS, A Beginner's Manuel.* During his years on life support, he achieved his lifetime goals of reading the entire Bible and the complete works of Herman Melville. He also saw his youngest son graduate from high school. He was fortunate to have the friendship of Adina Woodward, who helped him study the classical music that he loved. As the disease progressed, he wrote using a computer activated by an eyebrow switch attached to a headband. During the last five years of his life, he was unable to speak.

He was a man who could make people laugh and who could scare the living daylights out of them when he wanted to. But underneath his sometimes gruff exterior was a tender man with a passion for his family, for life, and for the written word. He overcame great sadness and struggles to become the kind of father who read his children to sleep with poetry, who invented songs while shaving, and who had the courage to fight for his convictions even when they weren't popular. One of his finest tributes was written by Gene Amole in the *Rocky Mountain News.*

Jane and Cecil's children are thriving. Hal teaches English at Centennial High School in Fort Collins; Caitlin (Caite) is married to Chris Clemens and they have a three year old, Claire. Cara is communications coordinator for the Human Resources Department and provides speech writing support for the President of CSU; Marcy finished a double masters in art history and library science at Indiana University and has accepted a job at the Art Institute of Chicago as a research librarian; Alex is a journalism major at Metropolitan State College.

Jane Neth has been a librarian at Cache Ia Poudre Junior High in Laporte for 18 years. Cecil had always loved the Bingham Hill Cemetery, and the burial of his cremains there is appropriate. Burial and setting of a VA memorial stone will be done in 1998 when the timing is right and when all the children can attend.

5. **Hope Dean** Died Nov. 20, 1992 Age zero

There's not much to say about little Hope except that she broke her parents' hearts. There can be a great deal of sadness involved upon the loss of an unborn child.

My oldest son, Alan Dean, and his wife, Kathleen Scheirman Dean, were looking forward to the birth of their second child in St. Louis,

Missouri, when in late November 1992, in the second trimester, something went wrong and the baby was miscarried. They brought the three-inch-long body when they came to Laporte for Christmas. Alan used a pickax to break frozen soil and buried little Hope in a jewelry box on Christmas Day near the large Memorial stone at the west end of the cemetery.

Two or three days later, Fr. Joseph Romero from Holy Family Church came to bless the gravesite. It was a dramatic scene. The sky was black, snow covered the ground, the wind was blowing, Father Romero's beret was askew and his jacket billowing. He said prayers for the dead and blessed the ground with holy water. The ceremony helped considerably and the parents felt more at peace after that.

The family has since moved to Fort Collins and Daniel Alan and Andrea Rose have joined big brother Max in the banquet of life and as members of that group who have a relative in the Bingham Hill cemetery.

Fr. Joe Romero himself died after a long and painful struggle with cancer at age 53, on March 13, 1998.

6. **Manuelita Gonzales + (P)** Died January 28, 1993 Age 82

Manuelita (Nellie) Gonzales was born November 10, 1910, in Albuquerque, New Mexico. Her parents were Luz Martinez and Nicolasa Libario. Her husband, Anselmo Gonzales, was buried at Grandview on August 12, 1969, at age 66. Nellie died in La Dera Americare Nursing Home in Albuquerque where she had spent the last five years of her life. Her photograph in this book is of her being honored as Queen for the Day.

Nellie Gonzales and her husband had two daughters, Margaret (deceased) and Frances; and four sons, Ambrosio, Jose, Tranquilino (Kino) and Floyd, who drowned at age 13, when a drunk driver who was helping the family move, drove his truck into an irrigation ditch. She has about 43 grandchildren.

Her son Jose said she was a great cook, often making 30 or 45 tortillas at a time, plus delicious green chili and red chili. He also remembers his mother's love for animals. She raised pigeons, chickens, pigs, goats, cows and sheep.

In their early married years, her husband was a sheriff in San Jose, New Mexico, the town where he was born. (Their son, my source of information, was named Jose after the town.) Nellie and her husband would ride horses together while he was out on his job. Jose said the family lived in several places, including Grants, New Mexico, where his dad was a lumberjack, and in the May Valley north of Lamar, Colorado, where he remembers his mother often being so tired from working in beet and onion fields.

Jose buried his mother's ashes in the Laporte cemetery on February 19, 1994, and later marked the spot with a headstone.

7. **Frances Ellen Ver Stratten + (P)** Died January 5,1996 Age 75
(The following tribute was written by Leslie Moore of Laporte.)

Frances was born July 6, 1920, in Healdsburg, California, to Lyn Ames and Ethel Gardner Ames. Her parents divorced when she was three, so Ethel brought her young daughter back to Laporte to reside with Ethel's mother, Eliza Bingham Tharp Gardner, on the family homestead (where the log house, red-shingled home and carriage house stand, next to the present-day post office).

On June 7, 1940, Frances married Wayne L. Ver Stratten (Ver Straeten was misspelled on his birth certificate) at St. Joseph's Church in Fort Collins. She was also baptized there prior to their wedding. Frances and Wayne settled down in Culver City, California, where they had three children: Diane Leslie, Janet Lyn and George Stanley. The family relocated in 1952 to Tulsa, Oklahoma, due to a job transfer by Douglas Aircraft.

In the summer of 1940, her mother, Ethel M. Ames, married Jake D. Holtz. They remained on the home place where Ethel ran her beauty shop and Jake tended the apple orchards for many years. Holtz was always an important part of the family.

In 1964, Frances and Wayne divorced. He later remarried and then passed away in May, 1972, at the age of 54. When Frances passed on, she was survived by two daughters and a son, nine grandchildren and three great-grandchildren: Leslie Moore and son, Sam Scruggs; George Ver Straeten and children Lindsey and Travis; and Janet Iverson and her six children: Shelly Randazzo (and two offspring, Giordan and Vincent), Jamie Laut (and daughter Kayla), Chad, Jody, Matt and Keri Iverson.

Frances also left her longtime special friend, Marilyn M. Ethridge, with whom she shared homes in Laporte and Tulsa. They were both retired law enforcement officers.

When Frances was a young housewife, she was noted for her fine ceramics and the clothing she sewed for herself, her family and friends. Her later interests included coaching synchronized swimming and teaching youngsters how to swim. She left a lasting impact on those she touched in both her private and professional life. Local people remember buying apples from the abundant trees around her house in Laporte.

Her funeral Mass was officiated by Father Philip Meredith at St. Joseph's Catholic Church on January 9, 1996, and her cremains were interred at the Bingham Hill Cemetery in the ancestral plot surrounded by the concrete wall on September 21, 1996. Father Phil Meredith consecrated the ground and said a few words. Phil Carpenter prepared the site and George Ver Straeten encased the gravestone in cement. The monument had to be hauled by wheelbarrow, due to the fact that vehicles are no longer allowed.

When Mickey Ethridge knelt to place her friend's ashes into the rather large hole, she tumbled in along with the box, which caused a moment of apprehension over her state and then hilarity at the whole scene. When everyone was composed, George, the son, and Raybo Moore, the son-in-law, lowered the engraved stone into place. It was a sunny day, and the crowd of about 50 family and friends bid a final farewell by releasing lavender and green balloons into the afternoon breeze. It is believed that Frances probably enjoyed the whole affair, as she loved being the center of attention.

8. **Leroy Vigil** + * **(P)** Died July 4, 1997 Age 52

Leroy Vigil was born on November 15, 1945 in Fort Collins and was a lifelong resident. His parents are Florence L. Krickbaum Vigil of Laporte and William Vigil, who died in August, 1962, when Leroy was 17 years old. His five brothers are Bill of LaJara; Glen of Fort Collins; and Paul, Dale and Clifford of Laporte. His four sisters are Betty Tullos of Anchorage, Alaska; Edith Jones of Encampment, Wyoming; Dorothy Coy of Hermingston, Oregon; and Ilene Kimes of Potosi, Missouri. He has 18 nieces and nephews.

Leroy loved trucks and started driving cattle from Walden to Fort Collins for Shorty Swift when he was 14 years old. For most of his life, he was a self-employed truck driver. Leroy graduated from Poudre High School, then served in the U.S. Marine Corps from December 29, 1965, to December 6, 1967. Even in Vietnam, he drove trucks, probably his least favorite load—American troops to the front line at Da Nang.

On March 23, 1968, he married Marian E. Gemborys. Marian was born in Cuba and came to this country with her parents to escape the revolution. Leroy and Marian had two sons, Eric and Christopher. Chris was lost at age nine on April 30, 1978 on a hike on Grey Rock Mountain and is presumed dead. Eric graduated with a degree in mechanical engineering from Oklahoma Christian University in May, 1997, and works for Lockheed-Martin in Littleton. Since 1993, foster daughters Amy Sanchez and Denise Redmond have also lived with the family.

Marian wants everyone to know Leroy taught her to love unconditionally. He was known by all for his genuineness and gentle spirit. He loved to work and often put in 12-hour days. He also loved elk hunting and fishing. He had a Fourth of July outing in the mountains planned; his death, caused by a heart attack, was unexpected and untimely.

Leroy Vigil was highly regarded in the community. His body was brought to his home for a wake. His Memorial service was at the Pleasant Valley Church of Christ in Bellvue with Mr. Marty Trujillo officiating. Over 300 relatives and friends attended and the church and its basement overflowed with mourners; cars were parked all the way to Watson Lake. Military honors were conducted by the American Legion George Beach Post No. 4, the VFW and the Disabled American Veterans. He was honored at his funeral service by a convoy of trucks. His own "Green Beauty," a 1972 Kenworth 18-wheeler, was brought to the ceremony and her "train horn" blown at the end of the service.

The cremains of Leroy Vigil will be buried in Bingham Hill Cemetery near the grave of his grandfather, Donaciano Vigil, who died in 1918. A Veteran's stone has been ordered and will be placed by his grave.

IV

VOLUNTEERS

LONG BEFORE OUR FAMILY purchased the land bordering the Bingham Hill Cemetery in 1977, various individuals or school and community groups cleaned and did repair work every few years.

In 1936, Henry Josephson, who owned a quarry near Bellvue, "brought down red sandstone and a marker was put at each unmarked grave (2)." A 1941 article by David Watrous in the *Express Courier*, sent to me by Mary Emarine, describes the work of her mother, Miss Mary Gates, a "golden-haired junior student of the Laporte Consolidated school." She involved the Daughters of Union Veterans, the Indian Relic and Hobby club and about 30 boys and girls from the school in an energetic cemetery clean-up day in 1941. There are several items in the Bingham Hill Cemetery file in the local history room of the Fort Collins public library. A *Coloradoan* article (8/16/1959) includes a photograph of Charles Tharp, 84, of Grand Junction and his brother-in-law Jake Holtz of Laporte at the Bingham family lot; they had reset the headstones in concrete and built a concrete wall. Leslie Moore of Laporte remembers that this project took two months as the men mixed the concrete by hand a little at a time.

The May 29, 1966, issue of the *Morning Star* names the 4-H members (led by Mrs. Oscar Schmunk) who cleaned the cemetery and also tells of Dr. E.P. Evans and the Loveland VFW Cooties who did many repairs. This was all done, it was noted, with the cooperation of Mr. Roy Juhl, owner of the adjacent pig farm. In the *Coloradoan* (4/21/1974), there is a photograph of Campfire girls cleaning the cemetery. Dina Bath of Laporte said she helped mow in the late 1970s with Girl Scouts led by Max Getts and Ted Rhodes.

Despite these attentions, however, the cemetery had a reputation of being a weedy old place and, in fact, the majority of persons living around Laporte and Bellvue didn't even know the cemetery existed. What one encountered by 1987 were tall grasses hiding stones, Canadian thistle, leafy spurge, hundreds of cacti and bayonet plants, and worst, gnarly brush which had taken over the entire east end of the cemetery, even inside the Provost lot.

Something had to be done. During the fall of 1987 and throughout 1988, the part my own family played in the cemetery was tremendous. My husband and sons and I cut brush, mowed grass, built fence and gates, planted cottonwood trees and hauled barrels of water (although the trees died anyway), put up signs and entertained and instructed visitors.

There were soon other hard workers and great projects. In 1987 and 1988 **Leroy Davison** cut a mountain of brush and cacti, hand-winched several of the heavy sandstone Provost blocks from the Mercer ditch, made a wrought-iron gate for the Provost lot and a metal chair, repaired and photographed tombstones and deeply cared about the cemetery. Davison suffered a heart attack in 1997 but recovered and occasionally visits the cemetery.

Lafi Miller brought his jeep and winched six more of the Provost stones from the ditch. My sons, **Andy Dean, Jim Brinks** and **John Brinks**, lifted those heavy stones (about 300 pounds each) to rebuild the Provost enclosure.

Mary Trionfera and the **Rainbow Riders' 4-H Club** cleaned in the cemetery from 1987 until 1996 when the club disbanded—a long stretch of blistered hands. This is the same club responsible for the awesome task of trying to move the "J. Thomas" coffin and body to a new site—the beginning of the mystery as to his identity. These were also the good 4-H Dads who lifted the stones back onto their bases after vandals pushed them off in 1988.

Fireman **Rollen (Cap) Williams** (d. at 59, 8/6/1992) and his wife **Mary** burned piles of brush in 1987. **Theresa Brookman** and **Dottie Davis** planted hundreds of iris bulbs in 1990 which are in full bloom each spring. Both **Ron Rains** and **Aubrey Glahn** donated used lawn mowers for cemetery use.

Neighbor fireman **Dick Speiss** is often available for fix-up tasks which require woodworking skills and **Becky Douglas** tends the flowers she planted by the entrance steps.

Ri Dressen coerced friends to remake pickets for the fenced lot smashed by vandals in March 1998.

Harold "Red" and **Jonnie Jenson** not only donated $75 for the granite memorial, but also made and set ten white crosses at unmarked graves and put a wrought-iron fence around the grave of little Queenie Maud Adams.

Ron Dixon from Fort Collins Monument Works donated wood entrance signs and a granite replica of the Provost children's sandstone headstones which are becoming harder to read each year.

Michael and **Jodee Holzwarth** built a solid picket fence around the grave of Jennie McGaa Brown and committed themselves to caring for the gravesite.

Lisa de Victoria (now of Idaho), a granddaughter of the abovementioned "Miss Mary Gates," brought her Cub Scouts to repair and put fresh paint on one of the fences around graves in June of 1996.

Three significant stones were set:

(1) **Josephine Clements** and the **Cache la Poudre Chapter of the Daughters of the American Revolution (DAR)** purchased a granite historical marker and had it set October 6, 1987. Its wording is copied in the chapter "Markers present in 1998."

(2) A large two-piece light gray granite monument on the northwest edge of the cemetery was set May 12, 1990. It has names of every person known at the time to be buried at Bingham Hill—adults on the front and back of one slab and children on the front and back of the other. The memorial was paid for by the following organizations and individuals, many of whom have passed away since 1990: **Fort Collins Historical Society, Westerners International, Horsetooth Antique Bottle Club of Fort Collins, the Larimer County Genealogical Society, Holy Family Church, Waverly** and **Lopez Elementary Schools** ("Dear Mrs. Brinks, We earned this money from our factory that made and sold bird houses. We would like you to have this money for Bingham Hill cemetery, Sincerely, Anaic Mihalck, factory president, Mr. Sabas 4th grade, Lopez school); **Ilene Bykert, Tom Gleason, Ada May Guard, Adele Brown Treis, Adelphia Glass, Louise Aragon, Red Jenson, Jacqueline Michie, Laura Jeanne Wunch,** and the four daughters of Frank E. Baxter, in whose memory they donated: **Leone Thayer, Lucile B. West, Norma Salisbury** and **Veda Hoepfer**.

Other donors were **Jim Brinks, Mac** and **Karen McDonald, Doris Bice, Florence LaBadie, Donna Metcalf, Jan Norman, Mary Humstone, Patricia Olsen** in memory of Frank Olsen, **Hazel Cuny, Allene Niehaus, Jim** and **Margaret Hyde, John** and **Darlene Nelson, Howard Thompsen,**

Glenn Pennock, Moe Mekelburg, Iola Pennock, Lois and Calvin Johnson, Jane Neth, Nina Bodenham, Jeramy Lowell, Karin Eberhart, Sally Ketcham, Wayne Sundberg, Liz Case, Joan Day, Loretta Wilson, Harlan Grummert, Steven and Sally Wilke, George and Mary Wallace, Coleen McNeil, Joe Stern, Marilyn and Arthur Gray, John and Anne Jordan, Loren Maxey, Chuck Terrell, Rick Bott, Pat Windmuller, Melvin Chubb, Richard Sweetman, Dr. Wilbur Miller, Andy Dean, Alan Dean, Jeanne Simpson, Daniel Martinez, Hobo Harry Fisher, Ray Stradcutter, Bob Mantle, Wanda Hoffman, Jay McCoy, Gunnar Jacobson, Ted Condos, Dr. Jim Gilman, David and Betty Hendricks, Bob Perry, Warren and Mary Riedesel, Ovie Johnson, Chris McElroy, Ellis Kingman, Dorothy Bath, Pauline Faillace, Harold and Wilma Camden, Michael and Jodee Holzwarth, John Quinn, Henry and Harriet Gronewoller, Ethel Schoondermark, Edna and Wendell Bragonier, Fred Heustis, Frances and Lyle Ver Straeten, Duayne Canfield, Lou Schmunk, Dr. Robert Pike, Myron Siefken, Margaret Potts and Bob Graves.

Also Nora Castellanos, Lorraine Vigil, Mary Dinkel, Stella Gallegos, Clara Pacheco and the Funkhousers of Idaho raised money within their families. With this kind of cooperation, it took only weeks to raise $2200.

(3) The third stone is for Alphonse LaRocque, the only French-Canadian settler who is buried in Laporte. Fort Collins Monument Company made an exact replica (except the thickness is three inches instead of the original, too fragile, two inches). The marble which was mined in Georgia cost $800 by the time it was shaped, lettered and set in the cemetery in July of 1996.

The Fort Collins Historical Society donated $400 and the balance came from the McGaa family, Sister Genevieve Cuny of Holy Rosary Mission, Pine Ridge, South Dakoka, Rheba Massey, R.H. Weber, R.J. LaRocque of Colonie, New York, Joy Poole, Jean Lamson, Diane Williams, a Gregston family and Harlan Grummert.

Whereas trucks brought the first two stones in 1987 and 1990 into the west end of the cemetery and directly to the sites, by 1996, vehicular entrance was not allowed, and employees of the monument company had a difficult time. In 1987, LaRocque's stone was in two pieces and flat on the ground; a volunteer fixed it and set it upright. Boys pushed and cracked it again, and with three breaks, it could not be repaired. Some misguided soul plopped the pieces in several inches of concrete which caused the heavy unit to sink and soon become covered with silt. The monument company had to wheelbarrow the 300 pound stone, and its base, down the path and truck it to their shop in order to reproduce exactly the several old types of print. When finished, they wheeled the new marble stone up the path and set it in concrete. For all this extra work, **Fort Collins Monument Company** deserves applause.

Bill Schneider walked the entire cemetery in 1995 with dowsing rods. Apparently earth disturbances, such as a grave, cause a dowser to sense these changes and the rods turn in his hands. Schneider placed flags on the four corners of over 200 rectangular areas, some with stones, but most with no markers at all. He found graves outside the west fence all the way to the large metal shed built in 1994. No one excavated at any dowsed site to prove the existence of graves, but since Schneider detected earth disturbance in places where he didn't know something had been buried, but I did, he might be right. If he is, there are closer to 300 graves in the cemetery than 150. Schneider also gave several dowsing demonstrations to groups visiting the cemetery.

In 1988, **Roy Juhl** and our hired man, **Ray Heldman**, pulled the embedded west wire fence from 18 inches of silt; neighbor **Art Wendel** (d. at 79, 1/5/1998) plowed and bladed; **Dave Gibson** leveled the fence line; **Henry Moore,** great-grandson of John Provost, donated money for part of a new tenon-joint fence.

Since 1986, there were eight outstanding Eagle Scout projects plus another project for a lesser award. **Eric Clark** and Boy Scout Troop 96 painted picket fenced lots, repaired wire fences, and repainted the BINGHAM HILL CEMETERY sign in September 1986. This was when the entire west and south boundaries of the cemetery were fenced with the most dilapidated barbed and woven wire fences imaginable.

Mark Nelson and Troop 90 built a retaining wall on the steep bank of the Mercer Ditch for the grave of J. Thomas in May 1989. This was a difficult project, and it has successfully prevented erosion.

On June 16, 1990, **Brian Gies,** Troop 90, landscaped the new memorial stone with rock, timbers and four juniper bushes. Three bushes died but one is thriving in 1998. **Bo Carlson**, also of Troop 90, built real steps which improved the dirt path leading to the cemetery path from Bingham Hill Road.

In February 1991, **Peter Stulz** of Troop 90 finished about 100 feet of the three-rail fence which was started in 1988. He also placed a 14-foot metal gate for vehicle entrance from the west. Also in 1991, **Ian McConica** of Troop 90, poured a cement foundation, built and painted a shed for storage of mowing equipment in the northwest corner of the cemetery. The purpose of both these excellent projects was stymied when Gary McDonald, a friend of Joan Welch, boarded the entire west end of the cemetery shut with hog and cattle panels so there could be no pickup entrance for either carrying out brush, or for bringing in monuments, mowers or any other equipment.

The three most recent Eagle Scout projects were completed by young men from Berthoud, Colorado, Troop 387. **Randall Harris** built a visitor stand and made a hinged box for visitors' signature notebooks in the summer of 1992. This was an outstanding project and more noticeable than many others. In the spring of 1994, his brother, **Brent Harris**, rebuilt and painted the largest picket fence surrounding unmarked graves. It had been rotting badly. These boys are from a Mormon family with eight children; all five sons received Eagle Scout awards.

Not related, but with the same last name and also from Berthoud, son of Doug and Judy Harris, is **Mark Harris** who built and placed two beautiful redwood benches on October 17, 1996. Mark Harris, too, was denied vehicular access, so he and his parents, before daylight that cold morning, were forced to carry the heavy benches all up way up the foot path.

Clara Pacheco and her daughter brought flowers every Memorial Day between 1988 and 1994 and placed them on her baby's grave and on almost every grave in the cemetery. This practice stopped in 1995 because Mrs. Pacheco is unable to walk the length of the path.

On January 29, 1994, nine-year-old **Lauren Helm** videotaped "A Tour at Bingham Hill Cemetery" for a project at Washington Lab School. Her videotape imparted knowledge of Laporte history to her classmates.

Jean Lamson, Diane Williams and **Erica Majoram** of Irish Elementary are the most diligent teachers in the district for bringing their fourth-graders each spring. Nothing impresses youngsters or gives them a sense of history more than a trip to the cemetery, and these teachers really care about history.

Steve Carr repaired three marble stones by drilling holes and setting internal rods in March 1997.

In the fall of 1997, **Mickey Ethridge** bought two 10-foot boards and painted a new BINGHAM HILL CEMETERY sign.

These folks were not exactly volunteers, but from 1991 through 1996, the Larimer County Parks Department, because of the urging of County Commissioner **Moe Mekelburg**, mowed and weed-whipped the cemetery three times each summer—before Memorial Day, the 4th of July and Labor Day. In 1997, because Ms. Welch who took over the Juhl land continued to refuse their entrance, the county crews in turn refused to pull their equipment any longer up the narrow walking path and said they will no longer mow the cemetery.

There were probably other good deeds done which I know nothing about or have forgotten. And there are those which didn't have to be done. To her credit, **Joan Welch** saw that the cemetery was mowed the summer of 1997. She preferred doing it that way rather have the county mow, and whether this will continue into the future is unknown.

Another task which shouldn't have had to be done was pro bono work by local attorney **J. Brad March** and the dozens of pro bono hours spent by Attorney **Matthew C. Colonell** from Denver who worked on regaining driving access to the cemetery. Colonell moved to California but forwarded a huge file of documents to be used in the future.

As for me, I don't do much physical work any more but still take groups through: fourth-grade classes, Brownies and Girl Scouts, Archeological Society, Questers, etc. I collect letters from people all over the country who inquire about their relatives, thank-you notes from school children and share all information with anyone who asks. I give talks and slide shows to clubs, and, of course, continue to expound on the value of the cemetery.

VANDALISM AND DISRESPECT

Most vandalism to the cemetery predates the 1980s. The worst offense was done by the New Mercer Ditch company when they dug and enlarged their ditch from the 1880s to the 1920s. On one or more occasions, caskets were pulled out of the ground and bones allowed to fall along the ditch bank. This information came from Laporte resident Jim Hyde who heard it from George (Chick) Nugent and also from Willis Morgenstern who had heard it from several people. Also Vic Tamlin said Reed Farrar had told him about skulls and bones in the ditch after work was done on the New Mercer. Ditch workers figured the cemetery had been abandoned and they "didn't give a darn," Tamlin said.

Disrespect for the cemetery goes on today. Attorney for the Mercer Ditch Company, Gene E. Fischer, wrote in a letter (10/10/1994) to Ms. Evans of the Larimer County Planning Department, concerning the Bingham Hill Cemetery: "This cemetery actually encroaches on the historic right-of-way for maintenance which the Ditch Company has by prescriptive use..." Does it sound odd to anyone else to hear complaints about "cemetery encroachment" when the cemetery was there long before the irrigation ditch? Combine the bullying personalities of early ditch company officers with their lack of respect for history and for the dead—and you can easily imagine ditchmen tearing up the slope of a cemetery and letting the bones fall where they may. It was a shameful episode.

There is one different story concerning casket removal. Peggy Simpson of Laporte said that her father, the late Harry Dunlap, told her that in the late 1920s, while the Mercer Ditch Company was digging into the cemetery, City of Fort Collins men stood by to move coffins to Grandview. His brother-in-law's father, William Hanawalt, Superintendent of Grandview from 1913 to 1932, reportedly stacked the excavated caskets before moving them. In one was only a "row of buttons and dust," according to Dunlap. Simpson pointed out a group of crowded tombstones in Grandview Cemetery along Laporte Avenue and said her father thought those were the Laporte burials. Phil Carpenter, present day Grandview supervisor, said those were actually graves moved from Mountain View Cemetery, not Laporte. I copied twelve names from those crowded tombstones (death dates from 1874 to 1886), looked up obituaries (most of which do not mention burial place), and finally found one, Duncan McMann (or McMahon) who died 3/2/1879 and was reported by the newspaper to have been buried at Mountain Home.

This seems to verify Carpenter's statement. I don't want to doubt Dunlap's story that bodies were transferred; there simply isn't anything in Grandview Records, in Mercer Ditch records or in the newspaper that tells of a mass removal of coffins from Laporte to Grandview in the 1920s or at any other time. It also does not negate the stories of so many Laporte old-timers about tearing out coffins.

As far as animal-related damage, from the 1940s to the early 1990s, hogs which were raised nearby occasionally got into the cemetery and rooted around. Hogs were fed old bread and thousands of bread wrappers blew all over the cemetery and beyond. Hog lot odor was often unbearable. There are, thankfully, no longer hogs fed or raised next to the cemetery. Other animals may have caused some damage. Before the 1940s, sheep and cattle often grazed freely, and some stones were pushed over by them. Any flat gravestone lying on the ground soon is covered with dirt. Vic Tamlin said he did a lot of muskrat trapping along the ditches and would often see babies' bones pulled up by skunks and badgers. He wasn't particularly religious or superstitious, he said, but didn't think varmints should dig up graves, so he trapped the skunks and kicked the little human baby bones down the holes and shovelled them full again. There are still one or two badger holes and occasionally we see rabbits or a large bull snake, but other than the holes, they don't cause damage.

Mrs. Mabel Burns, from whom we bought this farm, said that in the 1950s, she saw a man on a tractor with a blade push stones into the ditch. When we pulled ten of the large sandstone blocks which had been around the Provost graves from the ditch, their sheer weight and distance from origin made it obvious they did not fall there themselves. There is so much muck in the Mercer Ditch that volunteers worked in calf-high water, even off-season, as the ditch is never dry. The sandstone blocks were intact but any marble marker shoved into the water would soon disintegrate.

Bodies, especially those of children, were sometimes buried right along Bingham Hill Road, and Mrs. Clara Rodgers told me the area between the road and the cemetery was once white with tombstones. There are also graves west of the present fence. An arbitrary fence was built in the 1940s enclosing only 1.279 acres, not two full acres as "reserved" by Provost and Claymore, and many gravesites were left out. Outside graves have since been plowed over and any barbed wire or picket fencing around graves has been torn down and the land farmed. I consider that disrespect, if not vandalism.

Vandalism during my time in the area started in October 1988, when Juhl called to report that every stone in the cemetery had been pushed over. I was so distressed and so angry that I tracked down the culprits myself. With encouragement from a sheriff's deputy, the two ten-year-old Loveland boys apologized and each donated $50 to start the fund for the memorial stone. One of the boys said he hurt his back while shoving the tall Ida Keller monument. Good! Of all the stones they upset, only LaRocque's suffered irreparable damage and it was replaced in 1996.

On or about March 16, 1998, Ida May Keller's tall white obelisk was again toppled over by vandals, several pickets from one fenced lot were broken, the Virgin Mary's statue pushed over and beer bottles left behind.

For a few years, I left a copy of my book in the cemetery with a note urging visitors to use it as a guide but to leave it for others. After the fourth book was stolen, I quit that practice. Notebooks for visitors' signatures have been in the cemetery since 1987, but a notebook with about 2000 signatures from May 1992 to July 25, 1994 was stolen, and another notebook from September 1994 to June 20, 1995 was also taken. I began putting loose sheets in the guest box with the idea of bringing them home monthly, but even so, someone often beats me to them; signature sheets from August to December 1995, were taken, as well as others. It is discouraging and a shame because the signatures and the comments made by visitors and their relationships to buried persons also tell so much history. I would share all the signatures; no one needs to steal them.

In the summer of 1997, more items disappeared: the 13-inch crucifix from Don Vigil's grave, one of the white wood crosses, the heavy hand-doweled corner post which had been standing in the Bingham family lot for the past ten years, and the marble tombstone of Nellie Land. Nothing was left for Nellie Land but the sandstone block her stone sat on (see surveyor's legend) and her white marble footstone. It was later replaced.

Sometimes teenagers stop at our house and ask if they can sleep in the cemetery. I always say no, even though I think that a night amongst the dead might do some of the weirder ones some good.

At other times, young women who describe themselves as "wiccans" (pagan witches), tell about sitting in the cemetery at dusk. Kim Lofink and Jennifer Doermann are two who assure me that they "follow the old ways of nature and respect ancestors and spirits and would never harm the cemetery." To date, as far as I know, they have done no harm.

BRIEF LEGAL HISTORY OF THE CEMETERY
AND WHY THERE IS NO LONGER VEHICULAR ACCESS

AFTER THE ROCKY MOUNTAINS were through rumbling and forming themselves, this particular little knoll presumably sat peacefully for millions of years. Indian tribes roamed the river valley and maybe they buried some of their dead on the hill and maybe not. There is no evidence which indicates that they did, but some 1950s writers said colored cloth and beads were sometimes found (2).

Beginning in 1542, various European explorers claimed the surrounding lands for their respective monarchs in Spain and France and in 1801, the little spot which later became the Laporte Cemetery went along as part of the Louisiana Purchase. It was part of Missouri, then Nebraska, and finally in 1861, it became part of Larimer County, Territory of Colorado. The nearby town of La Porte was an important center between Denver and points north and was named the county seat.

Most of the following information was condensed from a book about the history of the Provost farm (1).

1858-1866: 160 Acres Claimed by Provost

In 1858 or 1859, several French-Canadian ex-trappers and their Sioux wives came either from Fort Laramie or from west of Loveland to found a town where the Laramie Road crossed the Cache la Poudre River. With them came Jean Baptiste Provost and his family.

All the couples claimed land but only Provost "squatted" south of the river. Before he even bought the land, he buried two children on the high spot which became Laporte's cemetery. He built a log cabin, ran a ferry across the river during the flood of 1864, sold liquor to troops guarding the stage line, used his home as a roadhouse and probably had other enterprises.

June 28, 1866: Land Purchased by Provost

The land was surveyed by the U.S. Government and on June 28, 1866, sold to John B. Provost for $200. It was the SW 1/4 of NE 1/4 and the SE 1/4 of NW 1/4 and the N 1/2 of NW 1/4 of Section 32, Twp. 8 N., Range 69 W., 6th P.M. The Cache la Poudre River ran through the northern part of the land; Bingham Hill Road later became part of its southern boundary.

August 6, 1866: Half-Interest Sold to Claymore

On August 6, 1866, John B. and Mary Provost sold half interest to

Benjamin Claymore (whose real name was Louis Benjamin Lessert) for $1000. Both Provost and his wife signed the warranty deed with X's—T.M. Smith and Sam Dion were witnesses. Claymore's half-Sioux wife, Emily, was not put on the deed as an owner.

Provost had built a bridge over the river at some earlier date and then sold it. Wayne Sundberg found a copy of a deed dated February 22, 1868, in which Nicholas O. Tuttle of Laporte, Larimer County, Colorado Territory, sold to Wells Fargo & Co, Glenn Talpey and the citizens of Laporte and vicinity for $300 "The Bridge now at Laporte across the Cache La Poudre situated on the land of John B. Provo. . .the Bridge being built by the said John B. Provo and John Wild, one half of which was deeded to John Wild by the said John B. Provo, and conveyed by the said John E. Wild to Nicholas O. Tuttle by Deed... May 15, 1867, and recorded in Book B. page 252..."

By 1879, several neighbors had buried their dead in the cemetery on Provost's and Claymore's land. Ben and Emily Claymore had five children but did not lose any while living near Laporte.

October 4, 1879: Provost and Claymore Sold to Webb

When Provost and Claymore (who came down from the reservation to sign the papers) sold to William Webb for $2100, a stipulation was put into the sale that two acres were to be **reserved as a burying place for the dead**. Unfortunately, the two acres were not defined, and that oversight has confused cemetery research. Selling price was $2100 which was not much appreciation for the 22 years the men owned the property. Claymore, especially, made nothing, since he had paid $1000 for his half-interest.

August 6, 1881: Webb Sold to Union Pacific

When Webb sold the land, no mention was made of the cemetery. During the railroad years, Fort Collins condemned a strip of land for a ditch which went along the edge of the cemetery, then to the pump house. This was done so downtown residents could have running water in their homes.

The acreage was bandied around between various railroad companies and track was laid through the center of the land and on to Bellvue.

From the *Courier*, 12/30/1886, "Mr. Rowland Herring and family, accompanied by Miss Cora Chapman, arrived in the city last Tuesday from New York. Mrs. Herring is a sister of the Garbutt brothers." Two of Mrs. Nettie Herring's brothers, Ed (Edward Nairn) and Irving (H.I.) were already prominent men here. Both were postmasters and also ran a mercantile store at Laporte, in addition to farming. Ed taught school and one newspaper article relates that he was county clerk, county treasurer, county assessor and clerk of the district court at the same time.

A few months after their arrival in Colorado, on April 13, 1887, Herrings moved into Provost's log house, which Nettie called the "railroad farm" (4b). During their 11-year rental period, Herring lost a baby (1891) and his wife, Nettie (1893). Herring buried the baby at Bingham Hill, then moved it to Grandview when his wife died.

January 3, 1898: Union Pacific Sold to Herring and Garbutt

Rowland Herring and his brother-in-law, H.I. Garbutt, paid $1800 for the farm in early 1898. H.I. Garbutt was the brother of Rowland's deceased wife. H.I. was a judge who raised Ted Herring after his mother died (old-timer Art Collamer remembered H.I. and thought he was Ted's father).

The place was then only 128.5, not 160 acres. All land east of Overland Trail had been sold off, the ditches took about ten acres, and the railroad right-of-way another ten acres. The cemetery sat in the middle of their land.

March 13, 1908: Garbutt Sold His Half-Interest

In 1901 Herring married Mary (Mollie) Garbutt, his first wife's sister-in law. They built a new barn in late 1904 and the log house was replaced by a new frame mail-order house in 1910-11. (When daughter Nellie Herring married Fancher Sarchet on January 6, 1908, the wedding took place in the log house, not the new one.) H.I. Garbutt sold his half-interest to his brother in-law, Rowland Herring, for $2500.

The Herring family possessed the farm longer than any other owners. Herring rented it in 1887, purchased it in 1898, died in 1935 and his estate sold it in 1944—a total of 57 years. Herrings owned the place in its heyday of plum and apple orchards, vegetables, sugar beets and alfalfa. Most Bingham Hill burials (over 100) took place during the Herring years and this family should be honored for fulfilling the dictate of Provost and Claymore that a certain two acres be used as a burying place.

The farm lost a few acres during the Herring years. Herring's son, Cam, opened the "Riverside Gas Station" on a comer of the farm, where Overland Trail meets the river. That was later sold and belongs to the estate of the late Harry Dunlap. Another son, Volney, built a house west of the main farmyard, along the river and that acre presently belongs to Edra Wentz. Herring also sold a parcel directly south of his house during the Depression. Ten homes now line that acreage along Overland Trail and Bingham Hill Road. Two ladies who lived across the river quieted title and took the half-acre "island" from Herring when he was near the end of his life—so they could prevent families from living on the island in tents during the summer months of the Depression. A total of about seven acres were sold or gifted by Herring.

June 3, 1944: Herring Estate Sold to Wood Hill
This sale was the beginning of the end for the cemetery as a viable repository. The land was split.

A. North of the Cemetery
Wood Hill was a land investor. He made some improvements and split the land into two portions—that south and west of the irrigation ditches, and that to the north of the cemetery.

The 100 acres to the north went to Allen and Mildred Clow on December 4, 1945, for about $11,500. **The surveyed boundaries did not include the cemetery.**

On September 25, 1948, Clows sold to Edgar and Fern Herring, a couple not related to Rowland Herring, for about $17,000. Edgar was a retired airline pilot and during his ownership, the Monte Davis family rented the house and operated a dairy. Herring remodeled the apple storage shed into a pine-paneled apartment, put in a septic tank for the house and apartment, poured a concrete floor in the barn, and made other improvements.

John and Mabel Burns purchased the farm in August 1952, for $24,000, and Mabel Burns sold to Jim Brinks for $200,000 on October 5, 1977.

The setting of the farm is beautiful, but the lay of the land is seductive. Much time, energy and money was spent by both Burns and Brinks trying to protect the integrity of the historic farm from entities which want to crisscross it. Early in its history, rights-of-way for three irrigation ditches had already been granted. Burns vigorously and successfully fought the building of a road through the middle of the farm, but allowed electric lines, a cable to the missile silo, a river inlet for Ideal Cement Company and a 27" diagonal water line for the City of Fort Collins. We spent months resisting Fort Collins bike trail easements along the river and down the railroad bed. In 1980, Platte River Power Authority considered our railroad right-of-way for monster-size transmission lines. Our daughter, Laura, then nine years old, wrote to President Reagan and the power lines went elsewhere. (She received a framed copy of her letter from Al Hamilton, manager of the electric company.) We also opposed huge water lines from Northern Colorado Water Conservancy but allowed easements for smaller water lines and for phone cables. On the plus side, after 15 years' negotiations, we regained the railroad right-of-way and the cement company also voluntarily gave up its easement to the river.

B. South of the Cemetery

Hostility toward the cemetery started at the time of the Wood Hill purchase. According to Jimmy Hyde, Wood Hill dug a basement in the middle of the dirt road leading from Bingham Hill Road to the cemetery. Hill moved a house to the location, then sold it and the 22 acres south and west of the ditches. When the land was sold, the boundaries went around but did not include the cemetery. **The cemetery was now in legal limbo.**

Hill sold to Philip and Una Ballard on May 6, 1946. The land went to James and Georgia Allison on April 23, 1947, and to Mona Nickerson on October 15, 1947. Charles and Olive Sandidge purchased the land on June 12, 1948, started a hog operation, and sold to Roy and Adele Juhl on November 21,1962.

None of the owners from 1946 to 1962 ever claimed to own the cemetery but one (or more) reportedly put in a big gate, told Harold Warren he could no longer conduct burials there, knocked down fences around graves near Bingham Hill Road, bulldozed some stones into the Mercer irrigation ditch, kept a mean dog and discouraged visitors. Attitude was better after 1962 when Roy Juhl purchased the land, and until 1993, he was amiable and helpful, especially with Scouts, and courteous about letting people drive past his house to the west end of the cemetery. It was the only way in.

In May, 1992, the widowed Roy Juhl deeded his farm to neighbor Joan Welch, according to a document which indicates he owes her $130,000. (A copy of this deed is on file [94-EX-0578] in the county planner's office.) Welch's significant other, Gary McDonald, built a large storage barn with a studio apartment directly west of the cemetery in the fall of 1994, cleaned up the hog pen mess, and even burned the old outhouse which had been in the cemetery. He also nailed hog panels along the entire west cemetery fence, blocked the gate a Boy Scout had recently finished, and piled large metal cattle panels against the cemetery fence. He said he was "keeping dogs in the cemetery from running on my land."

Welch applied to the county for permits to divide the land and build a house. At a Laporte meeting with county planners, it was made clear to Ms. Welch that only "limited access" was requested, approximately six to ten times a year—three for the county to mow weeds, two or three for 4-H or Scout projects, possibly two or three times for someone in a wheelchair or walker, or for someone who wanted to bring in a gravestone. Permission to develop was denied, according to county planners, both because Welch would not agree in writing to allow cemetery access and because she delivered no power of attorney from Mr. Juhl.

In late 1994, numerous letters came in to the County Commissioners from interested parties (Fort Collins Historical Society; Pioneer Association; Larimer County Historic Alliance; Hooker and Thomas Baker families; Kathy Wydallis; the Harris family of Berthoud whose sons earned Eagle Scout projects in the cemetery; Jerry Brown, a descendent of Jennie Brown; Mary Humstone; Doris Bice, a granddaughter of Rowl Herring; school children; and others). These are also in the Welch/Juhl file in the county planner's office. The letters advised and pleaded with the county not to allow the closing of the historic site.

Welch attorney Gene Fischer included in his December 10, 1994, letter to Carol Evans of the planning department "...the Ditch company will grant no access to the cemetery along its right-of-way...and will take whatever steps are necessary to prevent the use of its maintenance right-of-way by any attempted public access..." I believe they were trying to close even the walking path. However, the path is not on Juhl's land and no ditch maintenance was ever done from it anyway; to date, no further attempts have been made that I know of to close the walking path.

Through contacts of a McGaa relative, a volunteer attorney from Denver put in dozens of hours, and created a thick file about access which Larimer County can use when the time comes. In the meantime, the walking path is open and is adequate for the majority of visitors. However, those in walkers or wheelchairs cannot maneuver the path; the transport of the 300-pound stone for Frances VerStratten was difficult; the three VA stones going into the cemetery in 1998 will be a problem for the widows; and after six years of mowing, the County Parks Department stopped because of access problems in the summer of 1997.

Because there is reason to believe that bodies are buried all the way to the new barn, if not also under it, all legal happenings west of the cemetery are of interest to those caring for the cemetery. Welch and McDonald parted company and he sued her and Roy Juhl for the cost of his barn, utilities, improvements, etc. Welch said she preferred having the barn removed and the land restored. They were to be in civil court May 12, 1998 (Case# 96-CV-825-1), but according to Welch, McDonald settled out of court, not for the amount requested, which was in excess of $400,000, but for approximately $35,000. Apparently the barn stays.

I try not to criticize the county, because they did disallow a subdivision, but by "taking over the cemetery," it could solve the problem because access to every piece of "owned" land is mandatory. Commissioners reasoned that it might set a precedent and the county might have to take over other rural cemeteries. But there are no other cemeteries in the county without owners, and besides, the Pioneer Association said they would take over ownership, maintenance, and control from the county. The only county commitment was from Commissioner John Clark who said that when Mr. Juhl dies, and if the land passes to Joan Welch, that at that time, if she wants to subdivide, she will have to provide vehicular access to the cemetery.

In the meantime, Joan Welch and friend John Schmid mowed the cemetery in the summer of 1997, and she said they would again in 1998. Welch also removed the hog and cattle panelling from the west fence of the cemetery which greatly improves its looks.

In conclusion, there is no vehicular access because Joan Welch has unilaterally chosen not to give it. She said she feels "uncomfortable" with people driving through Mr. Juhl's yard.

Who Owns It? What Happened to the Full Two Acres?

The cemetery is an unusual piece of land in that it is not owned by either adjacent land owner or by any previous land owner. Irma Miller, a great granddaughter of Ben Claymore, filed a quit-claim deed of the cemetery to Jim Brinks to unite it in a symbolic way with its original land, but it is probably not a legally valid document. The State of Colorado could claim it, or the county could quiet title, but they have not done so.

A more intriguing question might be which two acres? The present fences enclose only 1.279 acres according to surveyor Mike Elliott. What happened to the rest of the two acres? The Mercer Ditch destroyed some of the burial plots and cemetery acreage. Unfortunately, no one fought for the cemetery (or for the rights of the relatives of the deceased) when the land was split and resold in the 1940s. It is not possible to reconstruct who did what and when, but when a south fence for the cemetery was built, it was definitely to the north of where it should have been and left many graves out. What is presently fenced certainly does not include the entire area used for burying which was probably more like five or six acres.

Whatever happens, future land development over burial sites even outside the fence should be prohibited. If the city or county bought the acreage east of Juhl's house, the access problem would be solved, room could be made for parking school buses of the students visiting the cemetery, and a pleasant park area between Bingham Hill Road and the cemetery would be available for picnics, etc. This land is adjacent to the historic water works acreage and would make a nice public parcel.

SUMMARIES, LOOSE ENDS AND MISCELLANEOUS

Size: The cemetery area as donated by Provost and Claymore in 1879 was two acres; the cemetery as fenced in 1998 is 1.279 acres. Encroachments have been made on all sides.

Number of bodies buried: There were at least 150 persons buried in the cemetery, and according to grave dowsing, possibly as many as 300 bodies lie inside and outside the cemetery fences.

Number of bodies moved: At least 15 bodies were moved from the Laporte cemetery to Grandview Cemetery and other places.

Access: Open driving access for burials (1862-1944); Variable access for maintenance (1945-1994); No access except walking path (1994-present).

Visitors: Over 10,000 people signed in between 1987 to 1998—from all 50 states and at least 20 foreign countries. By 2015, over 50,000 persons signed in. Many other visitors do not sign in.

Age at Death: 62% of burials were of children under 14; 38% were adults.

Nationalities: Before 1900, burials were approximately 1% French-Canadian; 6% American Indian-mixed blood; 80% Anglo.

After 1900, percentages of burials were 39% Anglo; 61% Hispanic.

Total percentages (1862-1998) are: 1% French-Canadian; 3% American Indian-mix; 28% Hispanic; and 68% Anglo.

Causes of death before 1900: unknown epidemics, 5; TB, 4; accident, 4; typhoid, 4; pneumonia, 4; stillbirths and premature births, 4; mothers at childbirth, 3; suicide, 3 (1 because of cancer; 1 because of pregnancy); heart problems, 3; croup, 2; cholera, 2; cancer, 2; diptheria, 2; old age, 2; murder, 2 (1 by Indians, 1 possible poisoning of a child); and at least 1 each: nosebleed, inflammatory rheumatism, umbilical cord around neck of infant, inflammation of brain, alcoholism, accident and measles during pregnancy (each killed one baby); unknown causes, 30.

Causes of death after 1900: pneumonia, 8; stillbirths and premature births, 6; typhoid, 5; old age, 5; scarlet fever, 4; TB, 3; heart problems, 3; influenza, 2; cancer, 2; and 1 each for "Ojo," umbilical cord around neck, congenital syphilis, skull deformity, whooping cough, summer complaint (dehydration), convulsions, stroke, meningitis, lightning, suicide, Lou Gehrig's disease; unknown causes, 18.

Months of death: March and September had the most deaths (15 each), whereas only 7 died in the month of June, and 8 in the months of May and October. The dates of death of 26 persons are unknown.

Ministers who aided at funerals: Rev. James Bailey, Rev. Bickerstaff, Rev. Hal Collier, Fr. Juan Fullana, Fr. LaJeunesse, Rev. McCutchen, Fr. Phil Meredith, Rev. Moore, Rev. Gordon Peterson, Rev. A.S. Phelps, Fr. Joseph Romero, Rev. Walter Shipp, Rev. C.H. Stone, Rev. Marty Trujillo, Rev. Morton Young (Fr. LaJeunesse is most often mentioned.)

Doctors who tended the ill and/or signed death certificates: Dr. E.P. Evans, Dr. Honstein, Dr. Little, Dr. O.W. Miller, Dr. R.W. Morrish, Dr. Platz, Dr. E.I. Raymond, Dr. Replogle, Dr.C.F. Wilkin, Dr. Taylor, Dr. Timothy Wirt (Dr. Wilkin is most often mentioned.)

Foreign born: Alphonse LaRocque, Mary McKillop McBride

Oldest person at death: probably Julia Learn, age 90

First Children Buried: Bazille Provost (1862), Susan Hardin (1865), Mary Provost (1866)

Last Children Buried: Maria Tamayo (1938), Baby Garcia (1939), Mary Inez Pacheco (1943)

First Adults Buried: Sarah Jane Hardin (1865), Julila Dennis (1873), Crawford Shaffer (1873)

Last Adults Buried: Florence Spragg (1933), Bill Howell (1940)

Adults after 1987 (Cremains Buried): Julia Learn (1987), Bill Alcorn (1989), Danny Allen (1991), Cecil Neth (1992), Manuelita Gonzales (1993), Frances Ver Stratten (1996), Leroy Vigil (1998)

Most Burials in one extended family: Don Vigil (more than 20); C.W. Howell (6), Bingham family (6)

Hopes for the future: Many "hopes" listed in the 1988 and 1990 editions of this book have come to pass—there is a large memorial stone with the names of those buried; the cemetery hasn't yet been destroyed by developers; Larimer County mowed weeds (from 1991 to 1996); two redwood benches were placed in the cemetery for the thoughtful and the weary; more names were found which were not known in 1990; a new tombstone for Alphonse LaRocque was placed in the cemetery and should last another 150 years; a few other souls have their first markers; I learned who J. Thomas was.

New hopes for the future include:

(1) That the next owner of the land surrounding the cemetery is more compassionate and less rigid and allows people who need to drive to the cemetery to do so, and without a legal battle.

(2) That the county or city form a large open space for the Laporte area by adding to the waterworks acreage on Overland Trail (already city-owned), the approximate five acres between Bingham Hill Road and the cemetery, and the cemetery itself, which would assure perpetural care.

(3) That vandals return the stolen Vigil crucifix and "Nellie Land" tombstone, then stay out of the cemetery forever. And that if Nellie's tombstone isn't returned, a donor will buy a new one.

Miscellaneous: Many people have said they would like to be buried at Bingham Hill—Dan MacArthur and Klaus Hoffman are two on the list. Hoffman said he didn't care about access; he had mountain rescue friends who would carry his coffin up the path.

An April 1, 1997, request from the family of Andy Howe from Delta, formerly from Bellvue, for full body burial was turned down by the the the adjacent landowner. Someone should set policy concerning access for maintenance, visitation and future burials. Should burials continue? Whole body? Cremains only? Do "new" burials contaminate the pioneer aspect of the cemetery? Was it meant to be a community cemetery and those who live elsewhere are not welcome? Should there be restriction on memorial stones? Is there a way to get the full two acres back? Who will mow grass and weeds each summer?

Before anyone—even a potential Laporte Cemetery Committee—can set standards and impose rules, ownership has to be established and this goes right back to the county's reluctance to claim ownership. The Pioneer Association has offered to take over if the county deeded it to them but the county has to quiet title first, or obtain a written guarantee of reasonable access, mutually agreed to by a surrounding landowner and cemetery caretakers.

PERSONS BURIED AT
BINGHAM HILL CEMETERY

BARBARA BINGHAM
(1857-1876)

JACOBO TRUJILLO
(1904-1920) and
ACACIO TRUILLO
(1865-1924)

LUCIA TRUJILLO
(1926-1927)
(With her mohter, Vitalia
Trujillo, seated, and aunt,
Magdalena Lujan)

ELIZA ANN ELIZABETH ROBERTSON (seated with baby)
(1853-1916)

Pictured in 1900 at Bellvue with (standing, left to right) Maggie and Samuel
Robertson, May (Robertson) and Bert Garnick, Emma and Andrew Robertson;
Front Row, Levi Robertson, Eliza's husband, sitting; the children, left to right,
Rose Beeson, Levon Garnick, Mabel Beeson, and two of Andrew's children.

DINKEL INFANT
(May 6, 1942)

181

CRAWFORD L. SHAFFER
(1849-1873)

WILL OUDERKIRK (DIED ca. 1895)
(With wife Nellie, and son Edward)

ABNER SPRAGG (1847-1923)
FLORENCE SPRAGG (1850-1933)

WILLIAM MARSHALL HOWELL
(1864-1939)

PERSONS BURIED AT BINGHAM HILL CEMETERY

IDA LOUISE MCNALLY
(1866-1883)

JENNY McGAA BROWN
(DIED 2/13/1878)
(Photograph may be of her daughter, Jessie.)

MARIA MARTINEZ (1912-1913)
(With her Godmother Sophia Martinez and parents Cleofas Aragon and Jose Valerio Martinez)

MARIA L. TAMAYO
(1937-1938)

DONACIANO VIGIL (About 1842-1918)
and his mother-in-law,
CRISANTA HERRERA (1846-1916)

183

PERSONS BURIED AFTER 1985

JULIA LEARN
(1895-1985)

DANNY ALLEN
(1953-1991)

MANUELITA GONZALES
(1910-1993)

FRANCES VER STRATTON
(1920-1996)

CECIL B. NETH (1924-1992)

VETERANS

LEROY VIGIL
(1945-1997)

WILLIAM ALCORN
(1949-1989)

1860s and 1870s

1880s and 1890s

AFTER 1900

HAND-CARVED STONES

NEW STONES IN THE CEMETERY

CHARLES W. HOWELL 1839–1894

BILL HOWELL JAN. 30, 1864 DEC. 30, 1939

ACACIO TRUJILLO JAN. 1, 1865 JULY 16, 1924

MARY INEZ PACHECO DEC. 24, 1942 JAN. 25, 1943

WINIFRED FARRAR 1885 — 1891

INFANT DAUGHTER OF MARTIN AND LOUISE ARAGON MAY 30, 1950

BELOVED MOTHER MANUELITA M GONZALES NOV 10 1910 JAN 28 1993

FRANCES E. VER STRATTEN JULY 16, 1920 JAN 5, 1996

MEMORIAL STONES

Above: Author Ed "Eagle Man" McGaa and Rose Brinks by the memorial stone set on May 12, 1990.

Left: Marker set by the Daughters of the American Revolution on Oct. 6, 1987

VOLUNTEERS

Left to right, top to bottom. 1. James Brinks and sons, John and Jim, cleaning brush from Provost children's lot. 2. John pointing out long-hidden tombstone of Jennie (McGaa) Brown. . Rose Brinks and Mary and Cap Williams burning brush. 4. Sam Harris and sign he donated. 5. Delivery of marker purchased by DAR. 6. Jim Brinks. 7. Twyla Surbeck and Mary Trionfera cleaning Bingham family plot. 8. Starr Quam and Joy Trionfera cleaning unknown child's lot. (Persons in last two photos belong to Rainbow Riders 4-H Club.)

Left to right, top to bottom. 1. Leroy Davison clearing brush near Jennie Brown's stone. (Compare area with top photos on previous page.) 2. Davison preparing to winch stone from Mercer Ditch. 3. Lafi Miller winching sandstone block. 4. Davison placing metal gate which he made onto original fittings. 5. Art Wendel plowing down bank of silt on west end of cemetery. 6. Roy Juhl who helped with several tasks. 7. Ray Heldman and Jim Brinks fitting new gate. 8. Ray Heldman building fence paid for by John Provost's great-grandson, Henry Moore. (Fence constructed in April, 1998.)

VOLUNTEERS CONTINUED...

Clockwise from top: 1. Michael Holzwarth building picket fence around Jenny McGaa Brown's grave. 2. Michael Elliott surveying cemetery. 3. Steve Carr repairing marble markers. 4. Rainbow Riders 4-H Club burning weeds and brush. 5. Bill Schneider dowsing for graves; Wayne Sundberg observing.

Landscaping memorial stone.

Two redwood benches.

Visitor stand.

**EAGLE
SCOUT
PROJECTS**

Rebuilt picket fence enclosure.

Tenon joint fence and gate. Storage shed.

VISITORS

Left to right, top to bottom: 1. Retired funeral director Harold Warren. 2. Frances (grand-niece of Ida McNally) and Wally Bujack. 3. Irene (great-granddaughter of Ben Claymore) and Blaine Perreten of Chadron, Nebr. and Ashley and Mary Scott of Littleton, Colo. 4. Edwin Brown from Louisville, Colo. by Jennie Brown's headstone (before repairs). 5. Henry Moore (great-grandson of John Provost) of Nebraska. 6. Joy Trionfera at grave of Don Vigil. 7. Sister Genevieve Cuny, descendant of Alphonse LaRocque and Adele Brown Treis, descendant of Jenny Brown. 8. Peri McGaa Strain from White River, S.D. visiting Jenny Brown's gravesite. 9. Irma Miller (great-granddaughter of Ben Claymore) of Westcliffe, Colo.

Provosts and Lesserts at the Bingham Hill Cemetery.

Charles "Cap" Provost, grandson of John Provost.

Priscilla and Amber Dressen, Jerry Brown, Pat Corrigan, Pete and Ri Dressen; all descendants of Jenny Brown.

Clara Rodgers and Jim Brinks visiting the graves of Clara's sisters and brother.

The 100th person to "sign in."

Sophia, Sam and Rex Dean from Boston, looking at new LaRocque headstone.

Jose and Judy Gonzales burying the cremains of loved ones.

Father Phil Merideth at the burial of the cremains of Frances VerStratten.

Ken Goldsberg and Russell Legg discussing access.

Fourth-graders on a field trip.

Larimer County employee.

Alan and Max Dean, Andy Dean, Jim Brinks and James S. Brinks—the pick-up crew who lifted the Keller oblisque onto the base after vandals pushed it over.

Daniel Dean visiting the cemetery.

CEMETERY SCENES

WHO WAS J. THOMAS?

Left to right, top to bottom. 1. Rainbow Riders 4-H Club, planning to move grave of J. Thomas. 2. The red-headed J. Thomas. 3. J. Thomas' leather coat. 4. Leg and sock of J. Thomas on its way to Dr. Michael Charney's office. 5. Dr. Michael Charney. 6. Boy Scout Troop 90, building retaining wall for J. Thomas' grave.

ADDENDUM: Rose Brinks, November 2005

In the past seven years, since the *History of the Bingham Hill Cemetery* was published in what was declared to be its third and last version, thousands more people have visited the cemetery. I gave tours to hundreds of school children, and several people stopped by our farm to tell new stories of those buried or of their descendants.

Two new Eagle Scout projects were completed to add to the eight already described on pp. 165-6 and they deserve mention. **Scott Potter** did a fantastic job with a 70-foot boardwalk leading up the path in December, 2002, and in 2005, **Christopher Low** and his troop from St. Joseph's did a general clean-up, paint, and repair job. Neighbor **John Schmid** has been faithful with mowing weeds several times each summer. That is no easy job. A few paranormal researchers tried to record night-time sounds and take photos of ghosts. The gigantic old cottonwood along the path is falling apart; two of its largest branches cracked off last month.

A month after this book came out, the cremains of **Ezra Samuel Travers**, a Cache la Poudre Elementary School student, were buried under a heart-shaped granite stone. Ezra was born February 10, 1988, and died in an auto accident on Christmas Day, 1998, at age 10. His classmates still bring coins and mementos to leave at his grave.

A particularly compelling story and photograph of a woman buried in the cemetery (early photographs are rare!) came to light, and that made me finally decide to republish this book, one *last* time—one additional page. Here is a synopsis of her story.

Josephine Alice Yockey Pyle (Pile)

On pp. 63-64, one reads that Sarah Yockey (40), died December 28, 1890, at the family residence near the Poudre canyon; and that her daughter, Josephine Pile (20) died a week later, January 5, 1891. Mr. Dave Yockey grieved, and put up a single marble tombstone (wording, p. 15; photo, p. 187). No cause of deaths was given. One assumed it was the end of the genetic line for 20-year-old Josephine.

One spring day in 2003, a phone call came in from a **Kay Wittman** of Lawrence, Kansas, who said she was the great-granddaughter of that 20-year-old woman and that she had just learned she was buried at Bingham Hill! The Fort Collins newspaper had not mentioned a child, but at the time of her death, Josephine Pyle did, in fact, have a daughter, Maude, about one year old. The child was taken to eastern Kansas to be raised by grandparents. This child grew up not knowing a nice monument stood on the hill by Laporte, Colorado, with her mother's and grandmother's names.

It is interesting, but not uncommon, to see names spelled in different ways. The name was spelled PYKE in the newspaper, PILE on the marble tombstone and in the *General Index* of this book (one assumes that if it is written in stone, it is accurate), but PYLE is the correct spelling.

A photograph of Josephine Yockey Pyle, her husband, and little Maude was furnished by Kay Wittman. It was taken in Kansas a few months before the death of Josephine. Wittman wrote: *"I don't know much about great-grandmother Josephine Pyle. I know that she was #3 of 7 children with her mother* (who was buried a week

201

before she was). *Her father remarried and had two more children with his second wife, Mary. I think she married John Pyle on Dec. 28, 1887 in Ottawa, KS. After she died as I was told John took Maude (my grandmother) back to Kansas and let Josephine's father take care of her and he left for parts unknown. He was murdered Aug. 1908..... I really wonder what happened to my great-grandmother and her mother...."*

From the *Atchison County Mail,* Sept. 4, 1908, Wittman sent a long article about the death of John Pyle, a retired horseshoer, a recluse who lived in a two-room cabin near the river and fished for a living, and was thought to have a hoard of gold. He was found with a bullet hole through his forehead. A rusty shotgun lying on his chest made it look suicidal, but since the barrels were filled with cobwebs, the general conclusion was that he was murdered. The news was also printed in the *Ottawa Herald.*

Little Maude grew up, married Erwin Hackett and had four children, Clinton, Lillian, Milton and Milo. She died in 1976 at the age of 87. Clinton had one daughter; Lillian had one son; Milo had two sons. Milton had five children including Kay Wittman who furnished this invaluable information. She and her husband Merle have three children, Terry, Brian and Alissa. Josephine Pyle's genes definitely still exist!

In the fall of 2003, Wittman and her husband drove from Lawrence, Kansas, to visit the Laporte graves of her great-grandmother and great-great grandmother, 113 years after their deaths. It was rewarding to experience another serendipitous unearthing of a poignant human story buried in this long abandoned but amazing little cemetery.

John and Josephine Yockey Pyle and daughter Maude. Photo taken in Quenemo, Kansas, 1890. Josephine died and was buried in the Laporte, Colorado, cemetery a few months later. John was murdered in Kansas in 1908.

Wedding photo of grown-up Maude Pyle and her husband Erwin Hackett, taken in Ottawa, Kansas, 1907.

ADDENDUM: Rose Brinks, July 2015

Ten years have passed since the last 500 copies of this book were printed and sold. Over 50,000 cemetery visitors have signed in by now, and since no books are available, I was asked to republish. It is not that easy, now that digital is the name of the game, but Gail Blinde of Fort Collins has the equipment and know-how to go from regular print to digital and to redo and add photos. There are nearly 50 new names in the 2015 addendum but just as with the 2005 Addendum, they have not been added to the General Index. Thirteen new names are added to the Index of Persons Buried on page 209.

Newly found information of old burials: Examining the historic newspaper files online, I found five burial notices which were missed when turning pages one newspaper at a time as I did in the 1980s. There are no tombstones for any of these people.

1. **Mrs. Mary Kirby** Died October 9, 1886 Age unknown
   Courier: 10/14/1886: "Mrs. Mary Kirby died at the residence of her son, James Kirby, last Saturday morning. The remains were interred in the Laporte cemetery Sunday afternoon."

2. **Ezra Honnold** Died November 17, 1893 Child
   Courier 11/23/1893: "The death of Ezra Honnold on Friday morning Nov. 17, created an aching void in the hearts of many warm personal friends in Bellvue, and cast a deeper shade of gloom than usual over the entire community. Especially does the blow fall with crushing weight on the family circle. Though sick but a few short days it was plainly seen that one so small could not master the deadly disease, typhoid, which had so firmly fastened itself upon the victim. Rev. J.F. Coffman preached a short but comforting sermon and then after a view of the remains had been taken the procession moved to Laporte cemetery where the body was laid to rest." This was followed by a poem.

3. **Louis Honnold** Died August 30, 1903 Age 7 years
   Courier 9/2/1903: "Louis, the seven-year old son of Mr. and Mrs. Honnold died of typhoid pneumonia at the family residence at Bellvue on Sunday. The funeral was held at 2 o'clock P.M. today. Burial at Laporte cemetery."

The relationship of the above two children to Thomas Honnold who died about 1893 while chasing pigs (p. 69) is unknown.

4. **Brown child** Died May 19, 1907 Newborn
   Courier 5/2911907: "A child born to Oliver Brown and wife Sunday, May 19, died and was buried the following day in the Laporte cemetery. The mother is getting along nicely. Mrs. Oliver Brown's sister from Tie Siding is staying with her for a few days."

5. **Lizzie Cordova** Died Oct. 6, 1908 Age 2 months

Courier: 10/7/1908: "Lizzie Cordova, the two months' old daughter of Edward Cordova, a Mexican living at Laporte, died yesterday after a lingering illness. Burial took place this afternoon in the Laporte cemetery." Note (p. 118) that her brother, Jose de Ia Luz Cordova, was buried in 1912.

More recent burials:

All recent burials are of people with relatives buried long ago in the cemetery or have long-time Laporte or Bellvue connections. There is a memorial stone for the child Chris Vigil and one for Vigil ancestors. **Ezra Travers** and **LeRoy Vigil's** deaths were mentioned in an earlier edition but headstone photos were not available until now. **Jerry Brown** and **Pat Corrigan** both helped with information writing the earlier edition and are now buried in the cemetery.

1. **Jenny McGaa Brown relatives.**

There are 3 granite stones for descendants of Jenny McGaa Brown—all close to her grave: **Jerry Brown** (1933 to 2000), **Pat Corrigan** (1925 to 2008) and her sister **Toni Callan** (1921 to 1994). Jerry and Pat are pictured on p. 197. Pete Dressen buried the cremains of his mother and aunt.

2. **Vigil family.**

At the west end of the cemetery there are 6 new stones, 3 professional (2 military) and 3 handmade. One, placed by Lorraine Vigil, is dedicated to the memory of her ancestors, **Crisanta Herrara** and her son-in-law, **Donaciano Vigil**. Both people are discussed at length in the book and have individual stones.

There are markers for **Chubby (Paul) Vigil** (1948 to 2008), **William Vigil** (1930 to 2011), **Lois N. Blodgett** (1953 to 2009), and two stones for father and son: **LeRoy Vigil** (1945 to 1997, p 160) and **Chris Vigil** (August 24, 1968-?) who was 9 when he went missing on a family hike on Grey Rock Mountain on April 30, 1978 (p. 125). The four adult Vigils are children of William and Florence Vigil; William was a son of Donaciano Vigil and Ramona Herrara (p. 125).

3. **James Michael Jackson** Died July 17, 2009 Age 38 years

Information from the handout at his funeral: Jim was born in Long Beach, CA, on September 10, 1971 to Mike & Judy Jackson. He was a creative, imaginative and artistic little boy. When Jim was age 7, his family moved to Bellvue, CO and he began playing drums. As a teen, Jim played drums and sang in several bands. He inspired his sister Joy to start singing. He loved to draw and won several awards. He loved mountain biking, mountain climbing and backpacking with his friends up Long's Peak. He loved the ocean and treasured his time at the family cabin near Yellowstone.

Music was his life and he formed the band The Boondock Saints. He married Jodi Gregory in Malibu Calif. In March of 2005 an MRI revealed a cancerous brain tumor. After surgery and treatments, he was in remission for many months, but the cancer reoccurred.

Both Jim Jackson and Ezra Travers, who died Christmas Day, 1998, (p. 201) were organ donors.

4. **Larry Allen Lesser** Died June 15, 2004 Age 52
Larry Allen Lesser was born in Fort Collins October 24, 1951.

New Replacement Stone in the Cemetery:

At first, any headstone replaced was with the original type stone (marble or sandstone), style, size and printing. Those include Alphonse LaRocque (cracked), Nellie Land (stolen), and Mary Provost (stolen but returned after a replicate was made.) A badly cracked marble stone for Cora Flowers, however, was replaced in November, 2011, with granite which was less expensive and more durable. It was paid for by Jeanne Flowers of Ketchum, Idaho, and Lois Johnson of Fort Collins, both great-granddaughters of Jacob Flowers. As in the past, Fort Collins Monuments works (which had been in business since 1889 but recently closed) did the work at cost.

A Bit of New Information on a Mystery:

Nothing had ever been found in local papers of the person under the largest head stone in the cemetery, that of 19-year-old **Ida B. Keller** who died in 1882. Her parents were A.J. and S.A. Keller. The marble ball from its top has been stolen but the 6-foot stone and small cracked footstone remain. Who was she? I recently found references to Mrs. S.A. Keller in the *Routt County Republican* in 1916 and in the *Routt County Sentinel* in 1920. She made devil's food and angel food cakes, she was in Steamboat to attend Eastern Star, etc. There were many references in both newspapers to Kellers, apparently a prominent family, but none of an Ida B. I suspect that like Ida Louise McNally, Ida B. Keller was a resident of the North Park area and brought to Laporte for burial.

Recent Crew Keeping the Cemetery Mowed and Cleaned:

For the last five years, the Bellvue Historic Foundation has taken physical care of the cemetery. Gas mowers, weed whippers, shovels, hoes, and bare hands are all evident when they arrive. A list of volunteers would include: **Derek Daubert, Mike and Judy Jackson, Joy and Jeremy McLaughlin, Monica Clark, Marcus Jackson, June Roberts, Neil and Nancy Spencer, Cynthia Manuel, Craig Brodahl, Lisa Maser, Robert Maser, Deby Brandt, Diane Shalar, Denise Johnson, Padraic McAuliffe, Suzanne Enman, James Pritchett family, Dan and Max Dean, Eric Sutherland, Mike Moen** and more. They thinned irises which were out of control, trimmed elm branches, mowed grass, pulled weeds and made the cemetery presentable for visitors.

Judy Jackson, 970-482-5091, of Bellvue has taken over from Rose Brinks as the person to call about tours, projects, and general information.

New Eagle Scout Projects:

In November of 2011, **Jonathan Zuniga** of Troop 97, removed a broken grave enclosure on the west side of the cemetery and replaced it with a completely new one. His troop also did other minor repairs and cleanup.

In September of 2012, **Dillon R.F. Knackstedt** of Troop 83 completed a project titled: "Create online data base of gravestone information and link data to an Arc GIS map." The online sites can be found at http://coloradograves.org/cemetery.php?cemID=454&pg=1 and http://www.arcgis.com/home/webmap/viewer.html?webmap=ff6f55cbba8a465e9f 8ef27adc2ab76d

Scheduled for late August 2015 is a major Eagle Scout project directed by **Billy Allen** of Troop 90. With the help of his troop as well as his 4-H Club, "Cinch 'em up," he plans to accomplish the following:

(1) Add a 50- foot extension to the wooden walkway on the path from Bingham Hill Road into the cemetery. Eagle Scout **Scott Potter** built the first 70 feet in 2002.
(2) Stain the wood of the Visitor Center which was originally built in 1992 by **Randall Harris** of Troop 387.
(3) Install plexiglass display cases on the Visitor Center.
(4) Repair and replace broken boards and pickets on wood enclosures around unknown graves.
(5) Repaint the large Bingham Hill Cemetery sign which was last replaced and painted by **Micky Ethridge** in 1997.

MEMORIAL STONES

Chris Vigil

Vigil Family

HEAD STONES

William Vigil

LeRoy Vigil

Chubby Vigil

Lois Blodgett

207

Ezra Travers

James Jackson

Edwin Brown

Toni Callan

Pat Corrigan

Cora Flowers

INDEX OF PERSONS BURIED AT BINGHAM HILL

INDEX OF PERSONS BURIED AT BINGHAM HILL *continued*

GENERAL INDEX

213

218

REFERENCES

1. Brinks, Rose L. *From Provost to Brinks, A Certain 160 Acres, Laporte, Colorado, 129 Years of History, 1858 to 1987,* 1987.

2. Davis, Alreen, J. Miller and M. Beatty. Booklet: "Cemeteries of Larimer County" (especially an article by Ruth Hereim), 1972.

3. Gray, John. *Calvary and Coaches,* 1978.

4. Vertical Files, local history room in the Fort Collins Public Library.
   (a) Probate papers of Mary, Oliver and Lizzie Provost, donated by Henry Moore.
   (b) Letters of Nettie Garbutt Herring (1874-1894) donated by Ann Garbutt Ryan.
   (c) Diaries and Letters of E.N. Garbutt (1867-1894) donated by Harry Kingman.
   (d) "Fort Collins Hispanics," written and donated by Daniel Martinez.

5. *History of Larimer County, Colorado, 1911,* by Ansel Watrous
   The History of Larimer County, Colorado, Vol. II, 1987. Editors: Arlene (Briggs) Ahlbrandt and Kathryn "Kate" Stieben.

6. Fort Collins funeral home records: Reager, Allnut, and Warren-Bohlender.

7. Grandview Cemetery records.

8. Newspapers and microfilm, Fort Collins Public Library. Newspapers (1894 and 1899-1908) loaned by Wayne Sundberg.

9. Scrapbooks of Richard Baker, now in the care of Bill Schneider.

10. Larimer County Courthouse: Grantor/Grantee Books; Larimer County #1 Pauper Record; Coroner's Record, 1881-1946 (now in coroner's office in Loveland); Index to Marriages 1858-1910.

11. Personal interview or correspondence with children, parents, siblings, wives, and other relatives of the deceased.
    (See "Acknowledgements.")

THE AUTHOR

Rose Stehno Brinks was born in 1935 on a farmstead north of Stratton, Nebraska, and led a typical farm childhood—milking cows, driving a tractor, writing to big brothers who were overseas in WWII, hoeing weeds, playing with cousins, and reading. She graduated *magna cum laude* from the Creighton University in Omaha, and earned masters' degrees in zoology from the University of Kansas and in radiology/radiation biology from Colorado State University. She also briefly attended Arizona State University, the University of Wyoming, and Lamar State College of Technology in Beaumont, Texas.

She taught in secondary schools and college for several years in Omaha, Las Vegas, Los Angeles, Phoenix, and Ottawa, Kansas. Her favorite hobby of flying was given up after a plane crash and death of her husband Alan Dean in 1965. She married James S. Brinks, a beef cattle geneticist and professor of Animal Sciences in 1969.

Mrs. Brinks has seven children, five stepchildren, fourteen grand-children, and eight step-grandchildren.

Writing about local history, working with her four Arabian horses, playing with the grandbabies and hanging around the Laporte Animal Clinic (owned by her son and daughter-in-law) are her newest hobbies. She also sneaks off for quick trips to places like Andorra, Bali, Czechoslovakia, Denmark, Egypt, Finland, Germany, Hawaii, Israel. . . .

Made in the USA
San Bernardino, CA
16 July 2020

75607630R00133